HUMAN MOTIVATION

Commentary on Goal-Directed Action

HUMAN MOTIVATION
Commentary on Goal-Directed Action

NATHAN BRODY

Department of Psychology
Wesleyan University
Middletown, Connecticut

 1983

ACADEMIC PRESS

A SUBSIDIARY OF HARCOURT BRACE JOVANOVICH, PUBLISHERS

New York   London
Paris   San Diego   San Francisco   São Paulo   Sydney   Tokyo   Toronto

ACADEMIC PRESS, INC.
111 Fifth Avenue, New York, New York 10003

United Kingdom Edition published by
ACADEMIC PRESS, INC. (LONDON) LTD.
24/28 Oval Road, London NW1 7DX

Library of Congress Cataloging in Publication Data

Brody, Nathan.
    Human motivation. *etc*

    Bibliography: p.
    Includes index.
    1. Motiviation (Psychology) I. Title.
BF503.B76   1983   153.8   82-22654
ISBN 0-12-134840-7

PRINTED IN THE UNITED STATES OF AMERICA

83 84 85 86   9 8 7 6 5 4 3 2 1

To Paul Oppenheim

CONTENTS

Preface   ix

Chapter 1

INTRODUCTION:
PURPOSIVE EXPLANATION   1

Tolman and Purpose   4
Hull and Purpose   6
Hull's Formal Theory   10

Chapter 2

MOTIVATION AND PERFORMANCE:
THE DESCENT OF
THE HULLIAN TRADITION   15

Spence's Theory of Anxiety as Drive   15
Limitations of Spence's Theory   24
Drive Theory of Social Facilitation   27
Alternative Conceptions of the Influence of Drive on Performance   31

Critical Evaluation of Theory of Nondirective Energizers   44
Conclusion   55

Chapter 3
ACHIEVEMENT MOTIVATION: TOWARD A PURPOSIVE THEORY   59

Atkinson's Risk-taking Model   70
Theoretical Extensions of Atkinson's Model   85
The Theory of Action   93

Chapter 4
BEYOND GOAL ATTAINMENT: REINFORCEMENT THEORY AND OPPONENT PROCESS THEORY   111

Reinforcement Theory   111
Opponent Process Theory   121

Chapter 5
MOTIVATION AND COGNITION: IN SEARCH OF THE GHOST IN THE MACHINE   139

The Unconscious   140
The Rise and Fall of Cognitive Explanations of Motivated
    Behavior   165
Prophenomenological Research   188

Epilogue   209

References   211

Author Index   223

Subject Index   229

PREFACE

This book is for the most part about human motivation. Although the general theory of motivation encompasses research that deals with biological motivation and that uses animals, the explosion of knowledge and the increasing specialization to which we appear unfortunately to be prone has rendered a comprehensive treatment of the entire subject increasingly difficult. Accordingly, I have focused on a series of issues concerning human social motivation. My failure to deal with biologically relevant aspects of the study of motivation in this book is to be construed more as a failure of my knowledge than as a principled act of conviction.

In preparing this volume I have been guided by two concerns. First, I have attempted in the initial chapter of this book to sketch a simplistic model of a goal-directed action sequence that is derived from the usual layman's conception of a goal-directed action. Each of the chapters that follows may be construed as a discussion of the complications inherent in that model. Chapter 2, which deals with the Hullian tradition in motivation, argues that there is a body of evidence that requires an analysis of motivational phenomena in nonpurposive terms. Chapter 3, which discusses theories growing out of research on achievement motivation, examines an emerging conception of action that requires one to extend the analysis of goal-directed action beyond a consideration of particular action sequences to a consideration of the waxing and waning of action sequences and to a consideration of the relationships among disparate action sequences. Chapter 4, which deals with a theory of affective dynamics and recent applications of certain economic principles to human behavior, also relates these theoretical developments to the theory of action presented in Chapter 3 and argues that all of these theories agree in changing the focus of the psychology of motivation from a consideration of self-contained action sequences to a consideration of relationships among diverse action tendencies. Chapter 5 again suggests complexities in the commonsense view of action tendencies. Namely, the usual assumption that individuals are aware of the reasons for their actions and that individuals are aware of the goals toward which their actions are directed is challenged. Chapter 5 attempts to present a synthesis of research on cognitive influences on motivation.

Second, in writing this book I have attempted to address issues that are in a sense somewhat ahead of our mastery. Although the book is heavily empirical, replete with descriptions of the results of specific investigations, I have attempted to use these empirical results to address fundamental issues about the shape of the future of scientific psychology of motivation, and, where possible, I have alluded to emerging conceptions that may provide a framework for future developments. In short, I have attempted to prognosticate—and the future will undoubtedly serve as a corrective for the misconceptions of this book.

It is always a pleasure to acknowledge one's intellectual debts. I hope any reader of this book will detect the profound influence my teacher in graduate school, Jack Atkinson, has had on my view of motivation. Although we may disagree occasionally on specifics, I share his view that the psychology of motivation should be shaped by a systematic consideration of basic theoretical issues. My second debt is to a friend and scholar of another era, now deceased, whose kindness, persistent intellectual curiosity, imagination, and clarity of thought taught me many things. I am pleased to dedicate this book to that friend, Paul Oppenheim.

HUMAN MOTIVATION

Commentary on Goal-Directed Action

Chapter *1*

INTRODUCTION: PURPOSIVE EXPLANATION

Nothing is less problematic to the layman than the belief that the behavior of human beings is organized into goal-directed actions. We do not describe our behavior in terms of colorless movements and responses. I would not, under ordinary circumstances, describe my efforts to find a suitable beginning for this book on motivation as a series of movements made by my hand while holding a pen. Rather, I would describe my behavior at this moment as involving the act of writing a beginning to a treatise on motivation. Such a description implies that the flux and flow of physical movements made during the day may be segmented and described in terms of a series of actions. An action may be understood in terms of a goal toward which it is directed. The attainment of the goal brings the action to its end. Thus, human behaviors may be considered as a series of instrumental acts—that is, an action that, if successfully accomplished, will lead to the attainment of some goal or end point of the action. If the instrumental activity does not lead to the attainment of the particular goal, other actions or activities may be instituted in an attempt to attain the goal, or the goal may be abandoned, and a new action may be instituted in order to attain some new goal.

The explanation of human action involves the specification of the goal toward which an action is presumably directed, and this specification usually is what is meant in response to the question: Why did a person do a particular thing? Thus, the answer to the question, "Why did Mr. Smith walk across the street?" might be, "in order to buy a pack of cigarettes." The goal of the action—in this instance, the purchase of a pack of cigarettes—serves in ordinary discourse, as a reasonable explanation of the behavior of the person. If the behavior appears to be reasonably considered as instrumental to the goal sought, if the goal appears to be one that a person might indeed wish to attain, and if we do not suspect the person offering such an explanation of his action of being deceptive, demented, or for some other reason acting in such a way that we doubt his ability to render sensible explanations of his action, we are likely to assume that we understand his action and that we have been given a sensible explanation for the action when we know its goal.

The laymen's explanatory schema is fraught with conceptual and philosophical difficulties. Although nothing appears more obvious than the goal-directed explanations of human behavior, such explanations appear strained and unnatural when offered for the behavior of physical events. We are not inclined to explain, for example, the elliptical orbit of the planets around the sun by appeal to some goal toward which this particular behavior leads. Apart from theological views that presume that certain physical regularities provide evidence for a divinely ordained purpose in the universe, teleological (that is, goal-directed) explanations play little or no role in the natural sciences, and indeed, their use is considered suspect. The explanation of physical events is generally thought to involve appeal to general laws from which the particular properties of the event in question may be derived (see Hempel & Oppenheim, 1948). This hypothetical, deductive model of explanation appears on the surface to be conspicuously lacking in the laymen's purposive teleological explanations. Some psychologists and philosophers have argued that the appropriate form or type of explanations to be provided in dealing with human actions are different from those that are appropriate in the natural sciences (e.g., Peters, 1958; C. Taylor, 1964; R. Taylor, 1966). They believe that human actions are adequately explained in purposive goal-directed terms and that such explanations are essentially different in form from the hypothetical, deductive explanations used in the physical sciences. And such theorists have objected, in principle, to explanations of human actions that are nonpurposive. They have embraced the view that the attempt to explain human action by appeal to hypothetical physical events, such as those occurring in the brain, is impossible in principle. They have also opposed "mechanistic" explanations.

A variety of positions have been taken on these matters. Some theorists (e.g., Nagel, 1961) have held that teleological explanations are not fundamentally different from the explanations used in the natural sciences and that they may be rendered without essential loss of meaning in a nonteleological form. (For discussion of these issues see Bunge, 1959; von Wright, 1974;

Wright, 1976.) It has also been argued that the alleged incompatibility between mechanism and purpose is false. Cyberneticists have asserted that physical devices may be constructed that have purposive qualities. In the simplest case, a thermostat may be understood as a device that exhibits goal-directed actions. It maintains a given level of temperature and takes action (starting or stopping a heating or cooling system) in order to maintain some defined goal. More elaborate examples of goal-directed mechanisms can be given. One can construct mechanical devices that are designed to maintain a given level of stimulation on photoreceptors. Such devices may locomote toward or away from light sources, dependent upon the intensity of the light, or may swivel and change the spatial orientation of their receptors in order to maintain a fixed level of stimulation. It thus appears that automata can behave in a goal-directed fashion. Since the behavior of the devices derives from the particular structure of their mechanisms and is presumably adequately described in terms of the general principles of physics and the natural sciences, it would appear that the antinomy between purposive explanations and "mechanistic" explanations offered in the natural sciences is arbitrary. (For a contrary view of the adequacy of mechanistic nonteleological explanations of the behavior of mechanical devices, see Boden, 1972.) Although it may be argued (and not without controversy) that some teleological explanations are equivalent to nonteleological ones, this leaves a variety of other questions surrounding this possible equivalence undecided. Is it possible or indeed even desirable to replace ordinary purposive explanations of human action by nonpurposive explanations? Are there classes of human actions that are best explained in nonpurposive terms? Danto (1973) discussed the distinction between human behaviors that occur but do not appear to be the result of our intentions and those that appear to be voluntary and self-directed (see also Day, 1975; Ryan, 1970). Danto pointed out that an erection is something that occurs but is not usually intended, whereas the act of raising one's arm is usually intended. Furthermore, behaviors that are normally under voluntary control may occur in a nonvoluntary way. We can distinguish between the act of raising one's hand in order to answer a question asked by a teacher in a classroom from the admittedly peculiar but not unimaginable act of having one's hand raised involuntarily for reasons that appear to the actor to be obscure. The physical act, that of raising one's hand, is the same. However, we are at first inclined to offer quite different explanations for the same physical act in these two cases. The act of raising one's hand in order to answer the question asked by a teacher appears quite sensibly to be explained in a purposive fashion. The somewhat puzzling experience of finding one's arm raising, against one's will as it were, is not transparently a purposive action that may be explained in an obvious way by appeal to a goal. We might find physiological explanations, perhaps in terms of some disruption of centers controlling motor acts in the brain, more reasonable in this latter case. Thus the fact that we believe, rightly or wrongly, that actions are intended—that is, under the control of our own desires and volition, lends a compelling phenomenological, experiential foundation for the view that at least some of our actions are to be explained purposively. Where such a phenomenological justification for purposive explanation is lacking, we are inclined to be unsure of the appropriate form of explanation to be provided. It is partly for this reason that Freudian explanations may strike us as odd. Freud extended the purposive model of explanation to acts that appear to the actor to be unintended. A slip of the tongue appears to a person as a random, unintended event. For Freud, a slip of the tongue or a dream was to be understood as being an instrumental act that satisfies some unconscious motive. For Freud, behaviors not appearing to be instrumental acts engaged in to satisfy some goal were to be interpreted as instrumental acts whether apparent or not to the actor. (For a discussion of the generalization of the purposive model to such behavior, see Flew, 1978, Chapter 8; Peters, 1958.)

It is not my intention to provide a discussion of the vexed philosophical issues surrounding the issue of teleological explanations. This brief excursion is designed to indicate that there are many puzzling questions surrounding the seemingly obvious assertion that we may explain human behavior in terms of purposive explanations. To a considerable degree the psychology of motivation may be understood as the attempt to come to grips with the issue of goal direction and purpose in behavior. Historical antecedents for contemporary issues invariably appear to exist in an unbroken chain, usually extending at the very least to the ancient Greeks. The foundation for this study of contemporary issues will be views regarding purpose held by two psychologists, Hull and Tolman, whose formative ideas date from the third and fourth decades of this century. Both of these psychologists were behaviorists. They both believed that introspection and appeal to phenomenological events had no place in psychology. Furthermore, both of these psychologists used rats extensively in their research, and both were inclined to believe that a systematic science of psychology, adequate for the explanation and understanding of human behavior, could be constructed on the basis of research involving the study of rats in mazes (see Koch, 1954, 1959). Where they differed—and differed, arguably, most fundamentally for our purpose—was with respect to their attitudes toward purposive explanation in psychology.

Tolman and Purpose

In 1925 Tolman published two papers in which his fundamental position on purposive explanation in psychology was stated (Tolman, 1925a, 1925b;

see also, 1920, 1922, 1923). Tolman argued for a new version of behaviorism. The behaviorism he sought, like all behaviorisms, would eschew reference to the experience of organisms. This methodological abnegation was compatible with the preference for studying animals rather than humans. He argued against Watson's physiological and mechanistic explanations, which he derided as mere muscle twitchism (Tolman, 1922). He believed that appropriate explanations of behavior would involve the use of psychological, as opposed to physiological, concepts. Most fundamental for our purpose was his belief that behaviorism must become purposive and that there was no incompatibility between behaviorism and purposive explanations. For him the stream of behavior was segmented into a variety of purposive acts. It was necessary, he thought, to include reference to the goal towards which an act was directed in order to appropriately describe and understand the act. Tolman (1926) wrote, "Such a purpose is quite an objective and purely behavioristic affair. It is a descriptive feature immanent in the character of the behavior *qua* behavior. It is not a mentalistic entity supposed to exist parallel to, and to run along side of, the behavior. It is out there in the behavior; of its descriptive warp and woof [p. 355]." Purposive behaviorism involved an amalgam of the behavioristic position of the philosopher Perry (1918, 1921a, 1921b, 1921c), who was the first to suggest that behaviorism could be purposive, and of the nonbehavioristic psychologist, McDougall (1923a, 1923b), who had developed a definition of purpose. Tolman suggested that the purposive character of behavior might be objectively defined in terms of that feature that McDougall had identified as the hallmark of purposiveness, "the persistence until" character of behavior. Thus purposive behavior for Tolman entailed the observation of a tendency to persist using various instrumental acts until goal attainment occurs. It is this allegedly descriptive and observable fact that Tolman took as the essence of behavior and that justifies the development of purposive behaviorism.

Tolman (1932, 1938, 1948) developed a variety of more formal theories of behavior and introduced a number of complex theoretical constructs for explanatory purposes. However, his commitment to a purposive goal-directed version of behaviorism remained as a leitmotif of his work. He took as a central concept the notion that what organisms learned was an expectancy. The most thoroughly developed explanation of the concept of expectancy was developed by MacCorquodale and Meehl (1954), and Tolman essentially accepted this analysis. An expectancy had three conjoined components—an elicitor (S_1), a reaction class or response (R_1), and an expectandum (S_2).

An expectancy may be understood as being analogous to a belief that a particular response (R_1) in the presence of a particular situation or set of eliciting circumstances (S_1) would lead to the occurrence of some event (S_2).

The development of an expectancy is a function of the number of occasions in which the particular sequence of events has been experienced and the valence or value of the event (S_2) to the organism. In a simple T-maze experiment, a rat at a choice point can turn left or right. Assume that the rat is hungry and that the right side of the maze (and not the left side) has food. If the rat is given an opportunity to explore the maze and if the rat turns right, he will find food. Repeated experiences of this type will develop an expectancy that a particular response (right turn) in the presence of this particular set of eliciting circumstances $(S_1$ the T maze) will lead to a particular outcome (S_2) that has value for the organism. The growth of the expectancy not only depends upon the frequency with which it is experienced or occurs, but also on the valence or value of the outcome to the organism. In this formulation, S_2 is the goal for the organism. It should be noted that an expectancy is not the equivalent of a response. It is rather a cognition or belief assumed to be held by the organism. It is one of the determinants of action but not the sole determinant of the behavior of an organism. MacCorquodale and Meehl assumed that the tendency to perform a particular response is a multiplicative function of the value of the expectancy and the valence or value of the expectandum, S_2—that is,

Reaction potential = expectancy $(S_1 \ R_1 \ S_2)$
$\qquad \qquad \times$ the valence or value of the outcome to the organism (S_2).

This brief excursion into the more formal aspects of Tolman's theory is designed to indicate the central role assigned to the goal object in the direction of behavior throughout Tolman's theorizing. The expectandum, S_2, obviously refers to the goal object. Note that the goal object serves to direct behavior. Not only is the strength of the expectation itself a function of the valence or value of the goal object to the organism, but also the valence of the goal object acts as a multiplier that determines the strength of any given response or reaction tendency. Tolman's later theory is one in which the behaviors of an organism are determined by the value assigned to goal objects and the expectations or beliefs held by the organism with respect to possible attainment of the goal object as a result of a particular response. Thus a goal provides both an energizing and directional influence on behavior.

Hull and Purpose

Tolman's contemporary and theoretical rival, Hull, had a different approach to the purposive explanation in psychology, and this difference shaped his theoretical efforts. Like Tolman, Hull considered the purposive goal-directed quality of behavior as a basic truth with which a general theory would have to deal. He was particularly influenced by Darwin's writings. The principle of "survival of the fittest" suggested to Hull that organisms would have to perform actions that were biologically advantageous in order to survive. Hence, there must exist some rule or guiding principle that led organisms to strive for goals that were biologically advantageous. Hull and Tolman thus agreed in their belief that the explanation of the purposive behavior of organisms was the central task of psychology. However, Hull disagreed profoundly with Tolman with respect to the explanatory role to be assigned to the belief in the purposive quality of behavior. For the early Tolman, purposiveness was a fact that in and of itself had explanatory value. It was to be assigned a central explicit role in the explanation of behavior. Indeed, Tolman believed that a mere description of behavior without reference to the goal toward which it was directed was incomplete and inadequate. Hull eschewed any reference to purpose in his explanatory system. In a remarkable set of papers written in the early 1930s, he attempted to derive the presumptive purposive character of behavior from theoretical language and mechanisms that were utterly devoid of reference to purpose. He wished to explain the purposive dimension of behavior by appeal to a series of internal events that were described as if they were actual physical stimuli and physical responses. Hull's approach to the purposive dimension of behavior is aptly described by the titles of two of his earliest articles dealing with this question—"Knowledge and Purpose as Habit Mechanisms" (1930), and "Goal Attraction and Directing Ideas Conceived as Habit Phenomena" (1931). Hull's early approach to psychological theory was influenced by Watsonian behaviorism (Watson, 1919). Like Watson he attempted to explain behavioral phenomena by appeal to stimulus and response connections using principles derived from the study of conditioning. Hull believed that biological drives such as hunger were accompanied by a distinctive set of internal stimuli (e.g., changes in the stomach), which he called drive stimuli, s_D. Such stimuli, although technically unobservable and hypothetical, were given in his theoretical analysis the properties and characteristics of ordinary external stimuli. Drive stimuli would be present throughout a sequence of learning experiences when a biological drive was present. Hull believed that drive stimuli became connected to all of the responses in an instrumental sequence leading to goal attainment. Confronted with a sequence of stimulus events in this world, s_1, s_2, s_3, each of the stimuli would elicit a particular response. If drive stimuli were present, they too would be connected to the sequence of responses. Hull's schematic representation of these events is presented in Figure 1.1.

Hull's concept of redintegration implies that the response strength associated with the responses R_1, R_2, etc., depends upon the summative strengths of the connections between each of the stimuli present with a particular response. Thus both the external stimulus s_1 and the internal drive stimuli s_D

THE WORLD:

THE ORGANISM:

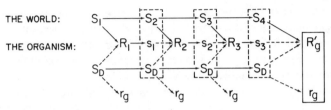

Figure 1.1. Hull's schematic representation of stimuli and responses that influence goal-directed action. (Adapted from Hull [1931].)

elicit the response R_1. Note that s_D is associated both with the responses that are instrumental to a goal and with the goal response (R_g) itself. In addition to the association between drive stimuli and the various responses in the sequence, there is a second set of stimuli internal to the organism that are associated with each response. Each response that occurs in a sequence gives rise to a distinctive proprioceptive stimulus, and through redintegration these stimuli also acquire the property of eliciting the next response in the sequence. Thus the response R_2 in the sequence is elicited by s_2—the external stimulus, s_1—the proprioceptive stimulus that results from the occurrence of the previous response R_1 and s_D, the drive stimulus. The response strength of R_2 represents summative influences of s_2, s_1 and s_D.

The drive stimulus is associated with the goal response, R_g, and with those responses that occur earlier in the sequence and may be conceived of as being instrumental to the goal. Since s_D is present throughout the response sequence, there is some tendency for s_D to elicit R_g prior to the attainment of the goal. However, in the normal course of events the response strength associated with the appropriate instrumental response early in the sequence is greater than the response strength of the goal response. At the point where s_2 occurs, stimuli eliciting R_2 include s_2 and s_1 as well as s_D, whereas the only stimulus eliciting R_g at this point is s_D. Thus the goal response is unlikely to interrupt the sequence prior to goal attainment. The possible invasive intrusion of the goal response is unlikely to occur where the goal response is genuinely incompatible or competing with the instrumental responses, since the greater response strength of the instrumental responses would prohibit the occurrence of an incompatible and weaker response. However, if there were components of the goal response that were not incompatible with instrumental responses, such components could occur early in the response sequence. For example, a hungry animal could perform some fractional weaker component of the goal response, such as salivation, while continuing to locomote toward the goal object. The fractional component of the goal response would be conditioned to the drive stimulus, which is present throughout the sequence, and its occurrence would not be incompatible with the occurrence of instrumental responses. The occurrence of a fractional and weak component of a goal response earlier in the sequence is called, by Hull, a fractional anticipatory goal response, r_g. Since r_g, although hypothetical, is theoretically treated as if it were an actual physical response, it is assumed that it is accompanied by its inevitable proprioceptive aftermath, s_g. This aftermath, s_g, acts as an additional internal stimuli and becomes conditioned to r_g giving rise to what is called the r_g–s_g mechanism. Thus, the s_g becomes conditioned to an instrumented response and along with the sequence of stimuli, s_1, s_2, s_3 . . . serve to integrate the various sequences of external responses, R_1, R_2, R_3.

Hull's analysis permitted him to derive a number of features of purposive behavior by appeal to colorless stimuli and responses. Thus the tendency of an organism to behave as if it had knowledge and foresight and were aware that a particular response would lead to a desired goal is explained by reference to the occurrence of fractional anticipatory goal responses. The 'persistence until' character of behavior taken by McDougall and Tolman as the hallmark of purposive behavior is explained by noting that the occurrence of the goal object in the presence of a stimulus that had previously been associated with the goal object weakens the connection between that stimulus and the goal object and thus decreases the probability of the occurrence of the goal response in the presence of that stimulus. However, the s_D, and s_g and the stimulus associated with the previous instrumental responses will be present in the goal region and will tend to elicit R_g. In addition to both s_D and s_g have been conditioned to other responses that will be elicited even in the absence of the external stimulus that elicited R_g. Thus a variety of other responses that have been associated with goal attainment will occur when the s_3—R_g connection is extinguished. Thus the organism will employ a variety of appropriate instrumental responses to attain a particular goal.

What is the significance of this analysis for our current understanding of motivational questions? It is easy to note those aspects of the analysis that appear antiquated. It is no longer necessary to cloak explanatory concepts in the peripheralist imagery of internal stimuli and responses, and the use of principles of conditioning to explain complex behavior is certainly not a fashionable enterprise. Quite apart from the brilliant tour de force contained in these early Hull papers, it can be argued that they are of enduring relevance in that they suggest an approach to motivation that remains viable in contemporary terms. Hull asserted that the occurrence of purposive behavior may, in principle, be explained without assigning a special explanatory role to purposive concepts. Moreover, Hull's commitment to a nonteleological or nonpurposive mode of explanation set the stage for him to advance a quite different sort of motivational construct. It is apparent that Hull took as his initial task in the 1930s the development of a nonpurposive explanation of purposive behavior. His use of nonteleological explanatory constructs was compatible with his subsequent development of a theory of motivation that was, in a radical sense, nonpurposive.

Hull's Formal Theory

Hull became committed to a more formal mode of theorizing and sought to develop a hypothetico-deductive theory that would serve as a comprehensive general theory for psychology. Hull's (1943, 1952) formal theory was presented in 1943, and a major revision was published in 1952. The theory held a predominant influence in experimental psychology for at least a decade after its original promulgation. It continued to exert some influence for two decades, but as a formal theory, it has been of little importance in the last decade. With respect to motivation theory, the central motivational construct of the theory, drive, continues to be of importance. In fact, one relatively recent major treatise in motivation (Bolles, 1975), may be read as essentially a criticism of the Hullian theory of drive. Moreover, the issues the drive theory addresses are of enduring relevance, and although a comfortable integration of motivational issues centered around the concept of drive is no longer viable, it is by no means clear that the concept of drive may be totally dismissed as being without empirical foundation. What follows will explicate Hull's theory of drive.

Hull's theory of motivation is, in part, contained in the following equation:

$$D \times {}_sH_r = {}_sE_r$$

D, which stands for drive, is the essential motivational construct in Hullian theory. Drive is a hypothetical variable that, in principle, is assumed to have some quantitative value. The value of drive is assumed to reflect the sum total of all sources of motivation present in a situation. Drive has two components. One component that may be called relevant is typically conceived of as a monotonically increasing function of deprivation. Thus the value of D in a typical animal learning experiment employing hungry animals would increase as deprivation is increased. An animal deprived of food for 23 hours may be presumed to have a higher level of drive than one deprived of food for 3 hours. The second component of D represents the influence of alien or irrelevant sources of motivation. This component may be assumed to reflect the view that sources of drive not related to the particular goal-directed sequence effect performance. Thus a food-deprived animal that receives food for an appropriate response in a learning experiment may be assumed to behave differently if that animal is influenced by a second source of drive such as thirst, sexual deprivation, or fear. Hull assumed that the total level of drive represented the sum of all sources of drive, whether they were relevant or irrelevant in the particular context. Each source of drive or motivation present in a situation will combine with every other source, on this theory, to yield a total value.

The drive construct contains a number of implications for a general theory of motivation. First, within the context of our discussion of motivation as dealing with the issue of purpose in psychology, it is apparent that Hull's commitment to nonpurposive explanations enabled him to propose a theory of motivation that is nonpurposive in an extremely thorough and radical sense. Drive, since it represents the sum of all sources of motivation is a nondirectional and nonpurposive construct. It is sometimes said that drive is a nondirectional energizer; it does not impel an organism toward any goal. Too, Hull's formulation provides for the consideration of a class of motivational problems and experiments that are conducted totally outside the framework of purposive issues.

Before explicating the rest of the formula and the various complexities entailed by it, let us consider some of the suggestions implicit in the construct D per se. The assumption of additivity of different sources of drive permits one to derive hypotheses about experimental results in situations in which two or more presumed sources of drive are present. Second, one can design motivational experiments in which no relevant source of drive is present at all. For example one could study the influence of a totally irrelevant source of drive such as sexual motivation in an experimental situation in which a person was required to perform some cognitive task for a monetary reward. In so far as the theory of drive is valid, the apparently irrelevant source of drive, sexual deprivation, should influence the performance of the individual on the cognitive task.

Hull's theory assumes that drive has a multiplicative influence on $_sH_r$, the symbol for habit strength. Like D, $_sH_r$ is a hypothetical variable to which, in principle, a numerical value may be assigned. Hull assumed that drive has a multiplicative influence on all habits that are present in a situation. $_sE_r$ is a symbol for effective reaction potential. This hypothetical variable is assumed to have a quantitative value determined by the product of drive and habit. Variations in the $_sE_r$ value associated with a particular habit are assumed to influence observable behavior in a variety of ways. For example, as $_sE_r$ increases, the magnitude or amplitude of a response will increase; the probability of occurrence of that response will increase, and the resistance to extinction (i.e., the number of times the response will occur without reinforcement or reward) increases.

Let us consider a simple experiment that Hull used in developing the $D \times {_sH_r} = {_sE_r}$ formula. Perin (1942) and Williams (1938) had studied the behavior of rats in a Skinner box. Rats were deprived of food for 23 hours, and they were permitted to press a bar for reinforcement, food pellets. The rats in different experimental groups were permitted to press the bar a different number of times. Extinction procedures were then instituted. The rats pressed the bar without receiving reinforcement (food pellets) under different conditions of food deprivation varying from 3 to 22 hours. The number of bar presses prior to extinction was noted. Figure 1.2 presents some of these data. Note that resistance to extinction, which is assumed to be a measure of reaction potential, increased up to what is apparently an asymptotic value as the number of reinforcements increased. Note that the curves describing number of responses to extinction as a function of number of reinforcements at 3 and 22 hours of deprivation show increasing divergence. These data are compatible with Hull's assumption that the value of $_sH_r$ is not related to the level of drive present during acquisition. The divergence in the curves is related to the differences in value of D associated with differences in hours of food deprivation. Multiplication of a constant $_sH_r$ by a higher value of D would produce the divergence in the curves that is present in these data.

Perin and Williams in their studies had investigated the effects of various combinations of hours of deprivation and number of reinforcements on resistance to extinction. Hull extrapolated curves representing the number of responses to extinction for a particular number of reinforcements as a function of differences in hours of deprivation. When extrapolated these functions indicated that there would be some resistance to extinction at zero hours of food deprivation. Hull attributed this to the assumption that D was not zero, even though the relevant drive, hunger, at zero hours of food deprivation was assumed to be zero. The positive nonzero value of D was assumed to be related to the presence of irrelevant sources of drive.

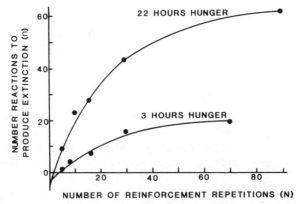

Figure 1.2. *The effects of number of reinforcements and drive on resistance to extinction. (From Hull [1943].)*

To account for the directional influences of motivation on behavior, Hull retained the concept of drive stimuli in his 1943 theory. Motivational deprivation was assumed to create distinctive drive stimuli. These drive stimuli (s_D) were, through past learning experiences, associated with various responses. Thus there exists a subset of habits present in any given situation that may be symbolized as $s_D H_r$. This symbol represents a habit or learned association between a particular drive stimulus and some response. The manipulation of motivation in an experimental situation by such procedures as deprivation of food has two consequences within Hull's 1943 system. On the one hand the deprivation increases the drive level, and as we have seen, drive acts to multiply or energize any and all habits present in a given situation. At the same time the particular drive stimuli associated with the motivational manipulation, hunger stimuli in the case of food deprivation, are introduced, and they elicit responses that have been associated with them. The class of responses elicited are those that have been rewarded or reinforced in the presence of the particular drive stimuli and hence are likely to be those that may be conceived of as being instrumental to the attainment of a relevant goal. Thus the presence of a motivational state is assumed to have both a directional (purposive?) influence on behavior and a nondirectional (nonpurposive) influence.

Chapter *2*

MOTIVATION AND PERFORMANCE: THE DESCENT OF THE HULLIAN TRADITION

This chapter will consider research on the relationship between motivation (conceived in a relatively nonpurposive fashion analogous to Hull's concept of drive) and performance. I will begin with a discussion of a research program that derives directly from an effort to test Hull's theory of drive using human subjects—Spence's research using the Taylor scale. Then research will be discussed that uses Hull's theory of drive as a basis for understanding the effects of the presence of another person (Zajonc's research). After dealing with research efforts based directly on a Hullian model, research will be examined that attempts to relate motivation to cognition pertaining to a class of problems that, for the most part, are not well formulated in Hullian terms.

Spence's Theory of Anxiety as Drive

The impetus to Spence's work was the development of a measure of individual differences in anxiety by J. A. Taylor (1951, 1953) called the Taylor Manifest Anxiety Scale (MAS). The Taylor scale was designed as a measure of drive in the Hullian sense. There are several lines of thought that converge in this conception. Many learning theorists in the Hullian tradition have thought of anxiety as a drive. Most of the research dealing with Hull's theory of drive had used animals, and in order to extend this research to the human level, it became necessary to develop a measure of drive in humans. Taylor turned to anxiety as an important drive and assumed that individual differences in anxiety would be indicative of individual differences in drive level. It was assumed that individuals who were high in anxiety tended to be chronically or constantly anxious and thus would be higher in drive level in any particular situation than individuals who were low in anxiety. Subsequent research tended to support a conception of the MAS as an acute measure of anxiety—that is, as a measure of the tendency to become anxious in certain situations.

The original research attempting to validate the MAS as a measure of drive in the Hullian sense dealt with eyeblink conditioning. The relationship between differences in drive level and eyeblink conditioning is derived as follows: In a simple learning situation in which a single habit is acquired, higher drive should lead to higher levels of excitatory potential than low drive, and this in turn should be reflected in higher levels of performance for the habit that is acquired. Accordingly, individuals who score high on the MAS should condition more rapidly than individuals who score low on the MAS. In addition, the assumption of a multiplicative relationship between drive and habit implies that conditioning curves for individuals who differ in drive level should show progressively larger divergence as conditioning proceeds. K. W. Spence (1964) surveyed the eyeblink-conditioning literature dealing with this problem. He found that, in 21 of 26 studies, subjects who scored high on the MAS showed significantly higher levels of performance than those who scored low. Representative results from two of these studies are presented in Figure 2.1. Note that the curves diverge over trials in accordance with the multiplicative assumption. Note also that conditioning occurred more rapidly when the unconditioned stimulus was higher. In Spence's theory, the magnitude of the unconditioned stimulus, which was assumed to be a noxious stimulus, determined the level of a hypothetical emotional response, R_e—the higher the level of emotional response, the higher the level of drive. Thus, differences in the magnitude of the unconditioned stimulus should have had a similar effect on eyeblink-conditioning performance as differences in scores on the MAS, since these differences each led to differences in emotional response, which, in turn, led to differences in drive.

Spence's review of the literature seems to indicate that the interpretation of the MAS as a measure of drive is supported by the eyeblink-conditioning studies. However, there are a number of qualifications that may be suggested. Scores on the MAS are not a major determinant of performance in this type of task. In order to obtain significant results, it is necessary to use a large number of subjects whose scores are at the extremes of the distribution of MAS scores. Typically, only those subjects whose scores fall in the upper and lower 20% of

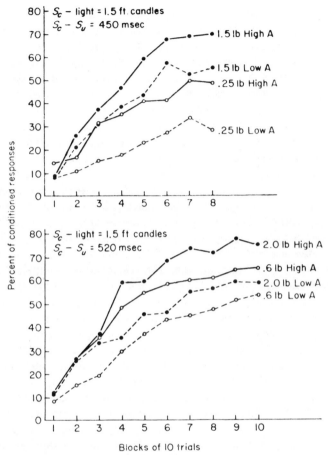

Figure 2.1. *Performance in eyelid conditioning as function of anxiety score and intensity of the unconditioned stimulus. (From K. W. Spence. A theory of emotionally based drive (D) and its relation to performance in simple learning situations. American Psychologist, 1958, 13, 131–141. Copyright 1958 by the American Psychological Association. Reprinted by permission of the publisher.)*

the distribution of scores on the MAS are included in the study. Actually, the question of the magnitude of the relationship between MAS scores and performance in an eyeblink-conditioning task is not crucial. In order to validate the theoretical assumption that scores on the MAS are related to drive, it is sufficient to find that the predicted relationship is obtained. There are more critical issues to be considered, however, in discussing the relationship between scores on the MAS and drive. If the MAS is a measure of drive then the same reasoning that leads to the prediction of superior performance for high scores on the MAS in eyeblink conditioning should suggest that individuals who score high on the MAS ought to exhibit superior performance in any classical conditioning situation in which the acquisition of a single habit is under investigation. Bindra, Paterson, and Strzelecki (1955) reported that differences on the MAS were unrelated to performance in a salivary-conditioning task. In this type of classical conditioning situation, the unconditioned stimulus is not noxious but is rewarding. J. T. Spence and Spence (1966) interpreted these results as indicating that the MAS measured acute anxiety— that is, that conditions of threat would be required to arouse anxiety. Hence, the MAS may be viewed as measuring the tendency to become anxious in threatening situations. Spence suggested on the basis of his review of the literature that relationships between MAS and eyeblink conditioning were maximized under conditions where subjects were made to be fearful and uneasy (for example, isolation of subjects, use of dimly lit rooms with complicated apparatus, etc.). Also, in support of the acute anxiety hypothesis is a study of Mednick (1957) who found no significant relationship between scores on the MAS and stimulus generalization for subjects who had served in several previous experiments. However, a significant relationship was found for those who were experimentally naive. Mednick's results were interpreted by J. T. Spence and Spence (1966) as indicating that subjects lost some of their potential to become anxious while participating in psychological experiments after repeatedly serving as subjects. These results suggest that the interpretations of the MAS as a measure of drive is valid only in threatening situations. K. W. Spence (1956) suggested that different rates of eyeblink conditioning as a function of Unconditioned Stimulus (UCS) intensity might be attributable to differences in the rate of habit formation rather than drive. The reasoning involved here is as follows: An eyeblink response serves to remove a noxious stimulus—the puff of air to the eye—and therefore is a response that is reinforced or rewarded. Under conditions of high puff intensity, the magnitude of the reinforcement is increased since the unconditioned stimulus produces more anxiety. If the growth of habit strength is a function of the magnitude of reinforcement, then the more rapid eyeblink conditioning that occurs when the unconditioned stimulus is high would be attributable to differences in the rate of development of habit strength rather than differences in drive. Subjects who score high on the MAS apparently have a greater capacity to become fearful than subjects who score low on the MAS. Therefore, the former subjects should receive greater amounts of reinforcement whenever they close their eye on the assumption that the puff of air is more noxious to them than to the latter subjects. Accordingly, the more rapid development of eyeblink conditioning among the subjects who score high on the MAS may be attributable to their more rapid development of habit strength.

An alternative explanation that does not refer to drive was advanced by Hilgard, Jones, and Kaplan (1951). They suggested that subjects who scored high on the MAS were worried, defensive individuals who came into the conditioning situation with strong response tendencies to blink and to wince. Since these responses were similar or identical to those that the experimenter wished to condition, they should have shown more rapid conditioning. This interpretation implies that the more rapid conditioning of the subjects who score high on the MAS is due to their initial advantage in habit strength. However, K. W. Spence (1964) found that the differences in performance in eyeblink conditioning between subjects who scored high and those who scored low on the MAS increased over trials. Since the differences were larger at the end of conditioning than at the beginning, it does not seem reasonable to attribute these differences to differences in initial level of habit strength.

This review of the research relating scores on the MAS to eyeblink conditioning indicates that the research has, for the most part, supported the interpretation of the MAS as a measure of drive in the Hullian sense. However, other interpretations that do not involve the drive concept can be developed to explain the relationship between scores on the MAS and eyeblink conditioning.

In addition to relating MAS to eyeblink conditioning, research has dealt with the relationship between the MAS and performance in a variety of other types of complex learning tasks. The term *complex* as used in this contest involves a single habit as in the classical conditioning situation. Predictions may be derived relating drive to performance on several types of tasks. The simplest extension of the Spence theory to a complex task involves a task in which several discrete habits are acquired and the various habits are acquired in isolation from each other. One type of task of this type is a noncompetitional, paired-associate learning task. In this task subjects must learn a list of paired associated—that is, the subject must learn to give the correct response each time a stimulus is presented. If the lists fulfill three criteria, unambiguous predictions can be made, to the effect that subjects who score high on the MAS will learn the list more rapidly than those who score low. The criteria are as follows:

1. The similarity among the stimuli must be minimal.
2. The similarity among responses must be minimal.
3. The intrapair relationship between stimulus and response must be minimal.

These criteria theoretically imply a situation in which the learning of each stimulus and response pair may be treated as the acquisition of a discrete habit that minimally interferes with or affects the acquisition of any other response pair. Furthermore, the third criterion creates a situation in which the initial habit strength for any stimulus–response connection is close to zero. Under these conditions, subjects who score high on the MAS (and who are therefore assumed to be high in drive) should learn the list more rapidly than those who score low. There should be little or no difference in performance at the start of the task when habit strength is close to zero. As the task progresses the difference between groups of high and low scorers on the MAS should increase with the group of high scorers on the MAS showing increasingly superior performance. Results in this type of learning generally supported these predictions (see K. W. Spence, 1958; J. A. Taylor, 1958; J. A. Taylor & Chapman, 1955). At least one study failed to support this prediction (Kamin & Fedorchaik, 1957).

It is also possible to design paired-associate tasks in which high drive should produce poorer performance than low drive. One such task involves a list in which some of the stimulus items are similar in meaning to other stimulus items. In addition some stimulus response pairs have high initial associative connections (e.g., tranquil–placid), whereas other pairs use stimuli that are related to stimuli in the high associative pairs but use response members which have low associative relationship to these stimuli (e.g., serene–headstrong). For these latter stimulus–response pairs, Spence assumes that, on the beginning trials of the learning situation, there will be a competition of response between the response acquired to similar stimuli on the high associative pairs and the correct response. The subject may be expected to acquire the correct responses for the high associative pairs more rapidly than the correct responses for the low associative pairs. This follows from the expectation that the initial habit strength for the latter responses is lower. Thus, for example, the subject ought to learn the response 'placid' to the stimulus 'tranquil' more rapidly than the response 'headstrong' to the stimulus 'serene'. During the early trials of the learning situation, these differential learning rates should create a situation of response competition. Thus, when confronted with the stimulus for a low associative pair, the subject should have a tendency to make one of two responses—the correct response or an incorrect response that is the response acquired to the similar stimulus in a high associative pair. In the early trials of learning, the habit strength associated with the incorrect response (e.g., "placid") could be higher than the habit strength associated with the correct response ("headstrong"). What would be the effect of differences in drive on the probability of saying the correct response? According to the Hull–Spence theory, drive multiplies all habits that are present in a particular situation. Therefore, in this situation the excitatory potential for both the correct and incorrect response would be higher under high drive conditions than under low drive conditions. However, the algebraic difference between the excitatory potentials increases as drive increases—that is, under high drive conditions, the differences between the excitatory potentials for habits that differ in their strength will be greater than under low Drive conditions. It follows from K. W. Spence's (1956, 1958) theory that the respective probabilities of making different responses are a function of the differences between their excitatory potential. If two responses have unequal habit strengths, then the probability of making the response whose habit strength is greater is increased when the difference between the excitatory potential for that response and its competitor is increased. Therefore, under high drive conditions, the probability of making that response whose habit strength is highest is greater than under low drive conditions. These considerations enable us to make predictions about the performance of subjects who differ in scores on the MAS in the paired-associate learning task. Subjects who score high on the MAS (and who are therefore high in drive) should make more incorrect responses than subjects low on the MAS during the early trials on the low associative stimulus–response pairs. During the later trials, as learning progresses, the habit strength for the correct response for the low associative pairs should become higher than the habit strength for the competing incorrect response. During these later trials the probability of a correct response for subjects who score high on the MAS on the low associative pairs should be higher than the probability of a correct response for those who score low on the MAS. Therefore, restricting the analysis to the low associative pairs we should expect superior performance on the early trials for subjects who score low on the MAS and superior performance on the later trials for subjects who score high. There is some evidence supporting the first part of the prediction (K. W. Spence, Farber, & McFann, 1956; K. W. Spence, Taylor, & Ketchel, 1956), and there is also some negative evidence (Lovaas, 1960).

Goulet (1968) presented a cogent analysis of the relationship between drive and verbal learning. He argued that many of the studies of this problem failed to adequately consider some of the variables that may influence performance on these tasks. He indicated that psychologists interested in paired-associate learning had treated this type of situation as one in which there were two functionally different learning tasks or stages—response learning and associative learning. The response stage involves the learning of the list of response units, and the associative stage involves the learning of the "hook up" of each response to its appropriate stimulus (Underwood & Schulz, 1960). This analysis implies that Spence's deduction that more incorrect responses would be given to low associative pairs early in learning by high MAS subjects is not necessarily valid. High drive should facilitate the response-learning stage—that is, under high drive conditions, subjects should have better learning of the separate responses. Competitional effects among responses would be restricted to the associative stage of learning. Thus, on the early trials of a paired-associate learning task, high drive should on the one hand facilitate the learning of the appropriate response units and then lead to poorer performance during the associative stage for the stimuli eliciting incorrect competitional responses with dominant response strength. Since differences in drive have opposite effects, no unambiguous prediction may be derived for this task.

A similar confounding exists with respect to some transfer-learning situations that have been used to test Spence's theory. One type of transfer experiment deals with the A–B, A–C paradigm. In this situation the subject learns a list of paired associates and is then presented with a second list consisting of the same stimuli but different responses. In one experiment designed to test Spence's theory, Standish and Champion (1960) gave subjects an A–B list consisting of pairs of high association value. The A–C list consisted of pairs of low association value. In this situation one would expect that, during the initial trials of learning on the A–C list, habit strengths for incorrect B responses would be higher than the habit strengths for correct C responses. This implies that subjects high in drive should show poorer performance during the learning of the A–C list on the early trials than subjects low in drive. Increasing drive should increase the probability of occurrence of the dominant but incorrect responses. As learning progresses on the A–C list, the correct or C response should eventually develop greater habit strength than the incorrect B response, and this should lead to superior performance for the high drive group later in learning. Using the MAS as a measure of drive, Standish and Champion obtained data supporting these predictions. However, Goulet (1968) pointed out that this deduction fails to consider the two-stage analysis of paired-associate learning that implies that high drive should facilitate the learning of the response units during the learning of the A–C list and that this factor should lead to superior learning for the high drive subjects early in learning. Thus, the deduction is in part confounded. Goulet presented several paradigms that permitted more refined tests of the relationship between drive and verbal learning.

There exists one study that provides a test of the Spence theory that avoids these problems. Spielberger and Smith (1966) studied behavior in a serial-learning task. Subjects were presented with a list of 12 nonsense syllables of low intralist similarity; they were required to anticipate the next syllable in the list and were given 26 trials in which to learn the list of 12 nonsense syllables. Spielberger and Smith analyzed the results separately for different trial blocks and for different syllables. They designated nonsense syllables in position 1, 2, 3, and 12 and easy words since these syllables elicited the smallest number of errors. Nonsense syllables in serial positions 6, 7, 8, and 9 were designated hard words, since they elicited the greatest number of errors. Note that the hard words are in the middle of the list. This agrees well with the usual results for serial-learning tasks in which items in the middle of the list are more difficult to learn than items at the beginning or end of the list. This finding is usually explained by assuming that items in the middle of the list are subject to greater competition than items at the beginning and end of the list. In this situation the following predictions can be made. For easy words (i.e., for words where response competition is at a minimum), there should be little difference between subjects who differ in drive during the early stages of the experiment since habit strength would be close to zero. As learning progresses and habit strength increases, subjects high in drive should exhibit increasingly superior performance relative to subjects low in drive. For hard words, subjects high in drive should show inferior performance early in learning. This follows from the assumption that response competition exists and that for these words incorrect competing responses are likely to be dominant (i.e., have higher habit strength) early in learning. As learning progresses the habit strength for the correct responses should become dominant and subjects high in drive should eventually exhibit superior performance on the hard words. Figure 2.2 presents the results obtained by Spielberger and Smith (1966). An examination of the data indicates that their results for subjects who differed on the MAS are in complete accord with the predictions.

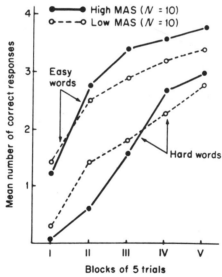

Figure 2.2. *Mean number of correct responses given by high and low subjects on successive trial blocks for easy and hard words. The easy words appeared in serial positions 1, 2, 3, and 12; the hard words appeared in serial positions 6, 7, 8. (From C. D. Spielberger and L. H. Smith. Anxiety (drive), stress, and serial position effects in serial-verbal learning. Journal of Experimental Psychology, 1966, 72, 589–595. Copyright 1966 by the American Psychological Association Reprinted by permission of the publisher and authors.)*

There have been a number of attempts to explain the relationship between scores on the MAS and performance in complex tasks without reference to differences in drive level. Child (1954) suggested that differences in behavior between subjects who differed on the MAS were to be explained not in terms of the effects of drive per se but in terms of differences in drive stimuli—that is, the characteristic stimuli associated with any drive state. Child argued that states of high anxiety have associated with them heightened autonomic responses and various covert verbalizations unrelated to the task. These drive stimuli detract from subjects attention to the task and are considered task-irrelevant. Accordingly, high anxiety subjects may be expected to perform more poorly in complex tasks requiring attention and concentration. This type of hypothesis explains the poorer performance of high anxiety subjects in complex tasks, but it does not, in any simple fashion, explain the superior performance of high anxiety subjects in complex tasks. Let us consider, as a concrete example, the findings of the Spielberger and Smith (1966) study. One could explain the initial superiority of the low anxiety subjects on the hard words by arguing that they were unable to adequately concentrate on these difficult items. Similarly, one could argue that the relative lack of difference in performance on the easy words at the beginning of the experiment could be explained by arguing that the distracting effects of the task-irrelevant responses had relatively little effect on the acquisition of easy words that did not require considerable concentration. Also, the relatively greater improvement in performance for the high anxiety subjects over trials might be explained by assuming that they become less anxious as the task progresses and therefore they are able to pay greater attention to the relevant aspects of the experimental situation. What *cannot* be explained by appeal to the drive stimulus theory is the superior performance of the subjects high in anxiety on both easy and hard words towards the latter part of the experiment. Task-irrelevant responses can detract from performance, but they cannot improve performance. Spence always accepted the possibility that differences in the MAS might reflect both differences in drive level and differences in drive stimuli. What has been at issue in the discussion of the literature relating differences in the MAS to performance is the possibility of dispensing with the drive construct completely. The review of the literature presented here suggests that appeal to the drive concept does provide a more parsimonious explanation of this total body of literature.

Limitations of Spence's Theory

Spence's research program failed to explore a number of additional possible deductions and complexities inherent in the Hullian theory. Kausler and

Trapp (1959) noted in a criticism of this work that there was no attempt to show that other sources of drive would influence performance on these tasks in the same way as scores on the MAS. The argument that the MAS is a measure of drive would be strengthened if it could be shown that other manipulations of drive produced differences in performance comparable to those produced by individual differences in the scores on the MAS. Ideally there should be a large body of established empirical findings that indicate the effect of manipulating different sources of drive on a variety of experimental tasks. Experiments involving the MAS have often simultaneously sought to establish what the effect of differences in drive would be in any given task and that the MAS was in fact a measure of drive. Since the effects of differences in drive on performance in any given task are ambiguous, it is not clear that the differences in performance of individuals who differ on the MAS invariably reflect differences in drive.

A study relevant to this issue was performed by Franks (1957). Franks found that subjects who had been deprived of food, water, and tobacco for 24 hours did not show more rapid eyeblink conditioning than subjects who were not deprived. These results suggest that traditional measures of drive (or at least those that are traditional in animal psychology, namely deprivation) do not relate to eyeblink conditioning. This implies either that drive is not related to eyeblink conditioning or that deprivation is not related to drive. In either case there is an ambiguity and a difficulty in the interpretation of anxiety as a drive.

Spence's research program neglected to consider additional aspects of Hull's theory that complicate deductions relating drive to performance. An important theoretical variable not considered was the concept of a threshold of response evocation. Increases in drive are assumed to increase the strength of the responses present in a situation. However, increases in drive do not change the threshold for response evocation. Therefore, increases in drive can increase the number of responses with response strengths above the threshold for response evocation leading to an increase in the number of responses present in a situation. Note that this influence of drive can operate in opposition to the tendency of high drive states to increase the probability of occurrence of dominant responses relative to all other responses. It is possible to define the kinds of experimental situations in which one of these two opposing theoretical mechanisms is likely to be dominant. In a situation in which only a limited set of responses are possible and in which all responses are above threshold level—that is, all responses have an initial probability of occurrence greater than zero—increases in drive should increase the probability of occurrence of dominant responses relative to all other responses. In a situation in which there are many responses that could occur but in which the set of all such responses includes many responses below a threshold of response evocation, increases in drive could, theoretically, increase the number of different responses above threshold leading to an increase in the number of responses observed and the possibility of a reduction in the probability of occurrence of dominant responses.

Brody (1964a, 1964b, 1971; Brody, Petersen, Upton, & Stabile, 1967) reported the results of studies using the Taylor scale that indicate that subjects who score high on the MAS may exhibit more variable responses than individuals who score low. For example, in one of his studies, subjects were presented 10 times with a list of stimulus words and were asked to write the first word they thought of in response to the stimulus word (Brody et al., 1967). The number of different words given in response to each stimulus word was noted. It was found that subjects who scored high on the MAS tended to use a larger number of different words in their repeated responses than those who scored low on the MAS. These results may be explained by Hullian theory as follows: Assume that there exists a large number of potential word associates for stimulus words for subjects in this situation. Many of these responses are below threshold. Increases in drive should increase the number of responses above threshold leading to an increase in response variability.

This interpretation would be buttressed if one could show that an additional source of drive, preferably an experimentally manipulated drive source, would lead to the same results. Brody et al. (1967, Experiment 2) used drugs as another source of drive in this experimental situation. They used d-amphetamine as a drug presumed to increase drive and arousal and meprobramate as a drug presumed to decrease anxiety and arousal. They found, in line with expectations, that subjects given meprobramate did indeed use a smaller number of different word associates than those given a plecebo. In addition, subjects given d-amphetamine used a larger number of different word associates than those given a placebo. These results suggest that sources of drive other than anxiety can increase the number of responses above a threshold of response evocation where a large potential pool of such responses exists.

Brody (1964a) was able to demonstrate higher response variability for subjects who scored high on the MAS than for the ones who scored low in another experimental situation. In this situation subjects were told that they were in an experiment dealing with subliminal perception and that they would be presented with either a circle or a square on each of 100 trials. Actually no stimuli were presented to all in order to study the influence of presumed drive effects on response probabilities in the absence of stimulus influences. Brody studied the probability of occurrence of each of the 32 possible sequences of a length of 5 contained in each subjects response series. He found that those who scored high on the MAS tended to have more random (more variable) response sequences than the ones who scored low. Subjects who scored low on the MAS scale tended to omit certain possible response sequences. These results may be interpreted by appeal to Hullian theory. If certain possible response sequences are below a threshold of response evocation, increases in drive could increase response strength and increase their probability of occurrence thus leading to more variable response sequences.

The research reviewed indicates that there are ambiguities surrounding the deceptively simple assertion that individual differences in anxiety may be conceived of as individual differences in drive level. The relationships between variations in drive and performance are not always clear. Complexities created by multistage conceptions of learning as well as the influences of threshold concepts tend to render a number of simple deductions complex.

Drive Theory of Social Facilitation

In 1898 Triplett found that individuals who performed a simple task with others present worked more rapidly than individuals who worked on the task alone. For the next four decades the problem of the influence of others on performance was a central topic in experimental social psychology. As is often the case in psychology, interest in this topic peaked, and little research dealing with this issue was performed from the late 1930s until 1965. The 30-year hiatus may have been prompted merely by almost inexplicable waxing and waning of fashion, or perhaps, more rationally, by a seemingly contradictory pattern of results that defied theoretical integration. In particular, studies of the influence of others on performance produced contradictory results sometimes leading to performance increments and other times leading to performance decrements.

In 1965 Zajonc reviewed this literature, and following a suggestion by Allport (1924) to the effect that the presence of others led to performance increments in simple tasks and performance decrements in complex tasks, he argued that this body of research might be integrated by assuming that the presence of others tends to increase drive in the Hullian sense. In other words, where the correct response in a situation was likely to be a dominant response in the habit family hierarchy, the presence of others should facilitate performance by virtue of an increase in drive that has a multiplicative relation to habits resulting in an increase in the probability of occurrence of dominant responses. Similarly, the presence of others while one is performing a task is likely to lead to poorer performance on a "complex task" in which the correct response is presumed to be nondominant in the habit family hierarchy.

Zajonc's hypothesis stimulated a large body of research dealing with social facilitation effects. Geen and Gange (1977) reviewed this literature and concluded that Zajonc's theory remains the most parsimonious single explanation (although perhaps not an all-encompassing one) of these phenomena (see also Weiss & Miller, 1971).

Research designed to test the drive theory interpretation of social facilitation is in one respect similar to Spence's attempt to test the hypothesis that individual differences in anxiety reflect differences in drive. That is, the empirical effects are not invariably robust, but in general they appear supportive of the theory. Several studies illustrate this somewhat inconsistent pattern of results. A particularly clear demonstration in favor of the hypothesis was reported by Zajonc and Sales (1966). They exposed subjects to a list of words. They varied the frequency of exposure to the words. They assumed, plausibly, that words that had been exposed frequently would have greater habit strength than words exposed infrequently. In the second part of their experiment, subjects were asked to recognize these words when they were presented briefly using a tachistoscope. In point of fact, the task was a pseudorecognition task since stimuli were not presented. If drive theory is correct, an increase in drive should increase the probability of occurrence of dominant responses. Hence those words presented more often in the initial phase of the experiment should have been used more frequently in the second pseudorecognition phase of the experiment. Figure 2.3 presents the results of the Zajonc and Sales study and indicates that the curve describing the increase in the response probabilities of words as a function of frequency of prior exposure exhibits steeper slope for subjects who performed the task in the presence of another rather than alone. This result is exactly what would be expected given the drive theory explanation.

A study that provides only equivocal support for the drive theory view was reported by Matlin and Zajonc (1968). They asked subjects to perform a word-associate task in which they were asked to give the first word they thought of in response to a stimulus word. They assumed that any stimulus word elicits a complex set of responses forming a habit family hierarchy. The dominant responses in the hierarchy were likely to be common frequent associates of each stimulus word. Therefore, they predicted that an increase in drive associated with the presence of another person would tend to increase the probability of occurrence of dominant common word associates. In their study each subject performed the task under two conditions: alone and in the presence of another. They found the predicted effect when subjects initially performed the task in the presence of another followed by performance alone. However, in the reverse or counterbalanced condition in which performance alone was followed by performance in the presence of another, the predicted increase in the use of common associates was not obtained (see also Blank, Staff, & Shaver, 1976).

One of the issues that has come to dominate more recent research in this area concerns the reason for the influence of others on presumed changes in

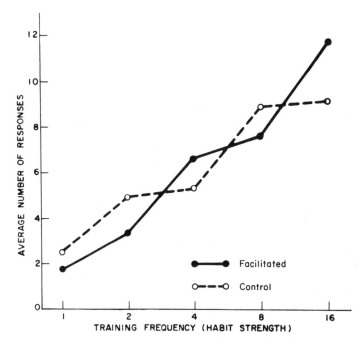

Figure 2.3. *Number of responses of different frequency classes emitted during the pseudorecognition series, averaged over subjects and over trial-blocks. (From Zajonc and Sales [1966].)*

drive. Cottrell (1968, 1972) argued that the presence of others leads to increases in drive only under conditions in which there is apprehension about the evaluation of performance. Thus, for Cottrell, the increase in drive is mediated by a cognitive variable and is not attributable to the mere presence of others. Zajonc, on the other hand, maintained that the "mere presence" of another is a sufficient condition for an increase in drive level even where evaluation apprehension and concern for performance is not present. Studies exist that support both of these contradictory positions. Cottrell, Wack, Sekaiak, and Rittle (1968) reported the results of a study in which subjects were presented with the pseudorecognition task used by Zajonc and Sales under three conditions. In one condition subjects performed the task alone; in a second condition they performed the task in the presence of an audience of two people; the final condition was designated a "mere presence" condition. In this condition the task was performed in the presence of two students who were wearing blindfolds to prepare themselves to participate in a perceptual experiment. Table 2.1 presents the results of this experiment. Note that the data indicate that the behavior of subjects in the alone and in the mere

TABLE 2.1
Slope of Function Relating Response Emission to Training Frequency for Three Conditions

Alone	Mere presence	Audience
.257	.292	.488

Source: Cottrell, Wack, Sekarak, and Rittle, 1968.

presence conditions was similar. The effects of hypothetical increases in drive on increased use of responses presumed to be dominant in the habit family hierarchy occurred only in the presence of others where the possibility for evaluation apprehension exists. These results support Cottrell's theoretical interpretation.

Markus (1978) reported a study supporting Zajonc's position. In her experiment, female subjects were required to put on clothes in preparation for an experiment in which all subjects were to be dressed alike. There were three conditions used that parallel those used by Cottrell *et al.* (1968). Subjects performed the task alone; they performed it while being watched by another person; or they performed it in a condition in which another person was present but working on some experimental apparatus with his or her back to the subject. Markus measured the time required to perform familiar acts of dressing and the time required to perform unfamiliar acts of dressing. She assumed that increases in drive would increase the probability of occurrence of dominant responses thus leading to more rapid performance of familiar overlearned acts of dressing and greater difficulty due to interference from dominant but incorrect responses in performing unfamiliar acts of dressing. Her results are presented in Table 2.2. Note that subjects in the condition representing mere presence ("incidental audience") demonstrated the theoretically expected effects of an increase in drive. Furthermore, their performance was comparable to that of subjects in the condition where evaluation apprehension could at least theoretically be presented although it was not likely to represent a powerful influence since the subjects were led to believe that the task they were performing was preliminary to the main experimental task.

Taken together the studies that have been briefly reviewed suggest that mere presence can at least occasionally serve as a sufficient condition for an increase in the level of drive. They also suggest that evaluation apprehension may independently increase drive level. Furthermore, all of the studies combined provide evidence for drivelike influences on performance independent of the question of the mechanism by which the increase in drive is indicated. The studies provide evidence for the influence of a nondirectional energizer that is the core meaning associated with the theoretical construct of drive. It is hard to see how a purposive conception of motivation can encompass these results. For example, the behavioral effects of the mere presence of another reported by Markus do not appear to be instances of goal-directed actions. Rather they appear as the diffuse consequences of the instantiation of a central state. At the same time these results do not address a number of central implications of drive theory. Although they provide evidence of a nondirectional energizer, they do not deal with the additivity of different sources of drive, and they do not derive implications dealing with some of the more complex potential influences of drive on performance (e.g., threshold phenomena).

Alternative Conceptions of the Influence of Drive on Performance

Although Hull's theory of drive continues to be used as a basis for such contemporary research efforts as the attempt to understand the influence of the presence of other individuals on performance, the theory also has been replaced to a considerable degree by different theories of the influence of nonspecific arousal states on performance. The historical roots of this descent of the "Drive × Habit" theory derive again from alternative formulations suggested by Hull and Tolman. In his article "Cognitive Maps in Rats and Men" Tolman (1948) asserted that excessive levels of motivation reduce the width of the cognitive map. Tolman's assertion suggests that motivation influences perception or, in more fashionably modern terminology, the information-processing capacities of an organism. States of high drive, on Tolman's formulation, lead to a narrowing of the focus of attention such that organisms fail to acquire the degree of information about the environment that they are

TABLE 2.2
Mean Time (in Seconds) to Complete Well-learned and Transfer Responses

	Alone (A)	Incidental audience (A)	Audience (A)	Difference (A) − (B)	Difference (B) − (C)
Well-learned responses	16.46^*_a	$13.49_{a,b}$	11.70_b	−2.97	−1.79
Transfer responses	28.85_c	32.73_d	33.94_d	3.88	1.21

Source: Markus, 1978.

$N = 15$ observations per cell.

*Means with different subscripts are significantly different from each other at the .05 level by Newman–Keuls test.

likely to acquire under lower drive conditions. Note that his generalization deals not with changes in response probabilities but rather with changes in what is learned or noticed about the environment. However, there is at least a superficial relationship between Tolman's and Hull's theories. As noted, increases in drive can increase the probability of occurrence of dominant responses leading to a reduction in response variability and to an increase in the repetition (i.e., a decrease in response variability) of behavior. Although the notion of the width of the cognitive map is metaphorically evocative and empirically vague, it is at least redolent of the notion that a reduction in width would be accompanied by a reduction in the variability of behavior. Tolman's theory addresses the cognitive basis of behavior, and Hull's theory addresses the behavior itself. However, both theories do appear to contain a similar theoretical notion.

Tolman's notion corresponds to a somewhat more precise theoretical statement developed by Easterbrook in 1959. Easterbrook asserted that the range of "cue utilization" is inversely related to arousal or drive. The reduction in cue utilization is assumed to be analogous to a shrinkage in the perceptual field leading to an increased focus on central events and the failure to attend to or be capable of receiving information about less relevant cues. Easterbrook's generalization is used to explain the oldest low-level empirical generalization in the psychology of motivation—the Yerkes–Dodson Law (see Broadhurst, 1959; Yerkes & Dodson, 1908), which contains two generalizations:

1. The relationship between motivation and performance on a task is an inverted U function. This implies that for any task there exists a level of motivation that is below the level of motivation required for optimal performance and that for any task there exists a level of motivation that is above the level required for optimal performance.
2. The optimal level of motivation associated with a task is inversely related to task complexity. This implies that a relatively high level of motivation could facilitate performance on a simple task and impede performance on a complex task.

Note that this second part of the Yerkes–Dodson Law is compatible with Hullian theory, whereas the first part of the law is not generally thought to be compatible with the theory. According to Hullian theory if a correct response is dominant and if all responses permitted are above the threshold of response evocation, drive is positively related to performance, and there is no level of drive that will lead to decreased levels of performance. Figure 2.4 presents a graphical representation of both aspects of the Yerkes–Dodson Law and indicates the type of relationship suggested by the combined version of the law. Easterbrook attempted to derive the Yerkes–Dodson Law from his

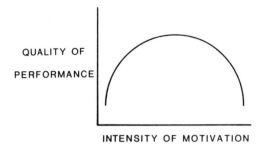

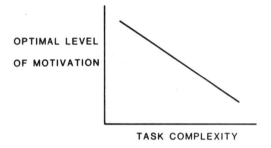

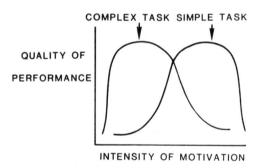

Figure 2.4.   *The Yerkes–Dodson Law.*

generalization by noting that at low levels of motivation or arousal, organisms would have a wide range of cue utilization including a high probability of attending to cues that were not task-relevant as well as cues that were task-relevant. The diffuse pattern of attention would interfere with optimal performance. As motivation increased, the reduction of cue utilization was presumed to proceed by the elimination of attention to task-irrelevant cues. The focus upon task-relevant cues improved performance. As motivation increased further, the reduction of cue utilization might include task-relevant cues, and the failure to attend to these cues reduced the quality of performance. Easterbrook explained the second component of the Yerkes–Dodson Law by appeal to the notion that task complexity was positively related to the number of cues required for successful task performance. Since simple tasks do not require an individual to pay attention to many cues for successful performance, relatively high levels of cue reduction attributable to high states of arousal will not necessarily adversely affect the quality of performance. Similar reductions in cue utilization will, however, lead to a reduced level of performance in complex tasks that, by definition, require an individual to use a large number of cues for optimal task performance.

Easterbrook's paper summarized a large body of evidence in favor of his generalization. A particularly vivid empirical result cited by Easterbrook is presented in a study reported by Bursill (1958). Bursill used a central task in which a subject was required to track a moving target by using a pointer that the subject attempted to superimpose upon the target. Subjects were also presented with a second task to perform simultaneously. The second task required them to report the occurrence of an occasional illumination of a series of six lights arranged around the display for the central task. Subjects performed the task when the room was at normal temperature or under conditions in which the room was heated to an uncomfortably above-normal temperature. Although performance on the central task was not appreciably affected by the presence of high heat, performance on the peripheral task was affected. In particular, Bursill reported that the probability of noticing the occurrence of those lights most removed from the central display was reduced. It was as if attention had narrowed to the central task and this "funneling" of attention rendered the individual incapable of responding to those aspects of the task that were peripheral.

Easterbrook's generalization, like Tolman's preceding generalization about the width of the cognitive map, appears to be focused on perceptual rather than response phenomena. However, the separation of perception and response is not made precisely; in fact, it is thoroughly confounded. Easterbrook (1959) defined a cue in terms of the occurrence of a response. He asserted: "A singular cue can be said to have been used when a related response has occurred. In multicue situations, a particular cue can be said to have been used if the ensuing response takes a form which it normally takes when that cue is present and normally does not take in its absence [pp. 188–189]." Thus it is apparent that on Easterbrook's analysis, cue utilization is inferred from responses and that a motivational influence of a nonspecific arousal state that influences responses is not conceptually distinguishable from a motivational influence on cue utilization that is inferred from responses. Thus the distinction between Easterbrook's generalization and the Hullian theory is not precise given Easterbrook's formulation of his hypothesis.

It is possible to design research that addresses this conceptual confounding between perception and the responses from which perception is inferred. One way of approaching this issue is to use an experimental task in which no stimulus is present at all. Changes in response probabilities under such circumstances clearly are not attributable to changes in capacity to process task-relevant stimulus information. Zajonc and Sales's study provides such an example. Another clear example of this type of study is one reported by Kuethe and Eriksen (1957). In their study subjects who differed in their scores on an individual difference measure of anxiety that was highly related to the MAS were presented with an extrasensory perception task in which they were required to guess which of the 11 digits, 1–11, was being presented to them. Actually there was no stimulus presented at all. They found that subjects who scored high in the test of anxiety tended to have less variable or less equiprobable response sequences than those whose scale scores on the anxiety measure were low. These results can be explained by appeals to the Hullian theory of drive, assuming that all of the response associated with the digits 1–11 were above threshold for subjects in the study. This assumption is warranted since subjects used all the responses at least once. Assuming further that the responses had unequal response strengths, Hullian theory implies that increase in drive would tend to increase the probability of occurrence of dominant responses leading to a more unbalanced or unequal set of response probabilities. Kuethe and Ericksen's results suggest that drive states can influence responses independent of the influence of information-processing capabilities. Thus these results are not readily encompassed by Easterbrook's generalization.

A second approach to the conceptual confounding that has been considered involves the attempt to design experiments that analytically isolate the influence of perceptual and response effects. Eriksen and Wechsler (1955) reported the results of such a study. In their study subjects were presented with a set of 11 squares differing in size. It is well known that subjects can reliably distinguish approximately seven objects differing in only one dimension. The squares were presented to the subjects singly, and they were required to say which of the 11 different-sized squares was being presented to them at that particular trial. Since 11 stimuli were used, the task exceeded the discrimination abilities of the subjects in the study. The subjects were assigned to one of two groups: a high-drive group in which they received electric shocks at random intervals and a low-drive group who did not receive the shocks. The experimental task permits the derivation of measures of perceptual capacity and measures of changes in response probability that are independent. The subjects in the shock condition did not differ in their perceptual discrimination performance from those in the nonshock condition—that is, the probability of accurate assignment of a stimulus to its correct response category was not affected by the presence of shock. However, when the response probabilities were examined independent of consideration of their respective relationships to the stimuli actually presented, it was found that the presence of shock tended to decrease the variability of responses leading to a less equiprobable distribution of responses. Evidently certain responses had higher initial response probabilities than others, and when a subject was in a state of uncertainty with respect to which of two or more stimuli had actually been presented, there was an increased tendency under the high-drive condition to resolve the uncertainty by choosing that response whose initial response strength was high. Thus the Eriksen and Wechsler study indicates that high drive can change response probabilities in a setting in which high drive does not influence an individual's ability to process information about the environment. It should be noted that the information-processing task presented to the subject is, in ways that may be important, different from the task presented to subjects in an experiment like Bursill's. In the Eriksen and Wechsler study, subjects were presented with a single stimulus and given ample time to examine the stimulus. The task did not involve the deployment of attention or the ability to notice diverse features of a complex array of stimuli. Rather, the perceptual task involved the ability to fractionate or discriminate among a set of discrete stimuli presented singly. In Bursill's experiment subjects were presented with a complex stimulus array that taxed an individual's ability to notice all of the relevant information. The task decidedly focused upon issues related to the deployment of attention.

Broadbent (1971) discussed the implications of a series of experiments designed to distinguish between motivational influences on stimulus processing and motivational influences on responses. Broadbent began his analysis with the discussion of a study by Glucksberg (1962). Glucksberg presented subjects with two words simultaneously for brief stimulus durations using a tachistoscope. Each word was printed in a different color. The subject was told to identify a word of a particular color. One word was relatively easy to identify (it was a common word and was printed boldly), and the other word was more difficult to identify since it was uncommon and printed less boldly. Glucksberg found financial incentives improved the performance of subjects on easy words and decreased the performance of subjects on difficult words. These results appear to support a Hullian theory, assuming that the presence of financial incentives increases motivation (drive). Subjects performing the task under relatively high drive conditions should have been more likely to use dominant responses that are, with relatively high probability, correct for the task of identifying the easy word and incorrect when the subject was required to identify the difficult word.

Broadbent reported that he and Gregory were able to essentially replicate Glucksberg's results using the presence of noise as a nonspecific source of motivational arousal. Broadbent described the results of a series of experiments involving variations on the experimental procedure used by Glucksberg. On a Hullian analysis of the phenomenon reported by Glucksberg, the use of instructions requiring a subject to attend to one of the two words printed in different colors is not a relevant feature of the task. Glucksberg indicated that the Hullian theoretical analysis implies that similar results would be obtained in a task that does not involve perceptual selectivity. If subjects were presented with the stimulus words used in his experiment singly, the influence of drive on responses should have led to better performance for the easy words and poorer performance for the task of identifying the difficult word. Broadbent reported that he and Gregory failed to find any relationships between the presence of financial incentives and the ease with which subjects were able to identify tachistoscopic presentations of common or uncommon words presented singly. These results do not support the Hullian analysis. Broadbent and Gregory went on to design a study in which the feature of perceptual selectivity was present in the absence of response biases. Subjects were presented with a mixture of red and white digits, and they were required to identify all of the digits of a particular color. They found that noise tended to decrease the quality of performance in this task. The effects of noise were not attributable to changes in response probabilities but appeared to be attributable to a perceptual influence. It appears that noise acted to prevent the subject from focusing on those stimuli that were defined as being correct. These results suggests, at least for the case of noise and financial incentives, and in this type of experiment, that performance decrements associated with motivational manipulation are more likely to involve perceptual effects rather than changes in response probabilities. Although changes in response probabilities in the absence of perceptual influences can be found in certain experiments, thus supporting a Hullian analysis, the Hullian analysis cannot readily encompass the perceptual phenomena associated with the stimulus-selectivity instructions used by Broadbent and Gregory.

G. R. J. Hockey (1970a, 1970b, 1970c) reported several studies using variations of the experimental situation used by Bursill in his demonstration that heat tended to lead to poorer performance in a dual-task situation in which the subject was required to track a moving target while reporting the occurrence of occasionally flashing lights arrayed in the periphery of the visual field. Hockey found that noise would influence performance on this task in a manner analogous to the influence of heat (that is, subjects who performed the task in the presence of noise tended to be less likely to report the occurrence of light flashes, particularly when those flashes were peripheral rather than in the center of the visual field). These results fit the Easterbrook's notions of a funneling of attention. Hockey (1970c) went on to show that the metaphorical interpretation of a narrowing or funneling of attention is not a sufficiently precise interpretation of these results. He designed a study in which subjects performed the dual task under conditions of noise and quiet, and he introduced an additional variable into the experiment—the probability of occurrence of the lights arrayed around the visual field was varied. In one condition the lights flashed with relatively equal probabilities, in the other condition the probabilities were nonequiprobable such that the lights in the center of the field occurred with higher probabilities than the lights in the periphery of the field. Table 2.3 presents the results of this experiment and indicates that the effect of noise on the latency to detect visual signals while performing a tracking task is dependent on the distribution of the probabilities of occurrence of the various stimuli. Note that the data indicate that, when the lights occurred with equal frequency across the visual field, noise induced a relatively constant increase in response latencies. However, under conditions in which central lights occurred with higher frequency than peripheral lights, noise led to a decrease in the time required to report the presence of the light when it was in the center of the visual field and an increase in the time required to report the presence of the light when it was presented peripherally. These results suggest a reinterpretation of the Easterbrook hypothesis. These results suggest that motivation (or noise, at any rate) acts to bias the deployment of attention such that attention is directed to signals with relatively high probability of occurrence. Note that Hockey did not perform the study that would have, with maximum clarity, distinguished between the funneling interpretation and the interpretation of biasing of attention—that is, an experiment in which the stimuli would have been presented in a biased manner such that the stimuli presented in the periphery of the visual field would occur with higher probabilities than the stimuli in the center of the

TABLE 2.3

Mean Detection Latencies for Central (C) and Peripheral (P) Sources, and Mean C–P Differences (in Milliseconds) over the Whole Task

		C	P	C–P
(A) Unbiased	Quiet	1136	1248	−112
	Noise	1181	1291	−110
(B) Biased	Quiet	1136	1346	−210
	Noise	1028	1393	−365
Difference (noise–quiet)				
(A) Unbiased		+45	+43	+2
(B) Biased		−108	+47	−155

Source: G. R. J. Hockey. Signal probability and spatial location as possible bases for increased selectivity in noise. *Quarterly Journal of Experimental Psychology,* 1970, *22,* 37–42.

TABLE 2.4

Mean Sensitivity for No-Shock and Shock Conditions over High and Low Degree of Focus of Attention on the Auditory Cue (HF, LF), and Immediate and Delayed Response (RI, RD) Conditions

Conditions	Sensitivity scores	
	No shock	Shock
HF–RI	3.02	2.63
HF–RD	3.32	2.61
LF–RI	3.13	2.30
LF–RD	3.61	1.60

Source: S. J. Bacon. Arousal and the range of cue utilization. *Journal of Experimental Psychology,* 1974, *102,* 81–87. Copyright 1974 by the American Psychological Association. Reprinted by permission of the publisher and author.

field. If Hockey were correct, then under these conditions, detection latencies would have been decreased for peripheral lights under noise conditions.

Our discussion of the results of Hockey's experiments suggests that experimental tasks may be decomposed into a variety of components that may be differentially affected by motivation. The effect of motivation on performance will depend upon the summative effect of the various component effects. There are three studies that illustrate this sort of analysis clearly. Bacon (1974) reported the results of a dual task experiment in which subjects were required to track a moving stimulus target and to report the occurrence of auditory signals. Motivation was manipulated by the use of random electric shocks. Subjects were instructed to focus their attention on the primary (tracking) or on the secondary task. In addition they were required to report the occurrence of auditory stimuli immediately or under delayed conditions. Table 2.4 presents the results of Bacon's study. When subjects were not asked to focus on the auditory stimuli (the low focus condition) and in addition when subjects were asked for delayed recall of the auditory stimuli, shock tended to impede performance and lower sensitivity. Bacon's results do not suggest a sharp diminution in total attentional capacity or ability to deal with demanding task requirements under shock conditions. Rather the results indicate that the subject's performance on the task was a complex function of task instructions and task requirements interacting with motivational variables. Note that under conditions in which the subject was instructed to attend to the auditory stimuli, the effects of shock were minimal and the requirement of delayed response did not lead to a deterioration of performance under shock conditions.

Only under conditions in which the subject was not instructed to focus attention on the auditory stimuli did shock lead to a deterioration of performance that was particularly marked under conditions in which the responses were delayed. Thus shock appears to have influenced the transfer of information to memory.

Motivational influences upon transfer of information to memory are clearly demonstrated in an experiment reported by Hamilton, Hockey, and Rejman (1977). In their study subjects were required to listen to a series of stimuli and were then asked to report, at unpredictable places, which stimuli had preceded the one at which the request for recall occurred. An examination of the data from their study presented in Figure 2.5 indicates that, irrespective of the rate of stimulus presentation, under noise conditions there was better recall for those stimuli that immediately preceded the stimulus and poorer recall for those stimuli that were more remote in the sequence. These results are in some respects similar to those reported by Bacon in that they indicate that under conditions in which motivation is high, there is a decrease in the retention of information in memory.

Hamilton, Hockey, and Rejman (1977) reported the results of another study that demonstrates differential influences of noise on different components of task performance. In this study subjects were asked to state which letter followed a particular letter in the alphabet. Subjects were asked to indicate the next letter or the second, third, or fourth letter following a particu-

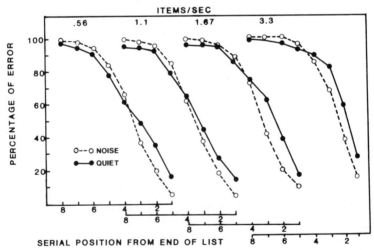

Figure 2.5. Errors in running memory span as a function of stimulus-input rate, serial position, and noise. (From Hamilton, Hockey, and Rejman [1977].)

TABLE 2.5
Storage and Process Conditions in the Closed-System Thinking Task, with Examples of the Task Performed

	Process instruction					
	Add 1		Add 2	Add 3	Add 4	
Storage instruction	Stimulus	Response			Stimulus	Response
Store 0	F	G	—	—	F	J
Store 1	—	—	—	—	—	—
Store 2	—	—	—	—	—	—
Store 3	FBRJ	GCSK	—	—	FBRJ	JFVN

Source: Hamilton, Hockey, and Rejman, 1977.

lar letter. This aspect of their experiment measured the rate required to perform mental operations where the results of the operations need not be stored or retained in memory. In addition they varied the task by presenting subjects with a single letter, two letters, three letters or four letters. Where more than one letter was presented, the subject could not give a response until all of the responses were given simultaneously. Thus the subject was required to hold in memory or store the results of intermediate processing. Table 2.5 presents an outline of the experimental conditions, and Figure 2.6 indicates the results of the experiment, presenting the ratio of the time required to complete the task under noise conditions to the time required to complete the task under conditions of quiet. Note that Figure 2.6 indicates that individuals were able to process information more rapidly under noise than in quiet conditions provided that the subject was not required to store information or retain in memory the results of previous information processing. However, as the retention components of the task became increasingly demanding, performance deteriorated in noise. The preceding studies on the effects of motivation on different components of information-processing inherent in an experimental task are related to other studies in which different possibilities for responding to stimulus material or processing it in different ways are inherent in the task. For example S. Schwartz (1974) presented subjects with lists of words that they were required to recall. The lists contained different semantic categories. Recall of the lists could proceed by recalling the words in the order in which they were presented or by clustering the words in terms of the several semantic categories present in the list. This latter strategy would require a subject to go beyond the information given—that is, to organize the list and to seek relationships among its diverse elements. (By contrast a

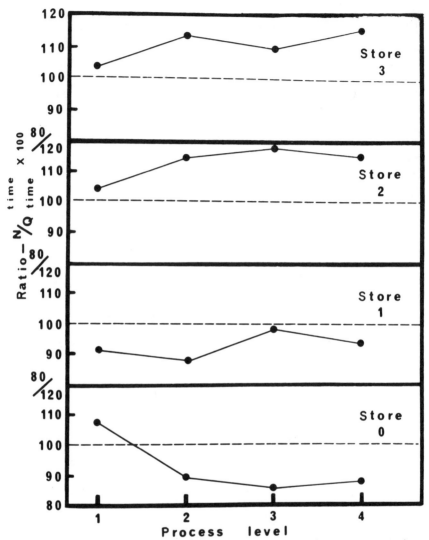

Figure 2.6. *Closed-system thinking performance in noise expressed as a percentage of time taken under quiet conditions. The four panels depict different storage levels. (From Hamilton, Hockey, and Rejman [1977].)*

strategy in which the subject would recall the words in the list in the order in which they were presented would not require the subject to note any relationships among the diverse elements in the list.) Schwartz found that under noise conditions subjects were more inclined to recall the list sequentially and were less likely to cluster the items in the list (see also Daee & Wilding, 1977; Hörmann & Osterkamp, 1966; Mueller, 1979).

It is apparent that motivational variables can affect performance in a variety of ways. Among the effects I have already noted are the following:

1. Motivation can increase the probability of occurrence of certain responses relative to other responses. The responses whose probability of occurrence are increased are presumably those whose initial probability of occurrence is higher than others—that is they are dominant in the habit family hierarchy.

2. Motivation can interfere with the tendency to direct attention to a particular part of the stimulus array.

3. Motivational influences can change the allocation of attention to various parts of the visual field. In particular, motivational variables tend to bias the allocation of attention to various stimulus sources increasing the tendency to sample from stimulus sources whose probability of occurrence is high.

4. Motivational influences may increase memory for stimuli over short periods but appear to decrease the tendency to transfer or hold information about stimuli in memory.

5. Not only does motivation appear to influence transfer of information to memory, but in addition, motivational influences may impede other types of processing of information subsequent to the initial reception and recognition of a stimulus. Schwartz's results suggesting a tendency for individuals to respond to recall stimuli in order òf presentation and not to cluster the stimuli suggests a reduction in the spontaneous processing of information under noise conditions.

The preceding summary is undoubtedly incomplete. In addition it is heavily weighted by a summary of studies that have used noise as a non-specific energizer as a motivational variable. Although some of the generalizations have been replicated or supported by studies using one or more additional sources of motivaion, it is undoubtedly the case that a consideration of a variety of motivational influences in each of the experimental situations that have provided evidence for these generalizations would lead to a situation in which specific generalizations would be modified or contradicted for other motivational variables (that is, all motivational variables do not influence information processing tasks in identical ways). In fact the available empirical literature does not permit the assertion that there exists any single other motivational variable whose influence on performance would, for example, duplicate the influence obtained for noise in a variety of experimental situations.

Critical Evaluation of
Theory of Nondirective Energizers

The discussion of the influence of motivation on performance has left undefined the nature of the diverse class of motivational influences that constitute the independent variable in generalizations about the influence of motivation on performance. In effect this chapter has been written as if any and all variables loosely defined as motivational, including individual differences in anxiety as measured by paper and pencil tests, noise, various drugs, heat, and financial incentives, were all variables that affected a central motivational state that, in turn, influenced performance in a uniform manner. This sort of undifferentiated conception of motivation is of course inherent in the Hullian concept of drive, and it is also contained in the Yerkes–Dodson Law and in the Easterbrook generalization about emotional arousal and cue utilization. One way in which all of these heterogenous manipulations and conditions may be subsumed under a common central motivational state is to assume that there is a unidimensional continuum of arousal ranging from states in which individuals are asleep to states of manic excitement. One might, to give this idea greater theoretical dignity, assume that there is a common physiological dimension of arousal that provides a foundation for the behavioral dimension. There are several difficulties with this view. First, current research has tended to emphasize the nonequivalence of different motivational states with respect to their influence on performance. Broadbent (1971) summarized several studies of different tasks that indicate that the effects of different stressors that are determined as having generalized performance effects are, when examined in detail, found to influence performance in subtly different ways. For example, he noted that Hockey found that the effects of noise and sleep deprivation to be diametrically opposed in a dual-task situation (p. 432). I have already indicated that noise tends to bias the scanning of the visual field such that individuals are more likely to attend to stimuli whose probabilities of occurrence are high. Sleep deprivation, on the other hand, has the opposite effect. Hockey (1970a) reported that individuals deprived of sleep were less likely than nondeprived individuals to attend to those signals whose probability of occurrence was high. Thus the latency of response was longer for stimuli presented in the center of the visual field than for stimuli presented in the periphery of the visual field. Another example of differential effects of different sources of stress discussed by Broadbent is seen on a task involving serial reactions to stimuli. In this task the subject was presented with a panel of five lights. The subject had to make a manual response by pointing to a particular light whenever it was lighted. The response triggered the presentation of a new stimulus. As subjects were required to work on this task, there was a tendency for long response durations to occur and for occasional errors in the choice of the appropriate response to occur. When subjects performed the task under conditions of noise, there was an increase in the number of errors of response. Sleep deprivation did not lead to an increase in the number of errors, but it tended to increase the number of reactions of long duration. Heat had still a different effect. Subjects who performed the task under conditions of heat tended to exhibit an increase of errors; however, the errors tended to occur at the beginning of the task rather than at the end of the task. Thus in this experimental situation, all three stressors tended to lead to a deterioration of performance but in idiosyncratic ways (see Pepler, 1959; Wilkinson, 1959).

Second, the notion of a unidimensional continuum of arousal that is related to an underlying physiological state is itself problematic. The physiological basis of such a central continuum of arousal was initially identified with the reticular arousal system (see Brown, 1961; Duffy, 1962; Hebb, 1955; Lindsley, 1957). However, this notion is no longer in accord with current physiological thinking. Physiological theorists have distinguished among states of arousal and have pointed to the fact that sleep itself contains states of physiological arousal. Lacey (1967) wrote an influential article dealing with the specificity of arousal states. Generalized arousal states might be indexed by a variety of different indices reflecting autonomic nervous system effects and cortical influences. Changes in the various indices of arousal in response to stimulation would tend to be uncorrelated or only minimally correlated. Thus a high level of response in one physiological indicator of arousal would not be likely to be associated with a high level of response in a second physiological indicator of arousal. Also, the relationship existing among various physiological indices of arousal might change over time and following different periods of time from stimulus onset. Furthermore, Lacey suggested that different patterns of physiological response might be associated with different types of cognitive tasks. For example, heart rate deceleration and increases in pupil diameter may occur following the initial presentation of novel stimuli. However, heart rate acceleration and increases in pupil diameter may be associated with mental operations that involve the transformation of input. In addition to the relative independence of different indices of arousal, it is also possible that they may reflect changes in arousal with different time lags. Humphreys, Revelle, Simon, and Gilliland (1980) discussed the relationship between changes in arousal as a function of time of day and various indices of physiological arousal (see also Eysenck & Folkard, 1980; Revelle, Humphreys, Simon, & Gilliland, 1980). They argued that various physiological indices of arousal might be related to a central state of arousal that varies through time of day with different degrees of time lag. This would tend to complicate any attempt to provide an independent physiological index of the arousal level of an individual. These complications have led theorists who postulate the existence of a central state of activation and arousal to differentiate between the hypothetical value of such a state and any single, combined, or derived physiological index. As a result such a state cannot be independently indexed with defined psychophysiological measures.

A particularly clear example of the independence of various indices of arousal is contained in a series of studies reported by Zuckerman (1979) on the psychophysiological effects of sensory deprivation. In these experiments subjects were placed in "sensory deprivation" chambers in which they were deprived of stimulation. The physiological effects of this experience varied as a function of time in the experiment. However, in those studies that measured responses over an extended period of time (typically for a period of days) a reasonably consistent pattern of physiological responses emerged. EEG indices of cortical arousal tended to decrease; there was a decrease in the mean frequency of the EEG waves. Autonomic arousal as indexed by the GSR indicated an opposite pattern of response exhibiting increases in skin conductance. Behavioral arousal, as indexed by the extent of restlessness during daylight periods, tended to increase over days of deprivation. The dissociation among various indices of arousal clearly complicates any attempt to define a unidimensional continuum of arousal. Moreover the particular pattern of dissociation found in these studies is not universal (that is, under other conditions these indices may covary positively or may be dissociated in still other ways exhibiting different patterns of interrelationship).

Third, the assumption that different sources of drive combine additively is not well-supported in the empirical literature. In fact, there are several studies that provide evidence contradictory to the assumption. A study by Brody *et al.* (1967) has been discussed that indicated that individual differences in anxiety as measured by the MAS and d-amphetamine both acted to increase the variability of successive word associates. These results were explained with reference to Hull's concept of a threshold for response evocation. On this theoretical analysis the subjects who scored high on the MAS and who were given d-amphetamine should have had the highest response variability if these two presumed sources of drive combine additively. Table 2.6 presents the results obtained in this study.

These data directly contradict the prediction derived from the Hullian expectation of drive additivity. Note that subjects with high scores on the MAS had lower variability scores under d-amphetamine than those who scored low on the MAS. Under placebo and meprobramate conditions, subjects who scored high on the MAS had greater response variability than the ones who scored low. There was a highly significant Drug × Anxiety interaction. These data suggest that the combined level of drive created by the presence of both anxiety and d-amphetamine is lower than the level of drive created by the

TABLE 2.6
Drugs, Anxiety, and Intrasubject Variability of Word Associates

Meprobomate		Placebo		d-Amphetamine	
High A	Low A	High A	Low A	High A	Low A
3.02	2.46	3.62	3.05	3.68	4.39

Source: Brody, Petersen, Upton, and Stabile, 1967.

presence of d-amphetamine alone. Thus, these results contradict the expectation of additivity of different sources of drive.

Brody (1964b) obtained additional evidence suggesting possible nonadditive combinations of individual differences in anxiety and an additional source of drive in an experiment on the variability of response sequences. Recall that subjects who scored high on the MAS tended to have more variable response sequences than those who scored low. In this study a second presumed source of drive was introduced—induced muscular tension created by having subjects squeeze a hand dynamometer while they were making their response judgments. Of 30 subjects who scored low on the MAS, 17 had more variable response sequences when their responses were obtained under conditions of induced muscular tension. Thus, induced muscular tension did not perceptibly increase response variability among subjects who scored low on the MAS. However, 21 of 30 subjects who scored high on the Taylor scale had lower response variability (i.e., less random response sequences) when their responses were made under conditions of induced muscular tension. Thus induced muscular tension tended to detract from the influence of anxiety as measured by the MAS. The results suggest the possibility that induced muscular tension may combine nonadditively with anxiety as measured by the Taylor scale. Therefore, these results may be interpreted in the same way as those of the Brody et al. (1967) study suggesting d-amphetamine might lower the drive level of subjects who scored high on the MAS.

The nonadditive interpretation of these results is buttressed by the results of the study by Kuethe and Eriksen (1957), who reported that induced muscular tension tended to interact with individual differences in anxiety. Subjects who scored high in anxiety in their study exhibited increased variability of their responses under conditions of induced muscular tension, and subjects who scored low on their measure of anxiety had decreases in response variability under conditions of induced muscular tension. Thus, the effects of induced muscular tension were opposite to the effects of anxiety (see also D. R. Meyer & Noble, 1958). These results are again compatible with the view that the introduction of a second source of drive may decrease the level of drive attributable to anxiety such that the total level of drive is lower when both individual differences in anxiety and the second source of drive are present than when one of these two presumed sources is present singly. Again these results contradict the assumption of additivity of different sources of drive.

Additional evidence for possible nonadditive effects of combinations of different sources of drive or arousal is contained in the experiments involving performance in serial reaction tasks. Wilkinson (see Hockey, 1979) reported the results of experiments using sleep loss and noise; sleep loss and incentive; and incentive and noise. Figure 2.7 presents the results of these studies. The data indicate that noise increased the number of errors made by subjects over time. Sleep loss considered by itself, in comparison to its absence, also led to an increase in the number of errors. However, the combined effect of both sources of stress was not additive. Note that, under conditions of both noise and sleep loss, subjects showed less increase in errors than under conditions of sleep loss in the absence of noise. The combined effects of sleep loss and incentive were similarly nonadditive. The presence of incentives led to a slight decrease in the number of long responses. Thus the effects of incentives, when considered by themselves, were opposite of the effects of sleep loss. However, when an incentive condition was combined with a sleep-loss condition, the results indicate that the adverse effects of sleep loss were counteracted by the presence of incentives. The combined effects of noise and incentive were also

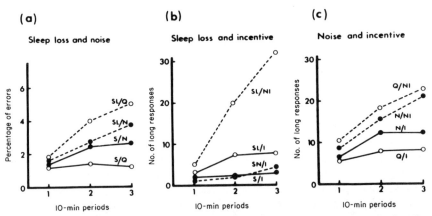

Figure 2.7. *Evidence for stress interactions on the 5-choice task. Abbreviations used in the figure are: S = normal sleep; SL = sleep loss; Q = quiet; N = noise; I = incentive; NI = no incentive. (From R. Hockey. Stress and the cognitive components of skilled performance. In V. Hamilton and D. M. Warburton (Eds.), Human Stress and Cognition. Chichester, England: Wiley, 1979. Copyright 1979 by John Wiley and Sons. Reprinted by permission of John Wiley and Sons, Ltd.)*

paradoxical. Noise in the absence of incentives tended to decrease the number of long responses. Incentives tended to dramatically decrease the number of long responses. Subjects given both noise and incentives tended to have more long responses than those who performed the task under quiet conditions in the presence of incentives.

Interactions between different motivational states have been reported in other experimental situations. Davies and Jones (1975) reported the results of an incidental learning experiment in which subjects were required to recall in order a list of words presented on slides. The words appeared at different locations on the slide. Subjects were asked to recall the location of the words on the slides. Both noise and incentive conditions tended to lead to poorer performance on the incidental task—the recall of the location of the words as opposed to the order in which the words were presented. However, under conditions in which both noise and financial incentives were present, they did not recall the location of the words more poorly than they did when the task was performed in the presence of noise without financial incentives. Thus the incentives did not combine additively with noise.

How are these diverse effects of the combination of different motivational variables to be interpreted? One possible way attempts to subsume many of them by postulating the existence of a unidimensional continuum of arousal or activation combined with the assumption of the inverted U-shaped relationship between level of motivation or arousal and performance postulated by the Yerkes–Dodson Law. Such an attempt assumes that the several sources of motivation, including the presence of incentives, will affect a common, underlying, central motive state analagous to Hull's drive concept. The nonmonotonic additive effects are to be explained by nonlinear relationships between the motive state and performance. (For a discussion of this type of argument, see Broadbent, 1971; R. Hockey, 1979; Revelle & Humphreys, 1980.) One could argue that sleep loss tends to decrease the physiological arousal level of an individual such that the individual is below some optimal level of arousal for performance on these complex tasks (see Corcoran, 1964; Wilkinson, 1965). Noise and incentives act to counteract the physiological deficit caused by sleep deprivation by increasing arousal level to the point where it is optimal for performance. The combined effects of noise and incentives might be attributable to the state of overarousal—that is, assuming an additive combination of motivational states and the Yerkes–Dodson Law, the combined effects of both motivational states would lead to a situation in which the subject is above the level of motivation required for optimal task performance. There are several difficulties with this sort of argument. The argument is in part ad hoc insofar as it represents an a posteriori ordering of complex patterns of results that would have been difficult to predict on an a priori basis. Also the argument does not do justice to the complexities of the experimental results. Note that with respect to their influence on sleep, both incentive conditions and noise conditions are treated as sources of arousal that have the capacity to offset the decrease in arousal attributed to sleep deprivation. However, if these two sources of arousal are considered individually their effects on the serial reaction task are not the same: Noise tends to increase errors; incentives, to decrease them. Thus the main effects of incentives and noise are not comparable. One could argue that incentive is not a motivational variable in the same sense that noise is. Noise acts as a nondirectional energizer, and its effects are not in any obvious sense tied to the purposive activities of an individual. Incentives, by contrast, are presumed to affect the purposes of an individual directly. In fact there are theorists who have treated incentives as being comparable with nondirectional motivational influences, and there are theorists who have tended to distinguish between the motivational influences of nondirectional states and incentives. Among the former group K. W. Spence (1956) modified Hull's theory by assuming that drive (D) and incentive (K) combine additively and that their sum has a multiplicative effect on habits. Other theorists, such as Revelle and Humphreys (1980), tended to distinguish between arousal and effort (see also Kahnemann, 1973). Presumably, incentives would influence the effort expended by an individual. Such a theory distinguishes between nonspecific arousal states and directed efforts. In terms of the present context, this latter type of theory would have to postulate an additional principle, namely, that incentives can increase arousal or that the increase in effort associated with the presence of incentives can improve performance despite the lowered arousal caused by such variables as sleep deprivation. Moreover, a dual theory must further assume that, in order to explain the effects of the combined motivational states in the serial-reaction task, the motivational influences attributable to effort states and the motivational influences attributable to arousal are additive with respect to their ability to lead to a state of overly intense motivation. It is apparent that the decision to differentiate between motivational influences of such presumed nondirective energizers as noise and incentives does not help to resolve the almost paradoxical complexities inherent in these results. Moreover, none of these speculations helps to resolve the effects of heat that apparently influence performance in a way distinct from the influences of sleep loss, noise, and incentive.

Revelle et al. (1980) reported the results of a series of experiments that they argued might provide support for the additivity of different sources of arousal. One of the arousal-related measures they used is an individual difference measure. They argued that introverts (low impulsive subjects) do not differ from extraverts (high impulsive subjects) in their chronic level of arousal but rather with respect to the time of day in which they are most aroused. They argued that nonimpulsive subjects (introverts) are likely to be highly aroused in the morning but not in the evening, whereas highly impulsive subjects (extraverts) are assumed to be low in arousal in the morning but high in arousal in the evening. Thus on this view, arousal due to impulsivity interacts with the time of day, which in itself is a variable used to study the effects of arousal on task performance since arousal is presumed to increase during the course of the day. Revelle *et al.* (1980) reported the results of a series of studies manipulating time of day; impulsivity, as measured by personality inventories; and caffeine, which they assumed to be a nonspecific energizer that adds to the overall level of arousal present in a particular subject. In their studies they gave subjects a variety of tests of cognitive abilities. Figure 2.8 presents the results of these studies and indicates that impulsive subjects given caffeine in the morning exhibited a clear improvement in task performance. Subjects low in impulsivity and who were assumed also to be high in arousal in the morning showed a clear decrement in performance when given caffeine in the morning. The opposite pattern of results was obtained in the evening—that is, caffeine increased the performance of those subjects low in impulsivity and led to performance decrements among those high in impulsivity and who were presumably at high levels of arousal in the evening. They interpreted this rather complex, but replicated pattern of interactions by appeal to the assumption that caffeine added to the arousal level of their subjects and that low impulsive subjects

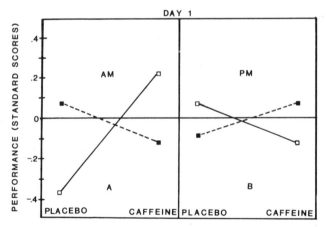

Figure 2.8. *Median performance (in standard scores) as a function of impulsivity, placebo or caffeine, time of day, and experiment duration for Revelle (1976), Gilliland (1977), and Experiments 1–5. (Low impulsives ---; high impulsives ————.) (From W. Revelle, M. S. Humphreys, L. Simon, and K. Gilliland. The interactive effect of personality, time of day, and caffeine: A test of the arousal model. Journal of* Experimental Psychology: General, *1980, 109, 1–31. Copyright 1980 by the American Psychological Association. Reprinted by permission of the publisher and authors.)*

who were highly aroused in the morning become overaroused when given caffeine and thus their performance deteriorated. The high impulsive subjects given caffeine in the morning were underaroused, and the addition of caffeine brought them to an arousal level that was optimal for task performance. Note that this analysis accepts the Yerkes–Dodson Law as valid. Eysenck and Folkard (1980) challenged this interpretation of these data (see also Humphreys et al., 1980). They indicated that the data indicating differences in arousal as a function of time of day for varying levels of impulsivity was by no means as clear-cut as implied by Revelle and his associates. In addition, they presented data that suggested that there was little or no difference in arousal levels as a function of time of day among subjects differing in impulsivity. Since Revelle and his associates did not measure the physiological responses of their subjects, their interpretation depends on the acceptance of assumptions for which the evidence is less than compelling. It is necessary to assume for example that the arousal attributable to caffeine is additive with the arousal attributed to diurnal variations in individual differences in impulsivity. Since there is less than compelling evidence for differences in diurnal rhythms of arousal among these subjects and no evidence for the additivity of arousal due to caffeine and the individual difference measure of arousal, it could be asserted with relatively equal accuracy that individuals who differ in impulsivity respond differently to caffeine at different times of the day. To complicate matters further, in another study reported by this research group (Craig, Humphreys, Rocklin, & Revelle, 1979), additivity of arousal between caffeine and differences associated with impulsivity was explicitly rejected, and in addition, in this latter article an argument was made that the additivity of caffeine effects and impulsivity effects on arousal was mediated by individual differences in another dimension of personality—neuroticism. It appears that the complex pattern of interactions cannot be explained by postulating simple additive models of different sources of arousal—particularly in the absence of agreed physiological indicators of the arousal state or of some other independent way of indexing the level of arousal that is present. Moreover the kinds of hypotheses that are introduced to explain these data even on an ad hoc basis point to the complexities of considering simple ways of manipulating arousal as being relatively clear-cut measures of arousal without additional complicating intervening consequences.

What conclusions can be drawn from this selected review of studies involving the manipulation of more than one source of drive or arousal? Although undoubtedly studies may be found in the human motivation literature that provide evidence for the additivity of several sources of motivation in a single experimental session, apparently other studies also exist that provide at best tenuous support for such an assumption, and there are still other studies that apparently contain negative evidence. Perhaps it is reasonable to conclude that the simple assumption of additivity is not an adequate representation of the complex pattern of results likely to occur in an experimental situation in which more than one source of drive or arousal is present.

Fourth, different sources of drive may have a number of elements associated with them that are distinctive to each individual source. In effect this is reflected in a Hullian theory by reference to the concept of drive stimuli. However, the drive stimulus concept fails to capture the nuances of the more general argument that any source of drive may have rather distinctive experimental consequences that are relatively independent of its assumed drivelike influences. Poulton (1977; 1979) argued that many of the effects of noise on performance can be explained by the possibility that noise may mask various auditory cues emanating from the apparatus that serves to assist performance in complex skill tasks. In addition, other detrimental effects of noise, particularly on tasks involving memory, may be attributable to interference with or masking of inner speech, which then interferes with verbal rehearsal in memory tasks. Poulton's position has been the subject of heated debate (Broadbent, 1978; Hartley, 1981; Poulton, 1981). A discussion of the numerous technical issues involved in the question of whether all performance decrements associated with noise are attributable to masking effects is beyond the scope of this discussion. However, it is apparent that noise considered as a nondirective energizer can have specific consequences that are peculiar to it.

There are other sources of drive used in research on nonspecific effects of arousal that can act as distractors. Experiments involving induced muscular tension require subjects to squeeze a hand dynamometer with a scale to calibrate force to specified levels of tension. The act of squeezing the dynamometer can act as a distractor and can occupy the attention of the subject. Experiments involving the use of heat also introduce a distracting agent. Individuals required to work on a task in heat may become aware of their discomfort and may think about their discomfort to the detriment of their performance on a task. Other sources of drive that involve the use of deprivation of drugs may introduce complications associated with drug deprivation as a source of drive. For example, nicotine and caffeine have been used as sources of arousal (see Andersson & Hockey, 1977). In such studies subjects are asked to refrain from using caffeine and nicotine for specified periods of time prior to the start of the experiment. The effects of the deprivation of a biological substance are not studied. Peculiarly, it is deprivation that classically, in the animal literature, is considered the standard method of inducing a source of drive. The deprivation of a substance for which there is a biological need should, in principal, serve to arouse an organism. Schachter and his associates (Schachter, 1977; Schachter, Kozlowski, & Silverstein, 1977;

Schachter, Silverstein, Kozlowski, Nerman, & Lieblin, 1977; Schachter, Silverstein, Kozlowski, Perlick, Herman, & Lieblin, 1977; Silverstein, Kozlowski, & Schachter, 1977) demonstrated that smoking acts as a biological addiction. Similarly, caffeine deprivation may be associated with irritability and restlessness. In experiments using nicotine and caffeine, it is the biological substances themselves that are considered the arousing manipulation. There is nothing inherently illogical or indeed empirically invalid in this assumption. It may, in fact, be that nicotine and caffeine ingestion following a period of deprivation of these substances may act as arousing agents. However, it is apparent that the experimental operations used to create the arousal state also include as part of the induction procedure the psychological consequences of deprivation that might exert special influences. It is apparent that the study of motivational influences within the context of a model of nonspecific arousal states serves to detract one's attention from the special characteristics associated with specific sources of drive. These idiosyncratic characteristics may account in part for the generalization that different sources of drive tend to influence performance in somewhat different ways and the suggestion that additivity of different sources of drive may be more the exception than the rule.

Fifth, experiments involving the use of nonspecific sources of motivation have tended to treat the contributions of those sources of motivation as being relatively constant throughout the experimental session. It may be the case that the influence of a particular source of drive varies over the course of an experimental session. Weiner (1966) reported the results of a very clear demonstration of this type of influence. Weiner (1972, 1980) argued that individuals who differ in anxiety tend to have different reactions to success and failure and to develop different attributions of the reasons for success and failure, which, in turn, lead them to respond differently to the experience of success and failure. This theory will be discussed in a subsequent chapter. Weiner suggested that individuals who are low in anxiety will work harder following success. Individuals who are high in anxiety, by contrast, will tend to do better on tasks in which they have succeeded than on tasks in which they have failed.

Weiner (1966) presented subjects with two tasks used by Spence in his analysis of the influence of variations of drive on learning. One paired-associate learning task used was an easy task in which high drive should have tended to improve performance and the other was a difficult task in which high drive should have led to poorer performance. The former task required the subject to learn a paired-associate list in which the correct response to the stimulus was likely to be dominant, and the latter list consisted of pairs in which there was a high probability of dominant responses in the list being incorrect. Accordingly, Spence would predict that subjects who were high in

TABLE 2.7

Mean Number of Trials to Criterion among Subjects Scoring in the Upper and Lower 25 Percentile on the TAQ

	Condition					
	Easy list (failure)			Difficult list (success)		
Anxiety	N	M	SD	N	M	SD
High	9	9.55	3.78	12	14.83	6.57
Low	12	7.08	1.85	10	20.10	7.35

Source: B. Weiner. The role of success and failure in the learning of easy and complex tasks. *Journal of Personality and Social Psychology,* 1966, *3,* 339–344. Copyright 1966 by the American Psychological Association. Reprinted by permission of the publisher and author.

anxiety (drive) would perform better on the easy task than on the difficult task; subjects who scored low on an anxiety test should have shown an opposite pattern of response. Weiner manipulated subjects' beliefs about their performance on these tasks: He led subjects performing the easy task to believe they were failing since their performance was worse than expected, whereas subjects performing the difficult task were led to believe that they had succeeded at the task since their performance was better than expected. Table 2.7 presents the results of this study and indicates that those who scored high on a measure of anxiety performed better on the difficult task and worse on the easy task—a pattern of results exactly opposite to those predicted by the assumption that individual differences in anxiety are a measure of drive. These results suggest that the impact of anxiety on performance is mediated by a subject's response to the outcomes of performance. Even where anxiety is aroused on a task, it may be incorrect to conceive of its influence in terms of the contribution of a fixed quantitative increase to overall drive level. Thus, Hullian theory cannot subsume influences of anxiety on performance that are modified by differential reactions to the outcomes of performance.

Conclusion

The study of nondirectional influences of motivation on performance is preeminently a Hullian concern. In this summary I will consider what if anything remains from the Hullian legacy in current attempts to understand the influence of motivation on performance. A review of this literature has indicated that there are problems in both aspects of Hullian theory embodied in the equation $D \times {}_sH_r \times {}_sE_r$. There are difficulties with the initial term in the equation, D, and there are difficulties in the conception of performance embodied in the equation. With respect to the concept of drive, among the difficulties that appear to beset that theoretical notion is the fact that there does not exist a clear specification of the class of variables that constitute sources of drive. Indeed those variables that have been used most prominently in the animal literature, such as food deprivation, have not been used much at all in the human experimental literature. Quite apart from the difficulty of specifying the nature of the class of variables that constitute sources of drive, there is considerable doubt that all members of what are taken as representative of the class of motivational variables or, in this context, sources of drive, have common effects either·with respect to some identifiable underlying physiological state or in terms of their influences on performance. In addition, although different sources of drive may in fact have similar performance influences, upon closer examination their respective influences on a particular task may be subtly different. Most critical of all, the most novel and idiosyncratic aspect of Hull's theory, namely the additivity of different sources of drive, has not been found to be a viable empirical concept. The concept may not be readily testable in light of the possible idiosyncratic influences of the particular sources of drive inadequately subsumed under the rubric, drive stimuli. Also, irrespective of the theoretical imprecision in the use of the concept, empirical results have not in general supported the necessity of postulating such a theoretical explanation. Although occasional patterns of results appear in the literature that support the notion of additivity, it is at least as likely, or perhaps more likely, to find results that are directly contradictory of the pattern either because the sum of two sources of drive is no greater than the influence of one or the other, or more dramatically, on occasion, because the possibility exists that the addition of a second source of drive may dissipate or decrease the influence of the original source of drive. Not only is it possible or even probable that the influence of any particular source of drive may vary as a function of the presence of other sources of drive, but also a single source of drive may change in its influence during an experiment. In classical Hullian theory variations in level of values of a theoretical variable over trials or time were analyzed in terms of changes in habit strengths. Drive was conceived of as a relatively enduring and static influence. However, the influence of a source of drive may change as an individual's interest in a task varies and as an individual receives feedback with respect to success or failure at a task. Thus the attempt to subsume all motivational influences under a common rubric and a single theoretical entity does not do justice to the complexities of current empirical efforts. Parenthetically, it should be noted that this criticism applies mutatis mutandis to other motivational generalizations such as Easterbrook's or the Yerkes–Dodson Law that assume a common influence of a single source of motivation.

Not only is it the case that drive as a single concept fails to capture the variety of motivational influences, Hullian theory encounters even greater difficulty when one considers the analysis of performance influences of motivational states. Although hypotheses derived from the Drive × Habit formulation occasionally are used in contemporary research efforts, such as those of Zajonc's, with respect to the influence of the presence of other individuals, it is the case that the testing of hypotheses derived using the Hullian theory of performance has receded from current work. There are two general reasons that can be cited for this phenomenon. First, the theory's analysis of performance influences is deceptively simple, and when such complications as different stages of learning and threshold effects are considered, the theory does not make predictions that are invariably clear-cut. Second, and of far greater significance, the Hullian theory of performance has been superceded by new developments in cognitive psychology that tend to decompose performance on a task into components that are separately measurable and that can be independently influenced by motivation. Such a componential perspective is illustrated by the experiments of Hamilton, Hockey, and Rejman (1977), demonstrating differential influences of noise on the rate of processing information when storage is not required, as compared to the rate of processing when storage is required. Contemporary analyses of performance have simply bypassed and rendered irrelevant the Hullian conception of changes in response probabilities. It is not so much that Hullian theory has been shown to be incorrect—its flaw is far more serious. It is uninteresting, or perhaps to be more precise, it has been rendered irrelevant by more sophisticated conceptions of cognitive processes.

If the Hullian conception of drive as a unidimensional motivation state is not viable and the conception of performance embodied in Hullian theory is outmoded, what if anything remains from the Hullian tradition? One could argue that the issue of nonpurposive or nondirectional motivation influences is quintessentially Hullian. Even at this point, a caveat is in order. The emerging conception of cognition is one of an individual who takes a more active role in the allocation of resources to different components of a task and, in addition, who determines the nature of the effective stimulus through attentional processes. Although such a conception stresses the role of the individual as an active participant, it does not necessarily entail purposive conceptions of motivation. There are several reasons to be quite cautious in postulating or introducing purposive conceptions. The allocation of resources to different aspects or components of a task is not necessarily a conscious decision of the organism. There is no evidence, for example, that when confronted with a high level of noise in an environment, an individual con- sciously decides to pay more attention or to monitor more frequently those elements of a task which occur with high frequency. The effects may occur quite involuntarily. There is nothing in the nature of the instructions given to a subject or in the nature of the motivational manipulations used that require subjects to show the sorts of changes that they do in fact show in order to accomplish the apparent purposive goal that all subjects, irrespective of the motivational condition to which they are assigned, presumably share—namely, to do well on the task. Thus there is no demonstration that the purposes of subjects are altered by the manipulation of such motivational variables as noise, drugs, or sleep deprivation. Thus we are left with the view that there are a class of motivational variables that can influence one or more central states of an individual and that these changes in central states can have somewhat diffuse effects on performance in a variety of tasks. What is per- haps the irreducible legacy of the Hullian tradition is simply this: These diffuse influences appear to be outside the framework of a theory of purposive behavior. The psychology of motivation cannot dispense with the notion of nonpurposive motivational influences.

Chapter 3

ACHIEVEMENT MOTIVATION: TOWARD A PURPOSIVE THEORY

We have argued that the psychology of motivation must encompass, for sake of completeness, a nonpurposive construct that, however conceived, refers to a change in the state of an organism that leads to rather diffuse influences on behavior. Of course, this does not preclude the inclusion of purposive conceptions of motivation in a general theory of motivation. This chapter traces the development of a purposive conception of motivation that develops, in large measure, from a program of research initiated by David McClelland and his associates in 1948.

McClelland (1958) noted that as late as 1948 there were no readily available measures of human social motives that would permit the psychologist to ascertain the presence of a particular social motive in a person. McClelland decided to develop such measures. His initial efforts were focused upon the need to achieve—defined as a desire to do well in competition with some standard of excellence. McClelland chose as his preferred method of measurement the Thematic Apperception Test (TAT), which had been used earlier by Henry Murray (1938) in an attempt to measure motivation by an analysis of the content of stories told about pictures. McClelland assumed that individuals would express their dominant motive tendencies in fantasy material. Although the conception of fantasy as a motivational source is certainly compatible with a Freudian view, it should be noted that in one sense McClelland's use of fantasy material was decidedly antithetical to Freudian notions. McClelland assumed that there would be a more or less direct relationship between the presence of a motive in a person and the content of the person's thoughts. Freudian theory has tended to argue that fantasy contents serve as indirect outlets for unconscious motivation. The theory tends to view fantasy material as inversely related to the underlying motive state. Thus an individual whose fantasy life is dominated by aggressive themes might be viewed as being incapable of the direct expression of aggression by Freudian interpretation.

McClelland sought to develop a test that would be capable of objective scoring. In order to do this, he developed a set of rules for the evaluation of TAT protocols. Individuals using these rules routinely obtain scores with reliability coefficients of .90 (see Smith & Feld, 1958). The categories used in the scoring system are as follows:

1. Achievement imagery—defined as a reference to a goal involving competition with a standard of excellence
2. Need—a stated desire to reach an achievement goal
3. Instrumental activity—reference to specific activities that are instrumental to the goal
4. Positive anticipatory goal state—the anticipation of goal attainment
5. Negative anticipatory goal state—the anticipation of failure to reach the achievement goal
6. Personal obstacle or block—a reference to an inability to achieve the goal
7. Environmental obstacle—a reference to some obstacle in the environment that makes attainment of the achievement goal more difficult
8. Positive affective state—a reference to a positive feeling associated with goal attainment
9. Negative affective state—a reference to unpleasant affects associated with failure to attain an achievement goal
10. Nurturant press—a reference to persons who assist someone in attaining an achievement goal
11. Achievement theme—this is scored when achievement imagery is assumed to be the dominant theme of the story

Note that this set of categories implicitly incorporates a goal-directed conception of behavior. The presence of a motive state is assumed to be reflected in a thought sequence that mimics actions of an individual engaged in goal-directed behavior in everyday life. McClelland, Atkinson, Clark, and Lowell (1953) included the usual categories of goal-directed activity as involving instrumental activity and persistence until the goal is attained including an attempt to circumvent barriers. In addition, the conception of goal-directed activity contained in this category system assumes that individuals are aware of the goal toward which their behavior is directed and anticipate the affective consequences of success or failure in attaining the goal. Thus the conception of motivation contained in this scoring system may be characterized as goal-directed and cognitive. This schematic scoring system can be used to measure other motives and in fact has been used to develop measures of need affiliation and need power. In this chapter I will concentrate on achievement motivation since it has been most extensively investigated and since the research on achievement motivation provides the empirical foundation for the development of a theory of purposive behavior.

The research on achievement motivation to be described has proceeded in two different directions. McClelland attempted to relate individual differences in achievement motivation to broad, socially relevant questions and to such things as economic growth and development. McClelland's best known student, John W. Atkinson (1957; Atkinson & Birch, 1970), attempted to develop formal theories based on research in achievement motivation. Both research efforts may be conceived of as attempts to demonstrate that the fantasy measure of achievement motivation is in fact a valid index of an important social motive.

How do we know that the measure of need achievement does in fact measure need achievement? Clearly, the question is not settled by fiat or by the act of naming the measure. McClelland *et al.* (1953) reported two kinds of investigations that tended to support this notion. First, they demonstrated that subjects given test instructions that were presumed to arouse achievement motivation tended to have higher need achievement scores. Of course, this demonstration merely establishes that the content of a person's fantasy changes but not that the fantasy reflects the presence of a motive.

Lowell (1950) reported one of the first studies that attempted to relate scores on the need-achievement measure to a measure of behavior. He reasoned that individuals who were high in achievement motivation would work harder on laboratory tasks. Lowell gave subjects such tasks as arithmetic problems and scrambled-word problems to solve. Data obtained by Lowell are presented in Figure 3.1. Note that Lowell found that subjects who scored high in an achievement tended to work harder on the task. Figure 3.1 indicates that both groups of subjects (those high and low in need achievement) started out with the same level of performance, but those high in need achievement improved their performance, whereas those low in need achievement exhibited performance declines.

The Lowell finding is not conclusive. One might argue that individuals who score high on need for achievement will work harder in a laboratory task, but this does not indicate that such individuals are really high in need for achievement in situations outside the laboratory. In fact, Lazarus (1961) expressed

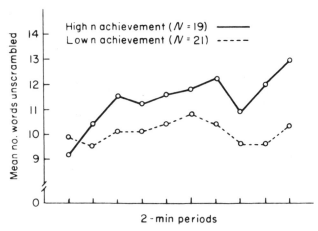

Figure 3.1.   *Performance of high and low need-achievement groups on scrambled word task. (From Lowell [1950].)*

the belief that scores on need for achievement can be inversely related to actual achievement motivation (that is, that the fantasy expression of need achievement is not a direct index of a person's achievement motivation but is rather a compensatory response for the failure to exhibit achievement motivation in everyday life). Results such as Lowell's do not really contradict Lazarus' contention since the laboratory expression of need achievement is not evidence of its expression outside the laboratory. However, there is some evidence that need achievement as measured by the TAT is related to a tendency to express achievement motivation in extralaboratory contexts. Crockett (1962), using a subset of 597 males selected from a larger random sample of males living in private homes in the United States, found a relationship between need-achievement scores and upward social mobility. He found that sons who were high in need achievement and whose fathers were in low or middle prestige occupations had greater occupational mobility than sons who were low in need achievement. However, no differences were obtained in intergenerational occupational mobility for sons differing in need achievement whose fathers were in the upper-middle or high prestige occupations. Crockett attributed the lack of relationship between need achievement and occupational mobility for sons of fathers in the upper-middle and high occupational prestige categories to the increased importance of education as a basis for upward mobility among these groups (see also Crockett, 1964; Littig & Yeracaris, 1965.)

The results obtained by Crockett do not unequivocally establish the validity of the need-achievement test as a measure of the tendency to express need achievement in extralaboratory contexts. Crockett's results tell us very little about the direction of influence of the social mobility and need-achievement variables. If one assumes that children who are high in need-achievement work harder as adults and are as a result more likely to be upwardly mobile, then Crockett's results do provide evidence for the validity of the need-achievement measure. However, there is another interpretation of Crockett's finding, namely, that when upward mobility occurs, need-achievement scores increase. Changes in mobility could lead to changes in the characteristic thoughts and preoccupations of an individual. The need-achievement score could reflect these changes.

Skolnick (1966) reported the results of a longitudinal study of achievement motivation extending over a 20-year period. She noted the social class position attained by the subjects in her study in adulthood and found correlations of .09 and .05 for boys and girls, respectively, between their social class position in adulthood and their need-achievement scores in adolescence. However, the correlations between need-achievement scores in adulthood and social class position in adulthood were .28 and .50 for men and women, respectively. These data suggest that the relationship between need-achievement scores and upward social mobility reported by Crockett should not be interpreted as indicating a causal influence of need achievement on social mobility. The direction of the relationship is more plausibly interpreted in the opposite direction—that is, changes in social position are likely to cause changes in the characteristic pattern of thought exhibited in test protocols producing higher need-achievement scores.

The most ambitious attempt to relate need achievement to extralaboratory changes is contained in McClelland's research. McClelland developed the hypothesis that achievement motivation is in part responsible for the economic growth of societies. The development of this hypothesis was described by McClelland (1961) as follows:

Forming the Key Hypothesis:
The Effects of the Protestant Reformation on n Achievement

It was actually a study by Winterbottom (1953) which first pointed to a possible link between achievement motivation and economic development. She was interested in trying to discover how parents, or more particularly mothers, produced a strong interest in achievement in their sons. She first obtained n Achievement scores on a group of 29 8-year-old boys and then conducted interviews to determine if the mothers of the "highs" had different attitudes toward bringing up children. What she found was that mothers of the "highs" expected their sons to master earlier such activities as the following. . .:

Know his way around the city
Be active and energetic
Try hard for things for himself
Make his own friends
Do well in competition

Furthermore, the mothers of the "lows" reported more restrictions: they did not want their sons to play with children not approved by the parents, nor did they want them to make important decisions by themselves. The picture here is reasonably clear. The mothers of the sons with high n Achievement have set higher standards for their sons: they expect self-reliance and mastery at an earlier age [Winterbottom, 1958, pp. 468–472].

An interesting historical parllel suggested itself. As we have seen, the German sociologist Max Weber (1904/1958) described in convincing detail how the Protestant Reformation produced a new character type which infused a more vigorous spirit into the attitude of both workers and entrepreneurs and which ultimately resulted in the development of modern industrial capitalism. If the Protestant Reformation represented a shift toward self-reliance training and the new "capitalistic spirit" and increased n Achievement, then the relationship found by Winterbottom may have been duplicated at a societal level in the history of Western Europe. The following diagram shows the parallel.

Weber's hypothesis

A ———————————————————————————————— D

Protestantism   Spirit of
(self-reliance values, etc.)   modern capitalism

Winterbottom's study

B ———————————————————————————————— C

INDEPENDENCE AND   n ACHIEVEMENT
MASTERY TRAINING   IN SONS
BY PARENTS

That is, the Winterbottom study suggests a psychological means by which the historical development described by Weber may have come about. The Protestant Reformation might have led to earlier independence and mastery training, which led to greater n Achievement, which in turn led to the rise of modern capitalism [pp. 46–47].

McClelland then proceeded to extend this hypothesis. He argued that differences in need achievement were responsible in part for the economic growth and decline in all societies. McClelland (1961) reported a number of studies designed to test his central hypothesis about the relationship of need achievement and economic growth. Two of these studies will be briefly described to indicate the scope and style of this major research effort.

In order to obtain a test of his hypothesis for countries in the modern world, McClelland needed a measure of achievement motivation and a measure of economic growth for a number of modern nations. McClelland decided to use children's readers as a basis for the measurement of need achievement levels in a particular country. McClelland assumed that the themes of the readers would reflect the motives and values of their cultures. He obtained a sample from children's readers for the period from 1920–1929 from 23 countries and a sample of stories from children's readers for the 1946–1955 period from 40 countries. McClelland then obtained a measure of economic growth for these countries. McClelland used three measures of economic growth over the period from 1925–1950 for the countries in his study. The first measure was based on Clark's measure, international units (i.u.) (Clark, 1957)—a measure of the income per capita expressed in terms of a common reference; McClelland also used a measure of electrical output—electricity produced in kilowatt hours per capita, and finally, McClelland obtained an index combining both of these measures. He obtained these measures for the year 1925 and the year 1950. For each of these measures, there was a relationship between 1925 levels and 1950 levels: Countries with relatively high rates of economic development in 1925 tended to have high rates in 1950. McClelland, therefore, correlated these scores and then defined economic growth as the deviation from the regression line predicting the expected growth. This measure indicated the degree to which a country had economic growth for the 1925–1950 period that exceeded or fell behind what would be expected on the basis of its 1925 level of economic development. These economic deviation scores were correlated with need achievement scores derived from the 1925 and 1950 readers. Table 3.1 presents these results. Need-achievement levels in children's readers in 1925 predicted economic growth for the 1925–1950 period. However, need-achievement levels in 1950 were not indicative of previous economic growth. The fact that high levels of need achievement predict future growth was taken by McClelland to indicate that need achievement influenced economic growth and not the converse.

Beit-Hallahmi (1980) reported the results of a replication of McClelland's study using, essentially, the same methods as McClelland. He correlated achievement levels derived from children's readers used in 38 countries in 1950, then used the McClelland index of growth in electrical output for these countries from 1952 to 1976. The correlation between these measures was .11, indicating that the predicted relationship between need-achievement levels and economic growth does not obtain for this historical period.

McClelland also attempted to test his hypothesis using historical data. In a

TABLE 3.1
Correlations of Reader Need-Achievement Scores with Deviations from Expected Economic Gains

Achievement level by year, n	I.U./cap 1925–1959, $N = 22$	Kwh/cap 1929–1950, $N = 22$	Both combined, $N = 21$
1925	.25	.53, $p < .01$	.46, $p < .02$
1950	−.10	.03	−.08

Source: McClelland, 1961.

study conducted by one of his students, Berlew, he attempted to relate changes in need achievement to the economic growth and decline of Ancient Greece. McClelland obtained indices of need-achievement levels by scoring samples of Greek literature from three periods, 900–475 B.C., 475–362 B.C., and 362–100 B.C., for need achievement. In order to obtain measures of economic development, Berlew, using considerable ingenuity, derived measures of trading area in square miles. These were obtained by studying the places where Greek earthenware jars (the containers used for much of their trade) of different periods were obtained. Figure 3.2 summarizes Berlew's findings. These data confirmed McClelland's expectation. Note that high levels of achievement motivation preceded economic growth and low levels of achievement motivation preceded economic decline.

A study by deCharms and Moeller (1962) related the frequency of achievement imagery in children's readers in successive 20-year periods from 1810 to 1950 to an index of the number of patents per one million population in the United States for the same time periods. The results of their analysis are presented in Figure 3.3, and an examination of the data indicates that there is an apparent congruence between these indices. Need-achievement levels in children's readers increased in the nineteenth century as did the number of patents issued. Need-achievement levels in children's readers declined in the first half of the twentieth century as did the numbers of patents issued.

McClelland's data are correlational rather than experimental. He did not measure need-achievement levels in a society and study the resultant changes in economic development. It is a truism of statistics that correlation is

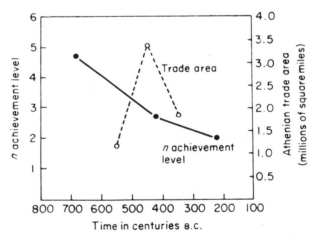

Figure 3.2.   *Average need-achievement level plotted at midpoints of periods of growth, climax, and decline of Athenian civilization as reflected in the extent of her trade area. (From McClelland [1961].)*

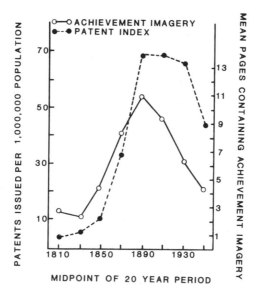

Figure 3.3. *Mean number of pages (out of 25) containing achievement imagery and the patent index. (From R. deCharms and G. H. Moeller. Values expressed in American children's readers: 1800–1950.* Journal of Abnormal and Social Psychology, *1962, 64, 136–142. Copyright 1962 by the American Psychological Association. Reprinted by permission of the publisher and authors.)*

not causation. One cannot infer the direction of causality from correlational data. If *a* and *b* are correlated, this could imply that *a* influences *b*, *b* influences *a* or both are influenced by a third variable. McClelland attempted to overcome this difficulty by noting the "time lag" in the relationship. Since changes in need achievement precede by an unspecified period changes in economic levels, then the changes in need achievement must be responsible for the changes in economic growth and not the converse. There is a possible criticism of this argument. The economic indices used by McClelland may have a certain time lag built into them. Consider, for example, electrical consumption. Electrical consumption should to some unknown degree reflect the economic growth that has preceded the consumption. Prior to any change in consumption, decisions would have to be made to expand production in many industries and to engage in entrepreneurial activities that would at some future date result in increases in electrical consumption. Therefore, it is at least theoretically possible that need-achievement levels in children's readers may reflect entrepreneurial activities that are simultaneously occurring. It is even possible that these entrepreneurial activities may occur prior to the occurrence of changes in the need-achievement content of children's readers. Such changes in the activities of members of a society might well be reflected in changes in the thematic content of the readers. This analysis suggests that, at least on this one central point, McClelland's data may not clearly indicate the direction of causality.

The argument that need achievement may not have causal relationship to economic growth in a society is buttressed by the findings of Skolnick (1966) and Beit-Hallahmi (1980). Beit-Hallahmi found that the relationship reported by McClelland between indices of need achievement derived from children's readers and economic growth was not present for the modern era. Skolnick found that social mobility was not predicted by adolescent need-achievement level and that social status related to adult need-achievement scores. These studies suggest that the relationship between need-achievement and indices of personal or social accomplishment may not be invariant and that the relationship may not invariably be interpreted as reflecting the influence of need achievement on economic and personal accomplishment as opposed to the converse or concurrent direction of influence.

McClelland (1965; McClelland & Winter, 1969), in his characteristically ambitious and bold manner, attempted to develop an experimental test of his hypothesis. In order to accomplish this, he developed a training program that purported to increase the need-achievement levels of adults. The approach to the inculcation of achievement motivation used by McClelland and his associates had several components. It included a description of the characteristics of the person with high need-achievement, the use of games and problems combined with an opportunity to discuss the characteristic behaviors of individuals who were high in achievement motivation on these tasks, and teaching subjects the techniques for scoring fantasy materials for need achievement. Need-achievement training sessions might persist over several sessions. It is apparent that motivational training was a complex quasi-therapeutic procedure involving social influence, monitoring of thoughts, and social modeling of appropriate behaviors. It is also apparent that such training would bias an index of need-achievement levels derived from subjects exposed to such intensive training. In order to assess the impact of need-achievement training on achievement motivation, one would have to observe behavioral changes in individuals exposed to the training. However, evidence for behavioral changes accompanying exposure to need-achievement training was ambiguous. It is not clear that the changes were attributable to changes in need achievement created by the training or to personal changes created by the entire experience of achievement training.

If the achievement training program were successful and if McClelland's hypothesis were correct, then the individuals who had been exposed to such programs should have engaged in activities that affected the economic development of their society. Kolb's (1965) article presented detailed information about an attempt to use this procedure to help underachieving high school boys improve their grades. Kolb started with a group of 57 boys who were placed in a summer school program. Of the boys, 20 of the 57 received achievement-motivation training. He found that the boys who participated in this training had greater improvement in their grade-point average 1 and 2 years later than did the boys in the control group. However, further analysis indicated that the improvement in grade-point average was restricted to boys in the achievement training group who were relatively high in socioeconomic status (see Figure 3.4).

Kolb's results raise some questions about the efficacy of achievement-motivation training. The finding that this training is seen to have significant impact on individuals with relatively high socioeconomic status suggests that the training may be efficacious only for individuals who return to a social situation that provides support and encouragement for achievement-oriented activities.

McClelland and Winter (1969) reported the results of a series of studies designed to create achievement motivation in businessmen in India. They found that achievement-motivation training produced a number of changes in the entrepreneurial behavior of the businessmen. Relative to a control group who did not receive the training, the businessmen who received the training were more likely to start a new business or to be involved in a major

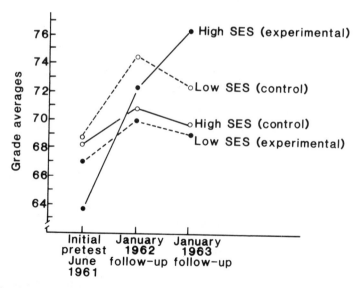

Figure 3.4. *School grade average in pretest and follow-up periods. (From D. Kolb.* Achievement motivation training for underachieving high-school boys. Journal of Personality and Social Psychology, *1965, 2, 783–792. Copyright 1965 by the American Psychological Association. Reprinted by permission of the publisher and author.)*

expansion of their firm. Also, the businessmen given this training showed significant increases in the number of hours they worked, in the number of people in their employ, and in the amount of money they invested in their businesses. The research reported by McClelland and Winter indicates that changes in achievement motivation produce the kinds of changes in entrepreneurial behavior that could lead to economic change and development. In addition, these studies establish that changes in achievement motivation do have significant consequences for behavior in extralaboratory settings.

Atkinson's Risk-taking Model

Atkinson's model treats need achievement as a theoretical variable that combines in specified ways with other theoretical variables. This relatively precise and formal representation of what is measured by the need-achievement test permits one to derive predictions of the expected behaviors of individuals who differ in achievement related motives. This model grows out of a synthesis of several "expectancy" theories (see Feather, 1959). Perhaps the most relevant theories are Tolman's (1955) expectancy theory and an analysis of the determinants of level of aspiration developed by Lewin, Dembo, Festinger, and Sears (1944). In Tolman's theory, the tendency to perform a particular act is a multiplicative function of three kinds of variables: a motivational variable representing the need or desire for some particular goal object; an expectancy variable that may be conceived of as a quantitatively varying belief that some particular act in a particular situation will lead to the goal object; and the incentive or the value of the goal object to the individual. Lewin's analysis of level of aspiration behavior considers variables that are conceptually similar to those used by Tolman. In Lewin's theory the choice of a particular task with a particular level of difficulty associated with it is a multiplicative function of the valence or value associated with success at the task and the subjective probability of success at the task. The valence of success corresponds to Tolman's incentive variable, and the subjective probability of success corresponds to Tolman's expectancy variable. In addition, Lewin discussed two motives that influence level of aspiration behavior, the hope of success, and the fear of failure. In summary, in theories developed both by Lewin and his collaborators and by Tolman, emphasis is placed on multiplicative relationships among motive, expectancy, and incentive variables.

Atkinson developed his risk-taking model, initially, to deal with level of aspiration or choice behavior. He assumed, as did Lewin in his analysis, that an individual in an achievement-oriented situation who must choose a task of a particular level of difficulty is in a conflict situation in which both a tendency to seek success (T_s) and a tendency to avoid failure (T_{af}) were involved. Each of these tendencies was assumed to be determined by a multiplicative relationship among motive, expectancy, and incentive variables. Thus, the tendency to seek success associated with a particular task is defined by the following equation:

$$T_s = M_s \times P_s \times I_s,$$

where M_s refers to the motive to achieve success, P_s to the subjective probability of success (that is, to the subject's expectancy that his performance on a particular task will be successful), and I_s refers to the incentive value of success (that is, the value of success on a particular task to the individual).

Atkinson (1957), following an earlier assumption of Lewin *et al.*, assumed that in achievement-related tasks (tasks in which success is related to a feeling of pride in competition with some standard of excellence) there is a special relationship between I_s and P_s. I_s is assumed to equal $1 - P_s$. This assumption implies that the incentive value of success at a task is related to the subjectively defined difficulty of the task. Thus, success at an easy task is assumed to have a lower incentive value than success at a difficult task.

Atkinson defined the tendency to avoid failure in a conceptually parallel manner, as follows:

$$T_{af} = M_{af} \times P_f \times I_f,$$

where M_{af} refers to the motive to avoid failure, P_f to the subjective probability of failure, and I_f to the incentive value of failure. Atkinson assumed, again in agreement with the Lewin *et al.* analysis, that there is a special relationship between P_f and I_f in an achievement-related task. The incentive value of failure is assumed to equal $- (1 - P_f)$. The negative sign in front of the parenthesis indicates that failure is a noxious event that is unpleasant for an individual and that he or she should attempt to avoid. The degree to which failure at a particular task is noxious or unpleasant is dependent upon the difficulty of the task. If the task is easy and P_f is, as a result, relatively low, then $1 - P_f$ will be relatively high, and $- (1 - P_f)$ will be a high negative number. On the other hand, if the task is difficult, P_f will be high; $1 - P_f$ will be relatively low; and $- (1 - P_f)$ will be a relatively low negative number. This simple algebra indicates the psychological basis of the assumption relating I_f and P_f—namely, that failure at an easy task is more unpleasant or noxious than failure at a difficult task.

It should be noted that Atkinson assumed that $P_s + P_f = 1$, and therefore, that $P_f = 1 - P_s$. Substituting in the equation defining the relationship between P_f and I_f, I_f is found to equal $-P_s$. Thus on an easy task, when P_s is high, I_f is high and negative, and on a difficult task where P_s is low, I_f is low and negative.

Atkinson's equations defining T_s and T_{af} imply that P_s and P_F, respectively, multiply I_s and I_f. The resulting products of this multiplication for different levels of P_s are presented in Table 3.2. An examination of Table 3.2 indicates that the products of both P_s and I_s and P_f and I_f reach their maximum absolute values when P_s is equal to .5, and the absolute value of the products decreases if P_s is increased or decreased. The product of P_s and I_s is positive whereas the product of P_f and I_f is negative.

Atkinson assumed that all persons have both M_s and M_{af}. Thus, for any achievement-related task, both T_s and T_{af} are assumed to be present. The total motivational tendency or resultant tendency is assumed to equal the combined effects of T_s and T_{af}. The resultant motivation associated with any task is dependent upon the relationship between M_s and M_{af} in a particular person. Table 3.3 illustrates resultant tendencies for tasks differing in P_s for different values of M_s and M_{af}.

An examination of Table 3.3 indicates the major implication of this model. Individuals in whom $M_s > M_{af}$ should have their highest positive resultant tendency associated with tasks for which P_s is at an intermediate level $-.5$. Individuals in whom $M_{af} > M_s$ should have negative resultant tendency associated with achievement-related tasks, but their negative resultant tendency should be highest for tasks where P_s is equal to .5. For these individuals, tasks that are very easy (high P_s) or very difficult (low P_s) should have lower negative resultant tendencies and should be preferred to tasks of intermediate difficulty. However, individuals in whom $M_s > M_{af}$ should prefer tasks of intermediate difficulty.

It is obvious that any empirical investigation of the implications of this theory requires a determination of the relationship between M_s and M_{af} for groups of individuals. Atkinson assumed that the projective measure of need achievement is a measure of the variable M_s in his theory and that the Mandler–Sarason Test of Test Anxiety (Mandler & Sarason, 1952) is a mea-

TABLE 3.2

The Product of P_s and I_s and I_f for Different P_s Values according to the Atkinson Model

P_s	$P_s \times I_s$	$P_f \times I_f$
.1	.09	−.09
.3	.21	−.21
.5	.25	−.25
.7	.21	−.21
.9	.09	−.09

Source: Atkinson, 1957.
Note: $I_s = 1 - P_s$; $P_s = 1 - P_s$; $I_f = -P_s$.

TABLE 3.3

Resultant Achievement Motivation ($T_s + T_{af}$) in Four Hypothetical Persons Differing in Strength of Motive to Achieve (M_s) and Motive to Avoid Failure (M_{af})

	Task	P_s	I_s	T_s	P_f	I_f	T_{af}	$T_s + T_{af}$
When $M_s = 3$ and	A	.90	.10	.27	.10	−.90	−.09	.18
$M_{af} = 1$	B	.70	.30	.63	.30	−.70	−.21	.42
	C	.50	.50	.75	.50	−.50	−.25	.50
	D	.30	.70	.63	.70	−.30	−.21	.42
	E	.10	.90	.27	.90	−.10	−.09	.18
When $M_s = 3$ and	A	.90	.10	.27	.10	−.90	−.18	.09
$M_{af} = 2$	B	.70	.30	.63	.30	−.70	−.42	.21
	C	.50	.50	.75	.50	−.50	−.50	.25
	D	.30	.70	.63	.70	−.30	−.42	.21
	E	.10	.90	.27	.90	−.10	−.18	.09
When $M_s = 3$ and	A	.90	.10	.27	.10	−.90	−.27	0
$M_{af} = 3$	B	.70	.30	.63	.30	−.70	−.63	0
	C	.50	.50	.75	.50	−.50	−.75	0
	D	.30	.70	.63	.70	−.30	−.63	0
	E	.10	.90	.27	.90	−.10	−.27	0
When $M_s = 1$ and	A	.90	.10	.09	.10	−.90	−.27	−.18
$M_{af} = 3$	B	.70	.30	.21	.30	−.70	−.63	−.42
	C	.50	.50	.25	.50	−.50	−.75	−.50
	D	.30	.70	.21	.70	−.30	−.63	−.42
	E	.10	.90	.09	.90	−.10	−.27	−.18

Source: Atkinson, 1964. By permission of Brooks/Cole Publishing Company.

sure of the variable M_{af}. These assumptions have usually led to a decision to assume that individuals who score high on need achievement (above the median) and low on the Mandler–Sarason scale are individuals in whom $M_s > M_{af}$. Similarly, individuals who score low on need achievement and high on the Mandler–Sarason are assumed to be individuals in whom $M_{af} > M_s$. These empirical identifications have permitted the test of several implications of the Atkinson model. These tests invariably rest on the simultaneous acceptance of two different kinds of assumptions. First, that the individual difference measures are in fact measures of the hypothetical variables M_s and M_{af} as defined in the theory. Second, that the theory contains a correct analysis of the determinants of behavior in achievement-related situations.

The earliest tests of the model concerned level of aspiration behavior. McClelland (1958) had obtained preliminary evidence that children who scored high in need achievement (as measured by Aronson's graphic procedure—see Aronson, 1958) tended to toss rings in a ring-toss game from intermediate distances whereas children low in need for achievement tended to avoid the intermediate distances. Atkinson and Litwin (1960) conducted an investigation of ring-toss behavior in subjects with different patterns of scores on the projective test of need achievement and on the Mandler–Sarason test. They assumed that individuals in whom $M_s > M_{af}$ should choose tasks of intermediate difficulty and should therefore tend to toss rings from intermediate distances. Individuals in whom $M_{af} > M_s$ should choose easy or difficult tasks and as a result in the ring toss game should elect to toss rings from long or short distances. An examination of Figure 3.5, which presents their findings, indicates that the results were in agreement with predictions.

Mahone (1960) extended this analysis of level of aspiration to occupational choice among college students. Mahone began his investigation by asking college students to estimate the percentage of college students who had the ability to succeed in various occupations. These estimates were highly correlated with sociological estimates of the prestige associated with various

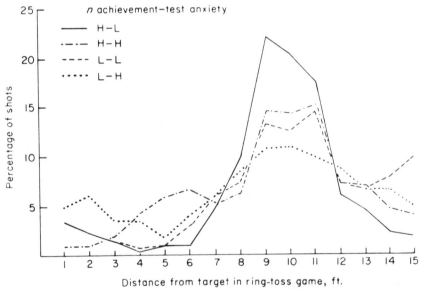

Figure 3.5. *Percentage of shots taken from each distance by college men in a ring-toss game. Graph is smoothed according to the method of running averages, for subjects classified as high or low simultaneously in need achievement and test anxiety. H–L (N = 13), H–H (N = 10), L–L (N = 9), L–H, (N = 13). (From J. W. Atkinson and G. H. Litwin. Achievement motive and test anxiety conceived as motive to approach success and motive to avoid failure. Journal of Abnormal and Social Psychology, 1960, 60, 52–63. Copyright 1960 by the American Psychological Association. Reprinted by permission of the publisher and authors.)*

TABLE 3.4

Effect of Individual Differences in Need Achievement and Anxiety on Subject Goal Discrepancy of Vocational Aspirations of Male College Students

Need achievement	Anxiety	N	Absolute goal discrepancy score (%)	
			Mid-third	Highest or lowest third
High	Low	36	50*	50
High	High	30	30	70
Low	Low	40	38	62
Low	High	28	18*	82

Source: K. H. Mahone. Fear of failure and unrealistic vocational aspiration. *Journal of Abnormal and Social Psychology*, 1960, *60*, 253–261. Copyright 1960 by the American Psychological Association. Reprinted by permission of the publisher and author.

*$p < .01$.

occupations. Certain occupational goals are more difficult to achieve than others. Accordingly, the choice of an occupation involves, in part at least, a choice among goals differing in the P_s values associated with them. The Atkinson theory thus implies that individuals in whom $M_s > M_{af}$ should choose occupations of intermediate difficulty and individuals in whom $M_{af} > M_s$ should choose occupations in which success was easy or difficult. Mahone argued that these predictions should be refined by a consideration of the subjective difficulty of the occupational choice—that is, an individual may choose a difficult occupation (for example, physician) that he or she believes, estimating his or her own ability, is easy for him or her. Mahone computed a subjective goal discrepancy score defined as the difference in the subject's estimate of his or her own ability relative to other college students and the subject's estimate of the ability required to achieve success at the chosen occupation. This distribution of goal discrepancy scores was divided into thirds. Mahone found that subjects who scored high in need achievement and low in text anxiety tended to have goal-discrepancy scores in the middle third of the distribution (see Table 3.4). Those with an opposite pattern of scores on the individual difference measures tended to have goal-discrepancy scores in the upper or lower thirds of the distribution. These results imply that subjects in whom $M_s > M_{af}$ tend to have relatively realistic occupational levels of aspiration. They choose occupations that are of intermediate difficulty for their assumed ability. Those in whom $M_{af} > M_s$ apparently choose occupations that are either relatively difficult or relatively easy for them, given their assumed level of ability.

The relationship between achievement-related motives and risk-taking preferences has been extensively studied, and a number of critical issues have been raised with respect to the relationship reported by Atkinson and Litwin. Although the preference for intermediate difficulty indicated in Figure 3.5 is clearly manifest among subjects in whom $M_s > M_{af}$, the data for subjects in whom $M_{af} > M_s$ do not indicate consistent preferences for tasks that are easy or difficult. Rather, the choices for subjects in whom $M_{af} > M_s$ tend to show some preference for tasks of intermediate difficulty—although the preference among these subjects for such tasks is less marked than among subjects in whom $M_s > M_{af}$. In fact, most studies dealing with risk preferences have reported comparable results—that is, a general preference for tasks of intermediate difficulty, which is somewhat more apparent or marked among subjects in whom $M_s > M_{af}$ than among those in whom $M_{af} > M_s$. W. U. Meyer, Folkes, and Weiner (1976) summarized data relating need achievement to risk preferences (see Table 3.5). These data tend to support the notion that there is a general preference for tasks of intermediate difficulty that is more readily apparent among subjects in whom $M_s > M_{af}$.

Atkinson and Feather (1966) explained these results by arguing that college students tend to be high in achievement motivation. However, Weiner (1980) argued that similar preferences for tasks of intermediate difficulty were found in samples of high school subjects who were obviously not selected for ability or achievement. Therefore, the phenomenon of preference for tasks of intermediate difficulty appears to be a somewhat general phenomenon present in most groups of subjects.

Trope and Brickman (1975) provided an alternative explanation for this phenomenon (see also Trope, 1975). They argued that there was a logical confounding between the difficulty level of a task and what they called the diagnosticity of a task. A task was said to be diagnostic when it provided an individual with information about his or her ability. The usual outcome of performance on easy or difficult tasks was success and failure, respectively. The individual who succeeds at either of these tasks does not receive much information about their personal abilities. Success at an easy task and failure at a difficult task may be attributable to task difficulty. However, success or failure at a task of intermediate difficulty where the outcome is uncertain may provide individuals with information about their personal characteristics and abilities. Thus preference for tasks of intermediate difficulty may be explained in terms of an affective model according to which subjects in whom $M_s > M_{af}$ maximize positive affect or by reference to an attempt to choose tasks that maximize information about an individual's personal characteristics. In the latter case some consistence preference for tasks of intermediate difficulty among subjects in whom $M_s > M_{af}$ would be attributable to a desire among them to receive feedback about their personal abilities. Trope and Brickman designed a study that attempted to separate the difficulty level of a task and its "diagnosticity." Consider a task with a P_s value of .5. If subjects are told that those of them with high ability to perform this task have a .6 probability of succeeding at the task and that those with low ability have a .4 probability of succeeding at the task, the task will be less diagnostic than one with the same P_s value for which all subjects are informed that the probability of success on the task for those with high ability is .8 and the probability of succeeding for those with low ability is .2. It is clear that difficulty level and diagnosticity of tasks may be independently varied. Trope and Brickman found that when given a choice between an easy task high in diagnosticity level and a task of intermediate difficulty level and low diagnosticity, subjects preferred the task with high diagnosticity rather than the task of intermediate difficulty, suggesting that the preference for tasks of intermediate difficulty is attributable to a general preference for diagnostic information about personal abilities.

Trope and Brickman's study did not include information about individual differences in achievement motivation, and as a result, their study does not provide a test of the notion that subjects in whom $M_s > M_{af}$ do *not* have a true preference for tasks of intermediate difficulty. Trope (1975) reported a study designed to test this notion. He used the Mehrabian test of achievement motivation (see Mehrabian, 1968) to classify subjects in motive orientation and presented them with tasks that were independently varied in both diagnosticity and difficulty. His findings were relatively unambiguous. First, he replicated the results reported by Trope and Brickman—that is, that subjects tended to prefer tasks of high diagnosticity to tasks of low diagnosticity. Second, this preference occurred at each of three difficulty levels (easy, moderate, and difficult). Figure 3.6 presents these preference data and also reveals a third finding. The clearest preference exhibited by subjects was for easy tasks rather than tasks of moderate or high difficulty. With respect to achievement motivation, the results were equally unambiguous. Subjects in whom $M_s > M_{af}$ exhibited clearer preferences for tasks high in diagnosticity than those in whom $M_{af} > M_s$ (see Figure 3.7). Subjects in whom $M_s > M_{af}$ did not have greater preference for tasks of intermediate difficulty than those in whom $M_{af} > M_s$. The Trope study, on the surface, appears to present an elegant experimental refutation of Atkinson's model—that is, that subjects in whom $M_s > M_{af}$ do not have a preference for tasks of intermediate difficulty, but rather, they have a preference for tasks that are high in diagnosticity.

Although the Trope study appears to be definitive, like most empirically decidable issues in psychology, the results are rarely unequivocal. Trope did not use the method of operationalizing the $M_s > M_{af}$ and $M_{af} > M_s$ distinction recommended by Atkinson. Rather, he used the Mehrabian test instead of the TAT measure of need achievement combined with the Mandler–Sarason Test Anxiety Questionnaire. Atkinson and Birch (1978) argued that paper-and-pencil tests of achievement motivation such as Mehrabian's might not be

78

TABLE 3.5
Risk-Preference Studies

Investigator[b]	Subjects	Task	P_s	Motive measure[c]	Choice distribution[a]	
					High n Ach	Low n Ach
Atkinson et al. (1960)[d]	Male, undergraduate	Shuffle board	Obj.	FTI	Quad.[e]	Linear (dif>int>eas)[f]
Atkinson and Litwin (1960)	Male, undergraduate	Ring-toss	Subj.	FTI, TAQ	Quad.	Quad.
Damm (1968)	Male, jr. high school	Ring-toss	Subj.	TAT, TASC	Quad./linear[g] (dif=int>eas)	Quad.
DeCharms and Davé (1965)	Male, grade school	Basket-shooting	Subj.	TAT	Linear/Quad.[h] (dif>int>eas)	Linear (dif>int>eas)
Hamilton (1974)	Male, high school	Ring-toss	Subj.	FTI, TAQ	Quad.	Linear (dif>int>eas)
Isaacson (1964)	Undergraduate	Major in school	Obj.	FTI, TAQ	Male=quad. Female=linear (eas>int>dif)	Linear[i]

Study	Population	Task	Type	Measure		
McClelland (1958)[j]	a. Kindergarten	Ring-toss	Obj.	Doodles	Quad.	Quad.
	b. Third-grade	Dot connection	Obj.	Doodles	Quad.	Linear (rectangular)
Moulton (1965)	Male, high school	Unspecified	Subj.	TAT, TAQ	Quad.	Quad.
Schneider (1973)[k]	Male, high school and under-graduate	Shooting	Subj.	TAT	Quad.	Quad.[l]

Source: W. U. Meyer, V. S. Folkes, and B. Weiner. The perceived information value and affective consequences of choice behavior and intermediate difficulty task selection. Journal of Research in Personality, 1976, 10, 410–423.

[a] The one best description as determined by visual inspection of the reported data.

[b] Relevant studies with insufficient data to be included are Mahone (1960); Morris (1966); Raynor and Smith (1966); and Kukla (1972).

[c] FTI = French Test of Insight; TAQ = Test Anxiety Questionnaire; TASC = Test Anxiety Scale for Children; TAT = Thematic Apperception Test.

[d] Data summed over five choices.

[e] Unless otherwise indicated, quadratic resembles a bell-shaped distribution. Often the authors combine difficulty levels so that the peak of the distribution cannot be determined.

[f] Greater choice of difficult than intermediate tasks, greater choice of intermediate than easy tasks.

[g] Distributions appear to be equally present.

[h] Two different TAT measures yield somewhat different distributions.

[i] Linear in three populations (includes dif>int>eas, eas>int>dif, and rectangular) and U-shaped in one.

[j] Two experiments.

[k] Summary of four experiments.

[l] Bell-shaped in three experiments, U-shaped in one.

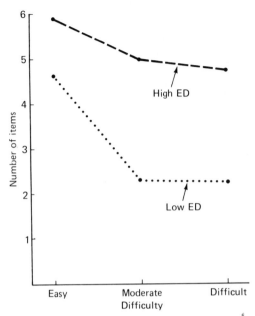

Figure 3.6.   *Mean number of items chosen from six texts varying in difficulty and expected diagnostic value (ED). (From Y. Trope. Seeking information about one's own ability as a determinant of choice among tasks.* Journal of Personality and Social Psychology, *1975, 32, 1004–1013. Copyright 1975 by the American Psychological Association. Reprinted by permission of the publisher and author.)*

a measure of the same construct as measured by the TAT and TAQ measures (p. 350). The Mehrabian test is based on research on the achievement motive. It asks subjects questions about their behavior in a variety of situations in which previous research suggests that individuals who differ in achievement motivation would behave in different ways. The validity of the test rests on the assumption that individuals' reports about their behavior are isomorphic with the actual behavior they would exhibit if they were exposed to the relevant situation. Also, the validity of the test is contingent upon the selection of appropriate behavioral manifestations of the underlying motive. More directly, Mehrabian (1968) reported that the correlation between his measure of resultant achievement motivation and a measure of resultant achievement motivation based on the combined score on the projective test and the TAQ was approximately .3. The positive correlation of .3 suggests that the Mehrabian test is only partially related to the combined projective method and TAQ procedure for defining the relationship between M_s and M_{af}. It would appear in light of the uncertainty surrounding the Mehrabian test as a measure of achievement motivation that Trope's study should be replicated with the use of the projective measure of need achievement. If the results of such an investigation using the projective test replicate Trope's results, it would appear that the risk-taking model would be clearly disconfirmed.

The concern expressed with respect to the method of measurement used by Trope in his study is buttressed by the results of an attempt to replicate his results in a German sample using another test of achievement motivation developed by Schmalt (1976). In Buckert, Meyer, and Schmalt's (1979) replication of the Trope experiment, they found, as did Trope, that subjects preferred tasks high in diagnosticity to tasks low in diagnosticity, independent of the difficulty level of the task. However, differences in need achievement were not related to preferences for tasks that differed in diagnosticity. These data suggest that differences in diagnosticity of tasks are not the sole or correct explanation of the greater preference for tasks of intermediate difficulty usually reported among subjects in whom $M_s > M_{af}$. Furthermore, in view of the questions about the identity of differing methods for the assessment of M_s and M_{af} used in these studies, there is as yet no conclusive evidence that individual differences in preferences for tasks of intermediate difficulty are to be

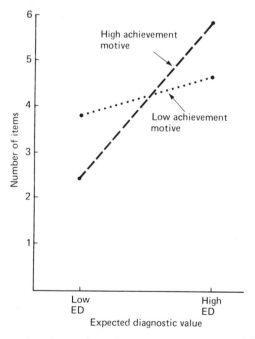

Figure 3.7.   *Mean number of items chosen from tests varying in expected diagnostic value (ED) by subjects varying in achievement motive. (From Y. Trope. Seeking information about one's own ability as a determinant of choice among tasks.* Journal of Personality and Social Psychology, 1975, 32, 1004–1013. *Copyright 1975 by the American Psychological Association. Reprinted by permission of the publisher and author.)*

explained in informational terms as a by-product of a desire for diagnosticity rather than in terms of attempts to maximize affective components as is implied by the Atkinson risk-taking model.

The previously described studies represent tests of relatively direct predictions derived from Atkinson's model. In what follows I will consider tests of somewhat more indirect implications derived from the model. These implications deal, respectively, with level of aspiration behavior, persistence, and performance.

Moulton (1965) was interested in the phenomena of atypical shift in level of aspiration. An atypical shift is the choice of a more difficult task following failure at an easier task or the choice of an easier task following success at a more difficult task. Moulton set up a level of aspiration situation in which subjects were required to work on a task of intermediate difficulty whose P_s value was assumed to be .5. The experiment was designed in such a way that the experimenter could manipulate success or failure at the task. One-half the subjects succeeded at the original task, and one-half failed. Subjects were then required to choose a task that was either easier or more difficult than the initial task chosen. Moulton quite reasonably assumed that success on the intermediate task would lead to an increase in the P_s values of all the tasks and failure would lead to a decrease in P_s values for all the tasks. The P_s values assigned by the experimenter to the easy and difficult tasks prior to subjects success or failure at the task of intermediate difficulty were equidistant from .5, $-.25$, and .75, respectively. Following success on the intermediate task, the P_s value for the difficult task should be closer to .5 than the P_s value for the easy task. Therefore, subjects in whom $M_s > M_{af}$ should have tended to choose the difficult task rather than the easy task. This choice would represent a typical shift—the choice of a more difficult task following success at an easier task. Subjects in whom $M_{af} > M_s$ should have tended to choose the easy task rather than the difficult task, because the P_s for this task is further from .5 than the P_s for the difficult task. This choice represents an atypical shift in level of aspiration. Following failure the P_s values on the easy task should be closer to .5 than the P_s values on the difficult task. Therefore, Moulton reasoned that subjects in whom $M_s > M_{af}$ should have a typical shift in this task—the choice of the easier task following failure, whereas those in whom $M_{af} > M_s$ should have an atypical shift—the choice of a more difficult task following failure. Table 3.6 presents Moulton's results. Examination of the data indicates that only the avoidance-oriented subjects (subjects in whom M_{af} was assumed to be greater than M_s) showed any substantial number of atypical shifts.

Perhaps the most elegant test of the Atkinson model deals with persistence. Feather (1961) derived hypotheses from the model about individual differences in persistence at tasks thought to be easy or difficult. Persistence is

TABLE 3.6
Type of Shift in Level of Aspiration as Related to Resultant Motivation

Resultant motivation	Type of shift		N
	Atypical	Typical	
Avoidance-oriented	11	20	31
Ambivalent	3	28	31
Approach-oriented	1	30	31
Total	15	78	93

Avoidance-oriented versus approach-oriented, $\chi^2 = 8.37^{**}$
Avoidance-oriented versus ambivalent, $\chi^2 = 4.52^*$

Source: R. W. Moulton. Effects of success and failure on level of aspiration as related to achievement motives. *Journal of Personality and Social Psychology,* 1965, *1,* 399–406. Copyright 1965 by the American Psychological Association. Reprinted by permission of the publisher and author.
   $^*p < .05.$
   $^{**}p < .01.$

usually defined in psychological research as the length of time a person continues to work on a task on which he or she fails to find an acceptable solution. Feather used insoluble puzzles in his study. He investigated persistence on these puzzles when subjects were told that the task was easy and when they were led to believe the task was difficult. Feather assumed that continued failure on the task tended to decrease P_s. If subject began the task believing that it was difficult ($P_s > .5$), failure on the task would lead to a situation in which P_s changes were moving away from .5. In this situation Atkinson's model implies that individuals in whom M_s is assumed to be greater than M_{af} should find themselves in a situation in which their resultant motivational tendency becomes less positive the longer they stay in the task. Individuals in whom $M_{af} > M_s$ should find their resulting motivational tendency becoming less negative the longer they persist on the task. If the subject begins the task with the expectation that it is easy ($P_s > .5$) and meets failure, changes in P_s should, at least initially, lead him or her to a P_s of .5. Under these conditions subjects in whom $M_s > M_{af}$ should initially find the task one in which their resultant motivational tendency is becoming increasingly positive. On the other hand, subjects in whom $M_{af} > M_s$ should find themselves in a task in which, at least initially, their resultant motivation becomes more negative as they persist on the task. Given this analysis, Feather was able to derive predictions indicating that those in whom $M_s > M_{af}$ would tend to persist more on easy than on difficult tasks and those in whom $M_{af} > M_s$ would tend to persist more on tasks defined as difficult than on easy tasks. Examination of Feather's results shown in Table 3.7 indicates that Feather obtained clear-cut support for his predictions.

TABLE 3.7

Persistence following Failure Related to Initial Expectancy of Success and Motivational Disposition of the Individual: Number of Subjects Who Were High and Low in Persistence in Relation to Stated Difficulty of the Initial Task and The Nature of Their Motivation

			Persistence trials	
Achievement, n	Test anxiety	Stated difficulty of task	High (above median)	Low (below median)
High	Low	$P_s = .70$ (easy)	6	2
		$P_s = .05$ (difficult)	2	7
Low	High	$P_s = .70$ (easy)	3	6
		$P_s = .05$ (difficult)	6	2

Partition of χ^2			
Source	Value	df	p
Motivation × Persistence	.12	1	n.s.
Expectation × Persistence	.12	1	n.s.
Motivation × Expectation × Persistence	7.65	1	<.01
Total	7.89	3	<.05

Source: N. T. Feather. The relationship of persistence at a task to expectation of success and achievement-related motives. *Journal of Abnormal and Social Psychology,* 1961, *63*, 552–561. Copyright 1961 by the American Psychological Association. Reprinted by permission of the publisher and author.

The last topic of consideration is the relationship between need achievement and performance using Atkinson's model as a basis for prediction. In the previous discussion of performance differences between individuals high or low in achievement motivation, little emphasis was placed on the conditions under which individuals who differ in achievement related motives will perform differently. Clearly Atkinson's model implies that optimal performance and effort would be exhibited by individuals in whom $M_s > M_{af}$ in tasks for which P_s is .5. Similarly, less than optimal interest and effort would be expected from individuals in whom $M_{af} > M_s$ when P_s is .5. O'Connor, Atkinson, and Horner (1966) tested implications derived from Atkinson's theory about the motivational implications of ability grouping in the schools. They studied the performance of sixth-grade children who were either switched from a fifth-grade heterogeneous classroom to a homogeneously ability-grouped sixth-grade or to a heterogeneous sixth-grade classroom. In a heterogeneous classroom there should be a large number of children for whom school represents a particularly easy or difficult situation. Children above average in ability should have, in comparison to others, found the school situation relatively easy, and children below average in ability should have found the school situation relatively difficult. Under conditions of ability grouping, most of the children in the classroom should have found themselves in competition with children of relatively equal ability. Accordingly, the school situation should have been defined as one of moderate difficulty for most of the children. This analysis implies that children in whom $M_s > M_{af}$ should tend to perform better in homogeneously grouped classrooms than in heterogeneous classrooms. Conversely, children in whom $M_{af} > M_s$ should tend to perform better in heterogeneous classrooms than in homogeneous classrooms. O'Connor *et al.* found that children in whom M_s was assumed to be higher than M_{af} did in fact perform better in homogeneous ability-grouped classes. They found that 79% of these children showed above median gains in arithmetic and reading in homogeneous classes. Only 40% of the $M_s > M_{af}$ children showed above average gains in the heterogeneous classrooms. No differences were found in performance among children in whom M_{af} can be assumed to be greater than M_s and who were assigned to homogeneous or heterogeneous classrooms. There was some slight evidence that these latter children showed greater interest in school when placed in heterogeneous rather than homogeneous classes. On the whole, the results of the O'Connor *et al.* study do extend the predictive range of Atkinson's model in that they show some of the conditions under which individuals who differ in achievement related motives may be expected to exhibit optimal performance.

Theoretical Extensions of Atkinson's Model

Feather's study may be viewed as the most elegant test reported of Atkinson's risk-taking model. It also suggests a conception of motivation that carries one beyond the risk-taking model. Atkinson's model specifies the relative strength of the tendency of individuals differing in hypothetical motive patterns to engage in a class of achievement related activities that differ in probability of success. The results of Feather's experiment do not derive from the model without some additional assumptions about the relationship between changes in achievement-related action tendencies and other activities presumably under the influence of other motivational tendencies in which individuals could be engaged. Thus, Feather used Atkinson's model as a basis for analyzing changes in the strength of the tendency to persist in a task. However, the model does not, strictly speaking, tell us at what point changes in the assumed underlying strength of the tendency to engage in this task will lead the individual to abandon the task. A person who is assumed to be high in need achievement may be assumed to have a positive motive to engage in the task even if he or she fails at a task assumed to be difficult. Of course the relative strength of the motivational tendency to engage in the task declines over time. In order to derive predictions about the cessation of activity, one must know something about an alternative motivational tendency to do something other than trying to solve a problem—which at some point in the sequence may be more attractive than persistence on the achievement-related task. This analysis suggests that a goal-directed theory of motivation cannot deal simply with the notion that behavior persists until a goal is attained. For, clearly, we do not always attain our goals, and at some point we must abandon them. Even when goals are attained, we substitute new goals for old ones.

In the research to be described, I will show a series of modifications of Atkinson's model and a series of new theoretical developments, each of which may be conceived of as extensions of the original theory involving the relationships between engaging in an achievement-related activity and subsequent activities.

Weiner (1965; see also 1972) reported one of the first studies that extended the Atkinson risk-taking model to consider changes in motivational tendencies that result from the attainment of a goal or failure to attain a goal. His analysis was based on ideas suggested by Atkinson (1964) and Atkinson and Cartwright (1964). They had argued that goal-directed tendencies persist until a goal is attained. The failure to attain a goal would leave a residue or "inertial tendency" that would persist through time and could influence behavior in a subsequent situation. (This notion implies that the effects of success and failure, with respect to subsequent motivational tendencies, are not symmetrical.)

Weiner (1965) argued that following success, the motivational tendencies both to seek success and to avoid failure are decreased. However, following failure, there is no corresponding decrement in these motivational tendencies (that is, goal attainment has not occurred, and there is a carry-over inertial influence present). Weiner applied this analysis of inertial influences to an experimental situation similar to that used by Feather (1961) in his study of persistence. In his experiment subjects either encountered success at an easy task (P_s = .7) or failure at a difficult task (P_s = .3). The task involved digit–symbol substitution (that is, subjects were asked to write a particular symbol for each digit appearing on a card). They were allowed to perform the task as often as they liked. Thus Weiner's experiment provides a measure of persistence. Also, by studying the time taken to complete 60 digit–symbol substitutions, the task permits one to obtain a measure of the quality of performance. Table 3.8 presents Weiner's data for the time taken to complete 60 digit–symbol substitutions on the initial attempt and on the second attempt following success at what subjects were led to believe was an easy task, or failure at what they were led to believe was a difficult task. There are several aspects of the results that are relevant to Weiner's theoretical analysis. Note first that the data indicate that the performance on the initial trial was essentially equal for both types of subjects ($M_s > M_{af}$ and $M_{af} > M_s$) in both types of situations in which the task was assumed to either be relatively easy or difficult. However, the effects of success and failure were not symmetrical. Failure tended to lead to slightly better performance among subjects in whom $M_s > M_{af}$ than success. (Note that shorter times to complete the task are indicative of better performance.) Failure clearly impeded the quality of performance of subjects in whom $M_{af} > M_s$. Weiner found that subjects in whom $M_s > M_{af}$ exhibited a slight but not statistically significant tendency to persist longer on the task following failure than following success. There were no differences in persistence at all among those in whom $M_{af} > M_s$.

Weiner interpreted his results as supporting the existence of inertial tendencies. Atkinson's risk-taking model assumed that achievement motivational tendencies are determined by the characteristics of the task which is presented to a person. Weiner assumed that success at an easy task ($P_s = .7$) and failure at a difficult task ($P_s = .3$) led to changes of equal magnitude in P_s in opposite directions. If the increment in P_s following success is roughly equal to the decrement in P_s following failure, subjects should have more or less equivalent motivational tendencies to engage in a task in the success or failure condition. However, success at the initial task decreases motivational tenden-

TABLE 3.8

Time (in Seconds) to Complete 60 Digit–Symbol Substitutions on Trial 1 and Trial 2

Condition		Motive classification			
		$M_s > M_{af}$		$M_{af} > M_s$	
		Trial 1	Trial 2	Trial 1	Trial 2
Success	N	19	19	12	12
	M	60.10	66.63	60.58	62.75
	SD	7.80	10.20	10.20	11.83
Failure	N	14[a]	14[a]	14	14
	M	60.93	64.33	60.93	70.43
	SD	9.06	8.45	8.83	13.0

Source: B. Weiner. The effects of unsatisfied achievement motivation in persistence and subsequent performance. *Journal of Personality,* 1965, *33,* 428–442. Copyright © 1965, Duke University Press (Durham, N.C.)

[a]Level of performance for one subject could not be accurately evaluated.

cies, and if failure does not diminish those tendencies, then the motivational tendency to engage in the task on the second trial may include an inertial tendency derived from the first trial following failure that is not present following success. This inertial tendency should add a positive component to the total motivation of subjects in whom $M_s > M_{af}$ following failure and a negative component to those in whom $M_{af} > M_s$. Also, given a choice permitting subjects to persist in this task, Weiner's analysis suggests that persistence should be greater following the failure condition among subjects in whom $M_s > M_{af}$ and persistence should be greater following success than failure among those in whom $M_{af} > M_s$. Although Weiner reports a significant interaction effect indicating that the effects on performance following the success and failure experience are not equivalent in both types of subjects, further analysis of the results indicates that the support for the analysis is somewhat equivocal—that is, that the hypothesized differences in performance are not statistically significant among subjects in whom $M_s > M_{af}$. They are significant in subjects in whom $M_{af} > M_s$. None of the differences were statistically significant for the persistence measures. Thus the only unequivocal support for the hypothesized inertial influence that Weiner found is a deterioration in performance following failure among subjects in whom $M_{af} > M_s$. Although this result is compatible with an inertial interpretation, it could probably be explained by any of a number of other theoretical accounts that are less elaborate. However, what is of great interest in Weiner's study, despite the somewhat equivocal empirical results is the analysis and empirical testing of a theoretical conception that is no longer "stimulus-bound" but that attempts to deal with carry-over motivational tendencies.

Raynor (1969, 1970, 1974; Raynor & Rubin, 1971) also extended the risk-taking model to a consideration of the relationships between several goal-directed actions. Raynor distinguished between goals that are sought as ends in themselves and goals that are perceived as subgoals or as contingent to other goals. In an achievement-oriented contingent situation, it is necessary to succeed at a particular task in order to be permitted to attempt to succeed at a subsequent task. Consider a student who plans to become a physician. Successful performance in a course in organic chemistry may be conceived as a contingent goal. Success at this task is required in order to be admitted into medical school, and, successful performance of classes in medical school is necessary to attain the ultimate goal. Raynor argued that the motivational tendencies to engage in a particular task are influenced not only by the characteristics of the task but also by the potential motivational effects of other goals that are contingently related to the successful performance on the immediate task. Raynor derived a number of predictions based on this theoretical analysis. If a successful performance at a particular task is perceived as being contingent to the opportunity to engage in other tasks, the resultant motivation to do well on this task should be stronger than if the same task is perceived as being noncontingent. Where the resultant motivation for a subject is positive $(M_s > M_{af})$ he or she ought to do better on a task that is contingent than one that is noncontingent. For subjects in whom $M_{af} > M_s$, the opposite prediction can be made if the task is one in which the quality of performance may reasonably be assumed to be positively related to resultant motivation.

Raynor reported several studies that provide data related to this analysis. In his initial study on this problem, Raynor studied grades in an introductory psychology course. He asked subjects to indicate whether or not good grades in the course were important to attain their long-term career objectives. He assumed that for subjects who asserted that the course grades were very important, good grades would act as contingent goals. This analysis implies that subjects in whom $M_s > M_{af}$ would get better grades if the goal of getting good grades was a contingent goal. Subjects in whom $M_{af} > M_s$ are assumed to get better grades where the goal of a good grade is noncontingent, since in the contingent goal case, the potential negative motivational consequences of subsequent tasks in the sequence detracts from the quality of performance on the present task. Table 3.9 presents the results of Raynor's initial study. An examination of the data in Table 3.9 shows a pattern of results that clearly supports the hypothesis: Subjects in whom $M_s > M_{af}$ clearly demonstrate better performance in a situation in which they assert that good grades are perceived as instrumental to success.

Raynor also reported a replication of this study in another introductory psychology class. The replication data are presented in Table 3.10, and the

TABLE 3.9
Study I: Mean Grades in Introductory Psychology as a Function of Achievement-related Motives and Perceived Instrumentality

N achievement test anxiety	Perceived instrumentality (PI-Psych)			
	N	Low	N	High
High–low	15	2.93	19	3.37
Low–high	11	3.00	17	2.59

Source: J. O. Raynor. Relationships between achievement-related motives, future orientation, and academic performance. *Journal of Personality and Social Psychology,* 1970, *15*, 28–33. Copyright 1970 by the American Psychological Association. Reprinted by permission of the publisher and author.

TABLE 3.10
Study II: Mean Grades in Introductory Psychology as a Function of Achievement-related Motives and Perceived Instrumentality

N achievement test anxiety	Perceived instrumentality (PI-Psych)			
	N	Low	N	High
High–low	21	2.95	20	3.50
Low–high	16	3.38	24	3.42

Source: J. O. Raynor. Relationships between achievement-related motives, future orientation, and academic performance. *Journal of Personality and Social Psychology,* 1970, *15,* 28–33. Copyright 1970 by the American Psychological Association. Reprinted by permission of the publisher and author.

data are not as clearly supportive of the analysis. In this case, the data indicate that subjects in whom $M_s > M_{af}$ obtain higher grades when they believe that grades are instrumental to subsequent career attainment. However, subjects in whom $M_{af} > M_s$ do not obtain poorer grades when they assert that the grades are instrumental to the attainment of their ultimate career goals. The statistical test for the interaction between motive groups and perceived instrumentality of grades did not quite attain the conventional level of significance ($p < .05$). Thus the replication data provides equivocal support for the analysis. Raynor also obtained information about the perceived instrumentality of other courses being taken by subjects in his study. He classified courses as being either high or low in their perceived instrumentality for subsequent career success, and he studied the grades in courses they asserted to be instrumental to subsequent career success. However, there was no significant interaction between motive groups and perceived instrumentality. Table 3.11 presents these data and clearly indicates that the pattern of results is comparable for both motive groups. Taken together, these studies provide only equivocal support for the theoretical analysis. There is little consistent evidence of an interaction between motive groups and perceived instrumentality of grades in determining grades.

Raynor and Rubin (1971) reported a direct experimental test of the predicted interaction between individual differences in motivation and performance in contingent and noncontingent path situations. In this study they informed subjects in one condition (contingent path) that successful performance at a task where the probability of success was .5 would be required in order to be permitted to work on a second task. In the other condition

TABLE 3.11
Individual Differences in Motivation and GPA as a Function of Perceived Instrumentality of Grades

N achievement test anxiety	Perceived instrumentality	
	Low	High
High–low	2.62	2.89
Low–high	2.71	2.84

Source: Raynor, 1970.

subjects were told that they would be given an opportunity to work on the series of tasks irrespective of the quality of their performance on the initial task (noncontingent path). The task consisted of a series of arithmetic problems. The data from the experiment are presented in Table 3.12 and indicate a clear pattern of results in support of the hypothesis. In addition there was a statistically significant interaction between motive groups and experimental conditions. Raynor's experimental study provides the clearest support for the notion that the quality of performance of a particular task is dependent on the relationship between a task and subsequent tasks. However, the study used a small sample and no replication of the results has been reported.

Raynor (1974) also used his theoretical analysis to derive hypotheses

TABLE 3.12
Mean Number of Problems Answered Correctly as a Function of Motive Groups and Experimental Conditions

	Condition			
	Noncontingent		Contingent	
Motive group	N	M	N	M
High-low	8	13.00	7	17.43
High–high	6	8.83	6	12.00
Low-low	10	12.70	6	11.33
Low–high	7	11.86	8	7.00

Source: J. O. Raynor and I. S. Rubin. Effects of achievement motivation and future orientation on level of performance. *Journal of Personality and Social Psychology*, 1971, 17, 36–41. Copyright 1971 by the American Psychological Association. Reprinted by permission of the publisher and authors.

about risk-taking behavior. He argued that subjects in whom $M_s > M_{af}$ should prefer easy tasks in contingent path situations. In a contingent path situation in which successful performance on a particular task is necessary in order to be permitted to continue on the path, the probability of successful attainment of the final goal of the sequence is the product of the several probabilities of success in each of the tasks. If individuals in whom $M_s > M_{af}$ would select three tasks with a probability of success of .5 in a contingent path in which successful performance of three tasks is required for final goal success, the probability of ultimate goal attainment would be .125. If subjects wish to insure a reasonable chance of ultimate goal success and if they wish to continue to strive toward an ultimate goal in an achievement-related situation, then they should gravitate toward easier tasks in contingent path situations. Subjects in whom $M_{af} > M_s$ should, on Raynor's analysis, avoid the choice of easy tasks in contingent tasks since the potential increase in the length of the path that initial success permits in effect adds to the total negative motivational influence. Raynor asserted that he conducted a series of seven studies on this issue. He found little evidence for the expected interaction between motive groups and contingent versus noncontingent paths in determining risk-taking preferences. According to Raynor his data indicated that all subjects, irrespective of motive groups, preferred easier tasks in contingent path situations. Raynor (1974) cited data obtained from an unpublished study by Wish and Hasazi that provided support for his hypothesis. In their study subjects were required to rate the difficulty level of attaining success in their chosen major. Subjects in whom $M_s > M_{af}$ preferred to choose majors in which the difficulty level was low; subjects in whom $M_{af} > M_s$ preferred majors where the difficulty level was high. Although this result conforms to the expectations for a contingent path situation, the results provide only equivocal support for the analysis since the study does not provide evidence of an interaction between the path contingency and motive groups (that is, this study does not provide evidence of a change in preference under different contingency conditions). Combined with Raynor's failure to find the predicted interaction in seven unpublished studies, it can be concluded that there is little evidence of an interaction between motive types and contingent versus noncontingent paths in determination of risk-taking behavior.

Examining the total set of results reported by Raynor, I find that, although there is occasional support for hypotheses derived from his theoretical extension of Atkinson's risk-taking model, the majority of the studies have not provided consistent empirical support for this analysis. What is perhaps of greater lasting interest in this body of research is the theoretical extension contained in the model—that is, that behavior on a particular task may be influenced by a subject's awareness of its relationship to subsequent tasks. Action tendencies may be hierarchically organized such that a particular goal-directed activity is not a final terminal goal but is conceived as a subgoal leading to a more distant goal. It would appear to be necessary for a goal-directed psychology of motivation to deal with the distinction of subgoals and ultimate goals.

The Theory of Action

The theoretical extension of Atkinson's risk-taking model that developed in the 1960s suggested a theoretical analysis of goal-directed action that dealt with the relationship among several goal-directed actions and the waxing and waning of motivational tendencies. In 1970 Atkinson and Birch published a comprehensive mathematical analysis of motivation that attempted to provide a theoretical framework for the consideration of problems of change in action tendencies.

The theory of action provides a formal (mathematical) treatment of the relationship among several action tendencies. It is assumed that individuals can engage in any of several action tendencies. The one that an individual is engaged in is strongest at a particular moment. However, the strength of a particular action tendency (as well as the strength of competing action tendencies) is presumed to vary over time. They are strengthened by the instigating forces that are elicited by various stimuli. Thus the sight of food may act as an instigating force (F) increasing the tendency of an individual to engage in eating behavior.

Consummatory forces (C) are those forces that weaken action tendencies and occur, inevitably, as a result of engaging in a particular activity. For example, eating tends to decrease the tendency to continue eating. Changes in action tendencies are dependent upon the effects of instigating and consummatory forces that act on the tendency over time. A tendency to engage in a particular activity will increase if the instigating force acting upon the activity is greater than the consummatory force acting upon it ($F > C$), and the strength of the tendency will decrease if $C > F$. Atkinson and Birch assumed that different activities that may be related to an action tendency will have different consummatory values (c).

For example, eating different foods might be considered as the expression of different action tendencies each having different consummatory values (c). Atkinson and Birch assumed that the strength of the consummatory force acting upon a particular action tendency depends on the consummatory value of the activity and the vigor or strength of the action tendency itself. They assumed that $c = C \times T$, where T is the strength of the action tendency. Note that this assumption implies that the strength of a particular action tendency will tend to vary over time and will tend to stabilize. If $F > C$, the strength of T increases. As T increases, however, c increases since $c = C \times T$. Similarly if $C > F$, the strength of a tendency will decrease, but as T decreases c decreases again leading to a state in which $C = F$, and the strength of the action tendency stabilizes. Of course if the environment changes and new instigating forces are introduced, the strength of the action tendency will change. Since the strength of an action tendency tends to stabilize, it is almost inevitable that at some point the strength of a competing incompatible action tendency that is increasing in strength due to the presence of an instigating force will eventually have a greater strength than the dominant tendency resulting in the emergence of a new action tendency. Note that consumma-tory forces do not decrease the strength of action tendencies that are not being expressed in behavior.

These assumptions suggest the formulation of a general principle of change in action tendencies. Consider a case in which A and B are incompati-ble action tendencies, and A is initially expressed and then B is expressed rather than A. It can be asserted that the initial strength of the tendency to engage in A is greater than the initial strength to engage in activity B, $T_{A_i} > T_{B_i}$. Similarly, when a change in action occurs finally at point F such that A is replaced by B then $T_{B_F} > T_{A_F}$. The time (t) taken for the change is dependent upon the initial difference in response strengths of A and B and the magnitude of consummatory and instigatory forces acting upon A and B respectively and may be expressed as follows:

$$t = [F_A/(C_A - T_B)]/F_B$$

Note that this equation suggests that the time required to change from A to B depends on the instigating and consummatory forces acting upon A and the initial strength of B divided by the instigating force acting upon B. Thus high values of T_{B_i}, F_B, and C_A all lead to rapid change in activity, and high values of F_A leads to persistence in an original activity.

There are a number of other theoretical concepts that are introduced in the theory of action. The analysis we have considered up to this point presup-poses that the action tendencies under consideration are mutually exclusive and independent. However action tendencies may themselves be related, and a tendency to engage in a particular activity may influence this tendency to engage in related activities. Displacement refers to the influence of an instigating force upon a group of action tendencies that are related in some way. Similarly, substitution refers to the influence of consummatory forces upon activities that are related to the activity being expressed in behavior. The presence of displacement and substitution can influence changes in the strengths of action tendencies.

In addition to the existence of instigatory forces that increase the strength of the tendency to engage in a particular action, there are environmental events that act in the opposite direction, and there are tendencies not to engage in a particular activity. Such tendencies are called by Atkinson and Birch, "negaction" tendencies (N), and they are assumed to act in opposition to tendencies to engage in a particular action. A resultant action tendency involves the combination of action and negaction tendencies. (Note the use of the term resultant action tendency is reminiscent of the terminology used in Atkinson's risk-taking theory where the term *resultant motivation* is used to refer to the combination of approach and avoidance tendencies.) A resultant action tendency ($\bar{T}$) is defined as follows:

$$\bar{T} = T - N$$

Corresponding to the existence of instigatory and consummatory forces, there are parallel forces that act on negaction tendencies. Inhibitory force (I) refers to the existence of an event that increases the strength of a negaction tendency. Resistance (R) is a concept that is analogous to consummatory force (C). Atkinson and Birch assume that the presence of a negaction tendency leading to a dampening or a suppression of an action tendency leads to the occurrence of a dampening or suppressive effect upon the negaction tendency itself. Just as the occurrence of an action tendency inevitably leads to the development of consummatory forces, so too the occurrence of negaction tendencies inevitably leads to the development of resistance that weakens the negaction tendency. Thus tendencies to engage or not to engage in an action inevitably wear themselves out as it were if they are expressed in behavior. Table 3.13 presents a summary of the several concepts that are basic to the Atkinson and Birch theory of action.

The strength of a negaction tendency depends upon the relative influences of the inhibitory force and resistance. Inhibitory forces—usually in the form of anticipated negative consequences of action—increase the negaction tendency. Resistance also decreases it. The magnitude of resistance is a positive function of the magnitude of the negaction tendency—that is, if the negaction tendency is very strong, then resistance will increase rapidly. If the inhibitory

TABLE 3.13

Analogous Concepts in the Treatment of Instigation of Action and Resistance to Action

Instigation of action	Resistance to action
Instigating force, F	Inhibitory force, I
Action tendency, T	Negaction tendency, N
Action	Resistance
Consummatory force, C	Force of resistance, R

Source: Atkinson and Birch, 1970.

force is strong leading to the development of a strong negaction tendency, then resistance will grow rapidly. Thus, in an environment providing a constant inhibitory force, resistance will eventually equal the inhibitory force, and the strength of the negaction tendency will stabilize. The consideration of the effect of negaction tendencies leads to revisions in the equations expressing the principle of change in activity. One version of this equation is as follows:

$$t = [(\bar{T}_{A_F} - T_{B_i}) + N_{B_F}]/F_B,$$

where $\bar{T}_{A_F}$ is the strength of the resultant action tendency A at the point at which action A is abandoned for B. T_{B_i} is the strength of initial action tending to engage in B; N_{B_F} is the negaction tendency acting upon action B at the moment of change from A to B; and F_B is the strength of the instigating force acting upon B.

This equation implies that the presence of a negaction tendency for B tends to increase the amount of time required to change from A to B. Evidently the presence of a negaction tendency for B leads to the development of resistance thus weakening the negaction tendency. The time required to dissipate N_B due to the development of resistance acting to diminish N_B acts to delay the expression of the B action tendency.

It should be apparent to the reader that the theory of action provides a comprehensive analysis of the forces that influence the waxing and waning of the tendency to engage in a series of goal-directed activities. In order to apply the theory, however, it is necessary to be able to assign numerical values to the several hypothetical variables that jointly determine the waxing and waning of action tendencies. For the most part, there is no available measurement procedure that permits one to assign values directly to these theoretical entities. This does not, however, lead to a situation in which the theory becomes a mere empty formalism. Several different strategies have been followed in an attempt to relate the theory to empirical phenomena.

Computer simulations for the theory have been developed by Seltzer (1973), and Seltzer and Sawusch (1974). These simulations have been used to derive hypothetical changes in motivational tendencies over time under a variety of different initial assumptions about parameter values for the several variables that are assumed in the theory to influence action tendencies. Such simulations permit one to derive information about such parameters as the time taken to initiate each of several particular activities, the time spent in the activities, and the frequency of engaging in the activities given differing assumptions about numerical values of the several variables whose influence jointly determines the strength of an action tendency. The use of computer simulation permits one to rapidly obtain solutions to the expected outcomes of hypothetical situations that would otherwise require enormous computational labor. The results of such simulations provide a picture of the complexity of waxing and waning tendencies. An example of such a simulation is presented in Figures 3.8 and 3.9. The figures indicate the strength of activities to engage in several different activities in two different settings—in an apartment and at a beach for two different individuals. The individuals differ in the strength of the instigatory forces to engage in several activities as well as in the

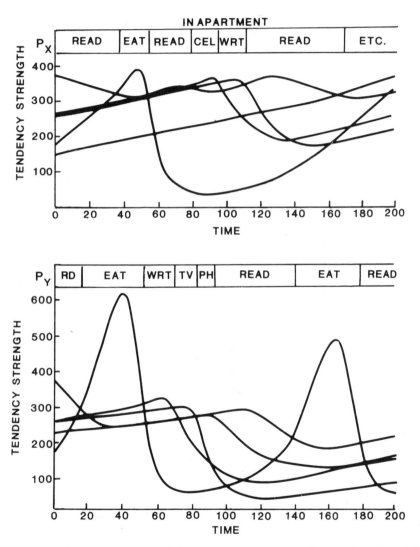

Figure 3.8. *Complexities in the underlying motivational structure of two students, P_x and P_y, over the course of a 2-hour interval in the constant environment of their apartments. (From Atkinson and Birch, 1978. By permission of Brooks/Cole Publishing Company.)*

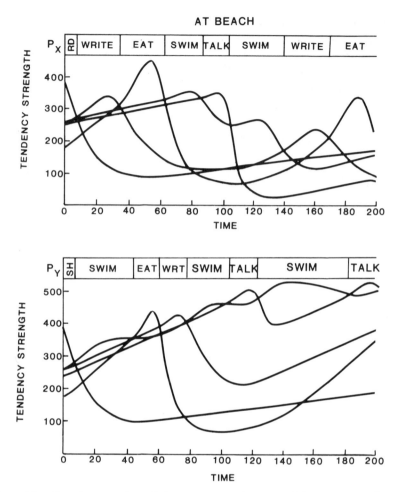

Figure 3.9.   *Complexities in the underlying motivational structure of the same two students,* P_x *and* P_y*, over the course of a comparable 2-hour interval at the beach. (From Atkinson and Birch, 1978. By permission of Brooks/Cole Publishing Company.)*

strengths of the consummatory forces acting upon them. In addition the forces that act upon them are different in different environments. Note that person X compared to person Y has a stronger instigatory force to read and person Y has a stronger instigatory force to eat than person X. The simulations in Figures 3.8 and 3.9 indicate that the initial activity of both persons X and Y in the apartment is reading. However, person X persists in this activity longer than person Y. It is obvious that this visual presentation is isomorphic with a tabular representation for this situation that permits one to obtain data with respect to the latency to initiate various actions, the duration of time over some period in which a particular action is engaged in and the frequency (i.e., the number of resumptions) of a particular action.

Atkinson and Birch also attempted to relate the theory in a general way to a variety of phenomena and issues in the literature. Two such attempts will be discussed here: An analysis of Weiner's research on "inertial" tendencies and a discussion of the relationships between the reliability and validity of projective measures of motivation. Atkinson and Birch (1970, Chapter 10; 1978, Chapter 4) presented an analysis of Weiner's research on inertial tendencies using the theory of action. They discussed theoretical expectations about changes in achievement-oriented action tendencies following success and failure at a task. They assumed that success at a task tends to reduce the capacity of the task to elicit an inhibitory force. They assumed that fear of failure acts as a negation tendency, whereas hope of success acts as an action tendency. The experience of success at a task changes the stimulus situation and reduces its potential to elicit inhibitory forces. This leads to a direct diminution of the negation tendency since the inhibitory force sustaining it is reduced. The magnitude of decrease in the negation tendency is dependent upon the strength of the negation tendency. It is reduced by resistance that is monotonically related to the strength of the negation tendency. Failure at a task leads to a different set of theoretical consequences. The occurrence of a failure experience increases the capacity of the stimulus to elicit an inhibitory force thus leading to a temporary strengthening of the negation tendency. Failure also reduces the capacity of the stimulus to elicit the instigatory force which sustains the action tendency. For subjects in whom $M_s > M_{af}$, there is assumed to be a minimal negation tendency; for those in whom $M_{af} > M_s$, negation tendencies are assumed to be relatively strong. Among these latter subjects the occurrence of a failure experience is assumed to increase inhibitory force leading to a momentary strengthening of the negation tendency. Success, by contrast, reduces the capacity of the stimulus to elicit an inhibitory force and thus reduces the negation tendency. Thus this analysis suggests that subjects in whom $M_{af} > M_s$ would show greater persistence and better performance following success than following failure.

Since subjects in whom $M_s > M_{af}$ are assumed to have relatively little negation tendency, the occurrence of a failure experience does not lead to a large increase in inhibitory force and negation tendencies. Also, the occurrence of a failure experience has little or no consummatory value for the positive action tendency to seek success, although the failure experience may decrease the capacity of the stimulus situation to elicit an instigating force thereby decreasing the strength of the action tendency. The occurrence of a success experience again has relatively little influence on the negation tendency, since such subjects are assumed to be relatively devoid of such tendencies. Success does have some consummatory value and hence results in a clear diminution of the action tendency to seek success. However, success may also strengthen the capacity of the stimulus to elicit an instigating force leading to a strengthening of an action tendency. Atkinson and Birch used this analysis to explain the theoretical expectations of an interaction between type of subject and response to success and failure. They asserted that subjects in whom $M_{af} > M_s$ should show greater persistence and better performance following success (presumably due to the reduction of the negaction tendency) than following failure and that subjects in whom M_s is assumed to be greater than M_{af} should exhibit better performance and greater persistence following failure than following success. (Presumably, this latter result follows from their relative lack of negaction tendency to be diminished by success.)

There are two difficulties with this analysis. First, an examination of Weiner's results provides, at best, equivocal support for this expected pattern of results. In addition, Atkinson and Birch do assert that the failure of subjects in whom $M_{af} > M_s$ to show less persistence following failure is not consistent with their analysis. Quite independent of the ambiguous empirical support for the theory, the derivations do not, strictly speaking, follow from the theory as stated unless one adds a number of additional quantitative assumptions about the value of the several variables that can be influenced by success and failure. The occurrence of a successful outcome reduces the capacity of the stimulus to elicit an inhibitory force and thus permits a diminution in the negaction tendency due to the operation of resistance. However, a success experience may also increase the instigatory force for success. Also success sustains a consummatory force that decreases the action tendency thereby leading to changes in the strength of the positive action tendency as well as the negaction tendency. Similarly the occurrence of a failure experience will increase inhibitory force thereby increasing negaction tendencies. However, the increase in the negaction tendency will also increase resistance. Also the occurrence of a failure experience can decrease the capacity of the stimulus to elicit instigatory force. It is apparent that success and failure have diverse effects on several variables within the theory, and although the scenario arrived at by Atkinson and Birch is perfectly plausible and perhaps even intuitively compelling, there exists various parametric values assignable to the theoretical variables influenced by success and failure that would provide quite different outcomes and predictions. This analysis indicates that in order to use the theory of action as a basis for explicit theoretical deductions some procedure will have to be found that specifies the permitted range of quantitative values assignable to the several theoretical variables contained within the theory.

The second application of the theory of action to phenomena in the literature of motivation derives from a controversy about the adequacy of the projective test of achievement motivation as a measure of motivation. The criticism was most forcefully stated by Entwistle in 1972 and was derived from the psychometric shibboleth that reliability is a necessary condition for validity. Reliability in the standard definition refers to the extent to which a particular test measures something consistent about an individual and validity refers to the extent to which the test is a measure of characteristics of a person it is presumed to measure.

It would appear to be correct to assert that tests that are not reliable cannot be valid although a test may be reliable and not valid. In practice, coefficients of reliability may be obtained by comparing agreements among parts of a test. For example a split-half coefficient of reliability indicates the agreement between scores obtained from two parts of a test taken at the same time (odd and even items). If the split-half reliability is low, one usually infers that the various items on the test measure different things and thus there is no consistent characteristic that is being measured by the several items. Coefficients of stability refer to measures of the consistency of response over a period of time and typically are based on correlations between test scores for the same individuals given the same test on two different occasions. If there is a high correlation between the scores, one typically assumes that the test is measuring some consistent characteristic of persons. Low reliability is viewed as being attributable to error, and error in psychometric theory is due to a random process. Thus tests with low reliability are not only seen as being invalid, but also as being incapable of consistent relationships with other measures.

Entwistle (1972) summarized available literature dealing with the reliability of the test, concluded that the test had unacceptably low reliability, and hence could not be valid. She estimated the reliability of the test to be approximately .3 or .4. She reported the results of a number of item analysis studies that buttressed her conclusions of low reliability. In item analysis, one studies the correlations between pairs of items. If the items measure the same thing, one should find that there is positive agreement among them. The low reliability based on item analyses indicates that a person's score on a particular item is not predictive of the score on another item. Thus if a person receives a high score for a particular picture indicating the presence of need achievement, this does not indicate that the person will receive a high score on the next picture. Entwistle concluded that the lack of reliability for the same measure implied that the test was not valid.

There are several possible rebuttals that can be offered in response to Entwistle's criticism. First, even if her argument were accepted at face value, it is not clear whether the lower bound value of .3 or .4 is so low as to render the measure invalid. Since most of the research using the projective test has involved the testing of hypotheses suggested by a theory rather than the attempt to attain predictions in applied setting, a test with a substantial degree of error might nevertheless have sufficient validity to be theoretically useful in group prediction even though the attempt to use the test would not be useful as a basis for accurate prediction about an individual.

It might also be possible that individuals are biased against repeating similar themes in their stories because of the typical instructions to consider the test as one of imagination. Winter and Stewart (1977) reported the results of an interesting study that supports this hypothesis. They assigned subjects to groups given one of three kinds of instructions before taking a projective test of motivation. (They obtained measures of need for power rather than need achievement [see Winter, 1973].) One group was told 1 week after writing stories to then write other stories similar in theme to the stories originally written. A second group was instructed to attempt to write second stories with different themes, and a third group was told to write whatever kinds of stories they wished, but they were informed that it was permissible to write stories similar to or different from those they had written previously. The test–retest coefficients of stability for the three groups were .27 for the subjects told to write different stories, .61 for the group told to write similar stories, and .58 for the group told it was permissible but not required to write similar stories. The correlation of .27 is comparable to the values typically reported in Entwistle's survey of the literature. These results suggest that subjects given instructions to conceive of projective tests of motivation as a test of imagination may in effect instruct themselves to write different kinds of stories on different occasions thus reducing the internal consistency of item responses and the degree of predictability of scores over time.

Atkinson, Bongort, and Price (1977) attempted to address the issue of the consistency of responses to pictures chosen to elicit need achievement using the theory of action. From this perspective telling a story containing achievement-oriented themes constitutes the expression of an achievement oriented action tendency. The expression of the response in behavior tends to have consummatory value and therefore will decrease the probability of responding to the next picture with another story containing achievement-oriented themes. Change in the strength of the action tendency to express achievement themes in stories is dependent on the ratio of instigatory to consummatory forces. Consummatory forces will decrease the action tendency only if it is expressed. The decrease in the tendency to continuously respond in the same way to different pictures should create a sawtooth pattern of response in which the fantasy expression of a particular motive decreases the tendency to respond in a similar fashion, and the increased probability of the expression of a different theme reduces the probability of continued choice of that theme permitting an increase in the probability of expressing the original motive.

Atkinson (1950) had in fact reported data suggesting the existence of such a pattern. Atkinson, Price, and Bongort used the computer simulations based on the theory of action to provide data about changes in the tendency to respond with a particular motive pattern given repeated opportunities to express the pattern. The theory of action implies that over a period of time the probability that an individual will engage in a particular action is dependent upon the underlying strength of the action tendencies. They assigned hypothetical values of the strength of action tendencies to mythical individuals. They then performed a variety of computer simulations indicating the way in which changes in responses to stimuli would occur over time as a function of the prior expression of a particular action tendency. The computer simulations permit one to ascertain the degree of agreement between responses to different item (pictures) and the degree of agreement between the final score based on the percentage of time in which need achievement scores were expressed over all occasions and the hypothetical score assigned to a mythical individual. Their computer simulation provided dramatic evidence of the theoretical disjunction between reliability and validity. Given certain parametric values, there can be very little agreement between item scores (hence low reliability) combined with high agreement between the overall probability of expression of a motive in response to pictures with the underlying true score. For example in one of their simulations, the measure of internal consistency, Cronbach's coefficient alpha was .08, indicative of virtually a total absence of reliability. The correct classification based on all responses to the correct third of the distribution was attained in 87% of the cases.

The use of computer simulations based on the theory of action demonstrates conclusively that the absence of reliability does not preclude validity given a theory of action tendencies that presupposes that the strength of such tendencies wax and wane with their expression over time. Moreover, the pattern of low reliability and high validity is theoretically expected. At the same time the computer analysis does not establish that the projective measure *is* valid, but only that it could be in the absence of reliability. A more convincing demonstration of the use of the theory of action in this context would involve the use of actual subjects. What would be required is some research effort in which subjects would be classified with respect to their motives, and the actual changes in their response patterns in a new test of achievement motivation would be predicted using the formal apparatus of the theory. The computer simulation of the independence of reliability and validity is a tour de force, but it is not quite the same as a program of empirical research demonstrating the value of the theory of action to predict the details of the behavior of individuals.

Although Atkinson and Birch used the theory of action to explain phenomena that were already in the literature, there have also been attempts to use the theory to derive new hypotheses. Kuhl and Blankenship (1979a, 1979b) used the theory of action to derive hypotheses about preference for tasks of different levels of difficulty in a situation in which an individual must repeatedly choose tasks. They assumed that the consummatory value of success at a task is greater than the consummatory value of failure ($c_s > c_f$), and consistent with the discussion of the theory of action analysis of Weiner's experiment, they assumed that resistance based on fear of failure is reduced more following success than failure ($r_s > r_f$). If a subject were forced to repeatedly choose tasks of different difficulty levels, the tendency to choose easy tasks would decrease over time. This occurs because the probability of success is, by definition, higher for an easier task than a difficult task, and the increased frequency with which success is encountered will tend to lead to the greater application of consummatory forces. Using a variety of values for the theoretical variables of the theory of action, Kuhl and Blankenship were able to use computer simulations to support this prediction. In addition, differences in motive patterns between subjects in whom $M_s > M_{af}$ and subjects in whom $M_{af} > M_s$ are related to theoretically expected differences in this type of experimental situation. The latter are assumed to have strong negaction tendencies. Success in a situation serves to reduce such tendencies. The sudden reduction in negaction action permits an increase in resultant motivation permitting the expression of previously dampened action tendencies, called, metaphorically, a bottled-up effect. Such an effect is not present in subjects in whom $M_s > M_{af}$. Alternatively, one could argue, as Kuhl and Blankenship explicitly did, that the value of resistance is greater following success than following failure. Although the shift toward more difficult tasks is expected for both types of subjects, the time taken for this shift is assumed to be different. The increased time for the emergence of dominance among the more difficult tasks is dependent upon the time required to overcome resistance caused by negaction tendencies.

Kuhl and Blankenship (1979a, 1979b) permitted subjects to repeatedly choose tasks differing in difficulty level with P_s values ranging from .8 to .1. They found that both types of subjects developed a preference for tasks of greater difficulty. The slope defining changes in preference for difficulty level over trials was .31 and .32 for subjects in whom $M_{af} > M_s$ and those in whom $M_{af} > M_s$, respectively. Note that the principal hypothesis of the development of a preference for tasks of increased difficulty was supported. However, these data obviously do not support the hypotheses based on the analysis of the influence of resistance, about the expected more rapid shift toward difficult tasks among subjects in whom $M_s > M_{af}$ than among those in whom $M_{af} > M_s$. Kuhl and Blankenship reported the results of some post hoc analyses that weakly supported this hypothesis. They noted that female subjects may be higher in fear of failure than males. Thus female subjects who tended to score high on the TAQ and low on the TAT measure of need achievement may be assumed to be the most clearly identifiable group of subjects in whom negaction tendencies are strong. This suggests that male subjects with the opposite pattern of scores on motive measures are the group in whom success tendencies are most clearly dominant. Kuhl and Blankenship noted that the males in whom $M_s > M_{af}$ had a mean slope of increased preference for difficult tasks of .43, and the female subjects in whom $M_{af} > M_s$ had a comparable slope of .22. However, the difference between the mean slopes of these two groups was not statistically significant at the usual .05 level. Thus, strictly speaking, the post hoc analysis still does not support the hypothesis of differences in the rate of development of preference for tasks of greater difficulty among subjects with different motive patterns. Quite apart from the lack of statistical significance, the comparison between the groups used for the post hoc analysis is questionable. It is based on the argument that "the failure-oriented groups, defined as those subjects with Thematic Apperception Test (TAT; Atkinson, 1958) rank minus Test Anxiety Questionnaire (TAQ; Mandler & Sarason, 1952) rank below the median, is not actually failure-oriented because most Michigan undergraduates are low in test anxiety [p. 149]." It should be noted that the theory of action requires only relative differences in action and negaction tendencies among the subjects being tested. Furthermore, to deny such differences is casually to sweep aside all of the research on individual differences in achievement motivation that provide one of the foundations of the theory of action itself. It is not my purpose here to belabor the use of an illegitimate post hoc analysis of results in an attempt to find support for a theoretical prediction that appears to have been clearly contradicted by the results of an experiment. Rather, I raise the issue of the apparent contradiction of the results as a basis for the discussion of a more general issue. Namely, to what extent do the results of empirical investigations in general, and Kuhl and Blankenship's study in particular, support the theory of action? With respect to the more particular issue the results provide at best only partial support. It is correct to assert that the theory has played a heuristic role in this research effort. The shift from a "static" conception of motivation in which the determinants of motive tendencies are defined by the interaction of personal dispositions and stimulus situations to a dynamic conception in which motive tendencies are assumed to vary over time as a function of their expression in behavior leads one to design experiments that address the consequences of repeated exposure to a situation and repeated opportunities to express a motive tendency. However, such a shift in perspective was already present in the research on inertial concepts. The detailed exposition and development of the complex theoretical structure with the opportunity to develop computer simulations of the theoretical concepts of the theory of action does not appear to be supported or rigorously tested by the Kuhl and Blankenship investigation. The quantitative details of the predictions are not developed, and one of the principal derivations is not supported. A preference for tasks of greater difficulty with repeated choice could be explained by any of a number of competing concepts without the use of a theoretical analysis of the complexity contained in the theory of action.

Blankenship (undated) attempted to test theoretical notions about substitution using simulations based on the theory of action. Her experiment had two phases. In the first phase, subjects in whom $M_s > M_{af}$ were presented with a nonachievement task (rating jokes) and an achievement oriented-task (a simulated target-shooting game using computer-presented problems in which the subject had to vary the angle of a hypothetical gun in order to hit a target). Subjects began with the nonachievement-oriented activity and were then permitted to shift whenever they pleased to an achievement-oriented activity that was either easy or difficult.

She found that the time taken to initiate an achievement-oriented task that was assumed to be easy did not differ from the time taken to initiate an achievement-oriented task assumed to be difficult. Since all subjects started with the same nonachievement-oriented task and since subjects were randomly assigned to an easy or difficult alternative task condition, it is reasonable to assume that instigatory and consummatory forces acting upon the initial nonachievement task were identical. Therefore, the lack of differences in time taken to initiate the new task implies, given the theory of action, that the force (F) to engage in easy tasks is equal to the force to engage in difficult tasks. Blankenship found that the initial duration of time spent on the easy task where subjects were given the opportunity to shift between this task and the original nonachievement-oriented task was shorter than the initial duration of time spent on the difficult task. This implies that the consummatory value of easy tasks must be greater than the consummatory value of difficult tasks.

Blankenship indicated that these results can be used to explain the data of the Kuhl and Blankenship experiment—that is, if the consummatory value associated with easy tasks is greater than the consummatory value of difficult tasks, then subjects presented with multiple opportunities to engage in achievement-oriented tasks of different degrees of difficulty should tend, over time, to develop a preference for difficult tasks since the greater consummatory force acting upon easy tasks will eventually decrease the strength of the tendency to engage in these tasks leading to a situation in which the strength of the tendency to engage in difficult tasks becomes stronger.

Blankenship's experiment had a second phase in which she used the data of the first phase and findings about differences in the consummatory value of engaging in easy or difficult tasks to derive hypotheses about substitution.

Recall that substitution refers to shared consummatory value among a group of related tasks. Blankenship was interested in the possible existence of substitution among achievement-oriented tasks differing in difficulty. She wanted to know if the consummatory forces generated by working on an easy task would spread to more difficult tasks and vice versa. She entertained four hypotheses about possible substitution relationships among different achievement-oriented tasks: (a) that substitution does not exist; (b) that the substitution does exist and that its relationships are symmetrical such that working on an easy task leads to the development of substitutions that spreads to more difficult tasks and that a comparable process exists that operates in the opposite direction (from difficult to easy); (c) that substitution exists and is asymmetrical such that working on easy tasks leads to greater substitute consummatory value for difficult tasks than the converse; and (d) substitution is asymmetrical with difficult tasks leading to greater substitute consummatory value for easier tasks than the converse. The experimental situation used by Blankenship to test these possible substitution relationships was one in which subjects who had participated in the initial task were permitted in the second phase of the experiment to choose between engaging in the original non-achievement-oriented task, the original achievement-oriented task (either easy or difficult), and a similar achievement-oriented task of intermediate difficulty. For subjects in the easy condition, the intermediate task would be more difficult than the original task, and for those in the difficult condition, the intermediate task represented an easier task. Blankenship believed that the most plausible substitution relationship among the alternatives considered was an asymmetrical relationship in which working on a difficult task provided more substitute consummatory force for working on an easier task than the converse asymmetrical relationship. Her intuition in this regard derived in part from the findings of the Kuhl and Blankenship study—that is, that such an asymmetrical substitution effect would tend to reduce the tendency to prefer easy tasks more than the tendency to prefer difficult tasks given successive experiences with such tasks even where the strengths of the initial tendencies were equal. This would occur because working on a difficult task would tend to reduce the strength of the tendency to work on an easy task more than working on an easy task would reduce the strength of the tendency to work on difficult tasks.

Blankenship used the results of the initial phase of her study that defined differences in consummatory forces for easy and difficult tasks combined with the computer simulation of the theory of action to derive outcome expectations for each of the four possible theoretical assumptions about substitution that she considered. Table 3.14 presents the results of these computer simulations indicating the latency of the intermediate task, the time spent engaged in this task, and the time engaged in the originally assigned task under each of four theoretical assumptions about substitution. Table 3.14 also presents the actual results obtained by Blankenship.

Blankenship argued that these results supported the pattern of results predicted by the assumption of asymmetrical substitution with greater sub-stitution from difficult to easy tasks than from easy to difficult tasks. She rejected the assumption of no substitution for these data arguing that the only pattern that predicted a large difference in latency to initiate the intermediate task with the easy group showing short latencies was Pattern 4. There are two difficulties with this reasoning. The obtained differences in latencies are barely statistically significant. In point of fact the differences were reported as signifi-cant only using a one-tailed test and would not have been significant if the appropriate two-tailed test were used. More critically, the obtained dif-ferences, 2 versus 3 minutes, appear conspicuously closer to the expected results under the simulation produced by assuming no substitution pattern (2.5/2.7) than they do to Pattern 4, which was accepted by Blankenship (2.5/7.8). In fact an examination of the obtained results in Table 3.14 indi-cates that they fit the expected results derived from the assumption of no substitution about as well as they fit the assumption of asymmetrical substitu-tion with difficult tasks substituting for easy tasks more than the converse. Thus it would appear to be the case that the fit between precise quantitative predictions—predictions whose robustness and invariance over different pa-rametric assumptions is not known—and obtained data are not sufficiently precise to permit one to use the theory of action to explain these empirical phenomena.

The discussion of Blankenship's results may strike the reader as overly detailed. The examination of these results was undertaken in order to again

TABLE 3.14
Simulations of Time Measures and Obtained Data

Substitution relationship	Latency intermediate task	Total time intermediate task	Time originally assigned task
1. No substitutions	2.5/2.7	7.0/6.3	5.4/6.8
2. Symmetrical substitution	6.7/7.8	4.5/4.0	6.1/7.5
3. Asymmetrical substitution E I D	6.7/2.7	4.4/6.8	7.0/5.7
4. Asymmetrical substitution D I I	2.5/7.8	7.5/3.6	4.1/8.4
5. Obtained results	2.0/3.0	8.4/5.0	2.8/6.5

Source: Blankenship (undated).

address the general issue of the bearing of empirical results on the probity of the theory of action. Also the analysis suggests that Blaneknship's research fails to convincingly coordinate the theory with empirical results and fails to distinguish among disparate theoretical interpretations of her data from the perspective of the theory of action. Parenthetically, it should be noted that her results might be explained equally well with a simpler theoretical apparatus.

Four different uses of the theory of action have been presented. Collectively they permit the development of an overall evaluation of the current status of the theory. Recall that the use of the theory to explain Weiner's study of "inertial" tendencies was only partially successful since the results on persistence did not fit theoretical expectations. The use of the theory to analyze the potential disjunction between reliability and validity, although theoretically valid, was not accompanied by a specific empirical research effort to provide empirical support for the disjunction. The Kuhl and Blankenship study provided only partial support for the theory. The expected results dealing with individual differences in motivation did not clearly emerge. In addition, Blankenship's analysis of substitution effects failed to clearly distinguish among alternative theoretical explanations. Considered collectively, these examples, which include the only studies designed as specific tests of the theory, indicate that the theory is relatively divorced from empirical results—that is, the problem of measurement remains unsolved. Although the theory contains a formal apparatus permitting the derivation of precise quantitative outcomes, the apparatus is rendered empty by the nonexistence of a procedure permitting one to assign precise quantitative values to the several variables whose influence jointly determines the waxing and waning of motivation tendencies.

Does this mean that the theory is not useful? Quite the contrary. The value of the theory lies in a number of conceptual advances. In particular, the theory spells out a number of implications of a goal-directed view of motivation that remained latent in previous theoretical efforts. Consider, for example, Tolman's definition of purpose as persistence until a goal has been attained. The definition leads inexorably to the absurd conclusion that a goal that cannot be attained will never be abandoned. In a sense the absurd consequence of the definition was circumvented by a research program that starved rats and created animals who could, with sufficient tolerance for error, be conceived of as monomaniacally pursuing a single goal. The conditions under which a particular goal might be abandoned for another were not addressed. Moreover, if behavior is conceived in goal-directed terms, then clearly the organism studied in an experiment must have had a goal prior to being assigned a task in the laboratory. Hence experiments involving single motive states must of necessity be conceived of as experiments involving motivational change—that is, the study of the process by means of which an organism changes its goal-directed activities. The emphasis on distribution of time spent in several activities and on latencies to engage in activities and the view of motives as latent states that influence such parameters are compelling consequences of the attempt to work out the inherent logic of a goal-directed view of behavior. Of course this general assertion of approval does not imply that the specific details of the theory will be retained. In particular, the use of action and negaction concepts with the inclusion of such parallel concepts as consummatory forces and resistance tends to lead to a situation in which there are a large number of parameters that must be considered in any situation in which the theory is applied.

The evaluation of the theory of action viewed as the theoretical culmination of research on achievement motivation can be related to a more general evaluation of the entire research effort in achievement motivation. The research has always had a stronger theoretical than empirical base. Many of the studies in the literature have relied on small samples and report weak results that may not be replicable. Consider several examples in the research reviewed here. McClelland's dramatic finding of a relationship between the content of children's readers and economic growth does not appear to be replicable for a more recent time period. Raynor's research effort on future orientation is riddled with negative results. Thus, although there are some findings that are clearly supportive of the theoretical concepts, the bulk of the research does not support the theoretical predictions that were derived. Because of the theoretical interest of the work, a number of books on motivation cite the positive results and leave out the negative findings. A similar example occurs frequently in the literature on achievement motivation; the body of research is marked by conceptual advances with occasional dramatic empirical support but not by a sustained empirical effort that leads to the development of a large body of unimpeachable empirical results.

Chapter *4*

BEYOND GOAL ATTAINMENT: REINFORCEMENT THEORY AND OPPONENT PROCESS THEORY

Chapter 3 traced the development of a conception of motivation that went beyond the study of a single goal-directed action tendency to a consideration of the relationship among diverse action tendencies and to the waxing and waning of action tendencies as a function of their expression in behavior. In this chapter I will discuss two theoretical developments that indicate analogous developments—reinforcement theory and Solomon's opponent process theory—and will attempt to relate them to the theory of action presented in Chapter 3.

Reinforcement Theory

Reinforcers are defined as stimuli that have the capacity to increase the probability of responses. A classic example of a reinforcer is the delivery of food to a hungry rat. In a Skinner box a lever that can be depressed is considered a response. If the response is followed by a reinforcer, the delivery of a pellet of food, the probability of bar pressing will increase. What is implicit and indeed ubiquitous in the classical account of the reinforcement process is the assumption that there exists a class of events that have the property of acting as reinforcers and that there exists a second class of responses that may be reinforced. Members of this latter class may be considered as instrumental responses leading to the occurrence of the reinforcer, which in a purposive conception of motivation, may be conceived of as the goal of the action sequence. From this conception it is obvious that the specification of the class of events that can act as reinforcers is equivalent to the specification of the class of events that can act as the goals of an action sequence. Considerable theoretical and empirical effort was expended on the attempt to define the essential properties of the class of events that acted as reinforcers. For example, Thorndike proposed in 1911 that responses that were accompanied by a state of affairs described as satisfying would be strengthened. Hull (1930) suggested that all reinforcers involved the occurrence of drive reduction.

The attempt to define one or more essential properties of the class of events that were reinforcers was criticized by Skinner (1938, 1953), who preferred a more theoretically neutral definition. Skinner refused to characterize reinforcers other than by their presumed operational effects as events whose occurrence increased the probability of occurrence of responses. However, such a definition of reinforcers is circular. A reinforcer is that which increases the probability of a response and that which increases the probability of a response is a reinforcer—and, it is generally recognized that circular definitions are not definitions at all. Meehl (1950) presented the classic defense of the Skinnerian definition. He pointed out that reinforcers were trans-situational. An event identified as a reinforcer would serve to reinforce any responses that would lead to or produce the reinforcer. Thus, food for a hungry rat would increase the probability of bar pressing, and it would also serve to increase the probability of such other responses as turning in a particular direction in a maze. Note how this concept of the transsituation of reinforcers is compatible with a purposive theory of motivation such as Tolman's. Tolman's theory contains such notions as variable means–end readiness and the docility of an organism—implying that the organism would adopt various means to attain a goal. Irrespective of whether reinforcement was defined in the pristinely neutral fashion of Skinner or with respect to any of several attempts to construct a theory of the common nature of all reinforcers, all of these positions implicitly accepted the division of the class of events studied into those that were instrumental and those that were the end states of purposive actions (i.e., reinforcers).

The first psychologist to challenge this neat dichotomy was Premack. Premack (1965) pointed out that the principle of reinforcement was rarely tested and the assumption that reinforcers were invariably transsituational was accepted as self-evidently true. Premack's approach to the definition of reinforcement involved a radical redefinition. He argued that reinforcement was to be understood and defined not as a property of events but rather as a property of the relation between different responses. In order to test this assumption, it is necessary to develop a metric by means of which different responses can be compared. Premack noted that most responses involve a particular duration that is relatively invariant. For example, rats lick approximately seven times per second. Since all observable responses endure for some particular period of time, different responses with grossly different topographies may be directly compared with respect to the amount of time that they endure. Over a particular fixed period of time, the duration of a response multiplied by the frequency of its occurrence gives one a measure of the probability of the response. Different responses occurring over the same period of time can be compared with respect to their probabilities. Premack argued that the reinforcement relation might be defined in terms of the relationship between the probabilities of responses over a time stretch having defined initial conditions. In particular, he asserted that a response whose temporary probability of occurrence is higher than a second response would act as a reinforcer. There are a number of interesting consequences of this particular definition. It is apparent that there is no class of responses that are invariably reinforcers. An event that occurs with a high probability under one set of circumstances will occur with low probability under another set of circumstances. In the former case it is more likely to serve as a reinforcer than in the latter case. Moreover, the same event can act as a reinforcer for those responses that occur with lower probabilities, and it can be reinforced by other responses that occur with higher probabilities in the same situation. The consummatory response of eating, which was used as a standard reinforcer, is a high probability response. The operant, or naturally occurring probability of bar pressing in a Skinner box, is a low probability response. Eating can therefore serve as a reinforcer for bar pressing. However, it is not hard to conceive of situations in which the consummatory response of eating would itself be subject to reinforcement. Such experiments were not conducted, perhaps because of the implicit acceptance of a hungry rat's eating as a biologically necessary act, which made it a suitable candidate for a reinforcer or goal object. The influence of a Darwinian model of survival clearly lurks in the background of the decision to select certain events as reinforcers and others as instrumental responses.

A consideration of some of his experiments will make Premack's notions of a reinforcement relation somewhat more explicit. In one of his studies (Premack, 1959), children were presented with a candy dispenser and a pinball machine wired for continuous operation. A new piece of chocolate was delivered to a child each time a child finished eating a piece of chocolate. In an initial session children were given free access to both the candy and the pinball machine, and the frequency of eating candy and the frequency of manipulating the pinball machine was noted. Premack indicates that the duration of each of these two responses was approximately equal and thus the frequency of each of these responses could be used as an index of the time expended on each of the responses during the experimental session. On the basis of their response frequencies, the children were classified into two groups—those who were "eaters" and those who were "manipulators." The former group were more likely to eat candy than to manipulate the pinball machine, whereas the latter group of children were more likely to manipulate the pinball machine than to eat candy. In a second session children were assigned to one of two contingency sessions in which pinball-machine playing was contingent upon eating or eating was contingent upon pinball machine playing. Premack found that for the children who were classified as manipulators, the probability of eating was increased if pinball manipulation was contingent upon eating (that is, if the experimental arrangement was one in which the child was required to eat a piece of candy in order to activate the pinball machine, the frequency of eating candy would increase, provided the child had been classified as a manipulator). However, if eating candy was the contingent response and children were required to manipulate the pinball machine in order to receive the candy, there was no increment in the frequency of eating for children classified as manipulators. For children who were classified as eaters, the probability of playing the pinball machine was increased if eating was contingent upon manipulation of the pinball machine. However, if manipulating the pinball machine was contingent upon eating, eating did not increase for these children. Note that in this study the consummatory response, eating, which is usually considered the reinforcer was itself capable of being reinforced. This experiment supports Premack's assumption that a more probable response will reinforce a less probable response if the occurrence of the former responses is contingent upon the occurrence of the latter response.

It is possible to question the generality of the results reported by Premack in this experiment. One could argue that manipulating a pinball machine is itself a highly rewarding act and thus the results do not pertain to just any two responses but are really peculiar to an experimental situation in which both responses are themselves goal objects. However, Premack (1963) was able to demonstrate that the reinforcement relation would hold between responses not usually considered rewarding in an experiment with monkeys. In this experiment four monkeys were exposed to an experimental situation in which four different responses were present: a lever, a plunger, a hinged flap on a door, and a horizontally operated lever. The response probabilities for these responses and various combinations under noncontingent settings were obtained for each of the monkeys. In subsequent sessions the monkeys were presented with contingent pairs of manipulanda. Since there were four possible manipulanda, there were six possible pairs that could be presented in a contingent relationship, and since each member of the pair could be made the contingent response, there were 12 experimental conditions in all. Premack predicted that the reinforcement relation would hold between responses that differed in base rate probabilities. If a monkey demonstrated higher base-rate probability of responding for one response over another then the response with higher base rate should be able to increase the probability of responding of the relatively low base rate response if the former response was made contingent upon the latter. The results were generally in accord with the predictions that were made. In one particularly interesting test of Premack's theory, one of the monkeys had relatively clearly defined differences in base rates of responses for the four manipulanda. For this monkey manipulation of the hinged door was intermediate in probability; manipulation of the horizontal lever was a high probability response; and manipulation of the plunger was a low probability response. For this monkey, manipulation of the hinged door was both reinforced and reinforcing. When operation of the door was contingent upon manipulation of the plunger, the probability of the plunger response increased. When manipulation of the horizontal lever was contingent upon manipulation of the door, the probability of occurrence of the door response increased. Thus the status of a particular response as a reinforcer or as an instrumental or reinforced response was relative to the response with which it was paired in a contingency relationship. This study suggests that the reinforcement relation postulated by Premack holds for any pair of responses and is not necessarily a property of the class of responses that have traditionally been considered as goal responses.

Premack's analysis of reinforcement relates to a goal-directed view of motivation in several ways. On the one hand the analysis may be read as challenging the traditional goal-directed analysis of motivation. Premack's theoretical language, which is devoid of reference to purposive conceptions and which seeks to break the theoretical dichotomy between instrumental acts and goal responses, appears to suggest, on the surface, that it is a mistake to think in terms of a purposive conception of motivation and that this commonsense notion has left the psychology of motivation with irrelevant intellectual baggage. Alternatively, one could attempt to reinterpret Premack's theory within the framework of a purposive conception of motivation. Premack's analysis suggests that there are no events that hold privileged status as the goals of action. Rather, any response that an organism can perform can, under some circumstances, act as a goal. Similarly all responses, including consummatory responses that are traditionally and uncritically accepted as goals for action, can be instrumental activities. It is thus fruitless to attempt to formulate theories that specify the common property of reinforcers or goals since the class of responses capable of acting as reinforcers is indefinitely large. Finally, Premack's analysis of reinforcement marks a shift in focus from an analysis of the influence of a particular goal object or single action sequence to an analysis of the distribution of several different activities. It should be noted that this change in emphasis parallels the change discussed in Chapter 3. Recall that our discussion of research on achievement motivation demonstrated a similar progression from research that dealt with the influence of a particular goal on behavior to research that dealt with the relationship among several different goal-directed activities and the abandonment of one activity for another. Note further that in both the theory of action and in Premack's theory, the duration of responding is taken as a critical variable. The distribution of actions and the relationships existing among them including their respective durations emerge as the paradigmatic motivational problem and replace a paradigm in which the effects of the influence of a single goal on an instrumental response are studied.

Premack's theoretical analysis of the reinforcement relation was challenged by Timberlake and Allison (1974). They argued that difference in response probabilities was not the critical variable that defined the reinforcement relation. They pointed out that most experiments in which reinforcement occurred were ones in which the opportunity to engage in a particular response at a desired frequency could occur only if an organism increased the probability of instrumental responding. Consider the standard Skinner box reinforcement experiment. Eating is a response that occurs frequently, and bar pressing is a response that occurs infrequently. In order for the rat to maintain its base rate of eating under the typical constraints imposed by the experimental situation in which eating is made contingent on bar pressing, the rate of bar pressing would have to increase over its base rate. Thus the typical experimental situation that demonstrates reinforcement contains both a probability difference in Premack's sense and a deprivation of the base rate of responding. Although these two conditions are confounded in most standard experimental situations, it is possible to design experiments in which these conditions are separated. Timberlake and Allison reviewed several studies that suggested that response deprivation was the critical condition for reinforcement rather than probability differences as suggested by Premack. Timberlake and Allison (1974) reported the results of an experiment in which rats were given an opportunity to lick a .4% or a .3% saccharin solution. Under baseline or noncontingency conditions, rats spent more time licking the .4% solution than the .3% solution. In order to create a condition of response deprivation under contingency conditions, they required the rats to lick the .4% solution for 80 seconds in order to gain access to the .3% solution for 10 seconds. If the rats performed the .4% response at the rate they performed it under noncontingency conditions, then response deprivation would occur for the .3% solution. Under these conditions Premack's probability differential theory would predict that the .4% response would not increase in frequency since it is more probable than the .3% response. However, if response deprivation is the necessary and sufficient condition for the occurrence of reinforcement, the .4% response should increase in probability of occurrence. One could say that the animal will increase the probability of occurrence of that response that is preferred in order to provide something closer to the preferred rate of response on the less preferred response. Timberlake and Allison's results supported the response deprivation assumption.

The results suggesting that response deprivation is the critical condition for a reinforcement relation are buttressed by other studies including one study with human subjects. Timberlake and Allison (1974) reported a study using saccharin-licking and running in an activity wheel as the two responses under investigation. In this study they used what is called a reciprocal schedule in which a certain amount of one response must be performed in order to have access to the second response, and one must then perform a certain amount of the second response in order to have access to the first response. In this type of schedule each response is, in effect, contingent upon the other. In one schedule rats were required to perform 30 quarter turns in a wheel in order to have access to the saccharin and 10 licks of the saccharin to have access to the running wheel. Under these conditions base-rate performance of the wheel running response would deprive the rat of base-rate performance of the licking response. Under these conditions wheel running increased. A second schedule was also used in this study in which 60 licks provided access to 5 quarter turns of the running wheel. Under this schedule the rat was response-deprived of running and the rate of licking increased. This study demonstrates that a reinforcement relationship can be manipulated by changing the schedule requirements that define the contingent relationships between responses.

Eisenberger, Karpman, and Trattner (1967) reported the results of a study with human subjects that supports the response-deprivation assumption. Subjects were presented with a lever and a knob that they were permitted to manipulate as they wished. Knob manipulation had a higher base-line probability than lever pressing. A contingency schedule was arranged in which knob manipulation was response deprived. The schedule was one in which baseline performance of the more probable response would deprive subjects of the opportunity to engage in baseline responding of the less probable response. Under these conditions the response rate for the more probable knob response increased.

Allison, Miller, and Wozny (1979) investigated the influence of variations in schedule requirements for instrumental responding and in the magnitude of the goal or contingent response received on changes in response probabilities. They suggested that there were six relationships that could be obtained in experiments that varies the number of instrumental responses required for reinforcement and the magnitude of the reinforcement received:

1. Increasing the requirement for instrumental responding would serve to increase the rate of responding for the instrumental response if the contingent response were deprived. (It should be noted that this generalization holds only over some range of possibilities. If the schedule requires an extremely large number of responses for access to the contingent response, the organism may cease responding. In point of fact experimental extinction is defined by an absence of the reinforcer following repeated occurrences of an instrumental response.)
2. The increase in response rate would not be sufficient to maintain the base rate of responding on the contingent response. As the requirements of the schedule increased, the reduction in the rate of responding on the contingent response would increase.
3. As the magnitude of reward increased, the total reward attained under a given schedule requirement would increase.
4. As the magnitude of reward increased, the rate of instrumental responding for that reward would decrease.
5. If a schedule led to response deprivation of a contingent response, the base rate of responding for the instrumental response would increase.
6. If a schedule led to response deprivation of a contingent response, the rate of increase of the base rate of the instrumental response would not be sufficient to maintain the base rate of response for the contingent response.

Allison, Miller, and Wozny (1979, Experiment 1) reported the results of an experiment that demonstrated all six of these relationships. Rats were given access under baseline conditions to a lever that could be depressed (the instrumental response) and to a spout that they could lick in order to obtain water (the contingent response). The rats were required to press for different amounts of time in order to have access to the spout for different amounts of time. Thus in this experiment both the instrumental requirements imposed by the schedule and the magnitude of the reward received for satisfying different schedule requirements were simultaneously varied. All six of the hypothesized relationships were obtained. Figure 4.1 presents the results of the study. Note that the amount of time spent performing the instrumental response increases as the schedule becomes more demanding. Note also that the amount of time spent performing the instrumental response decreases as the magnitude of the contingent response increases. As the amount of lever pressing required for access to drinking increases, the amount of drinking declines, and as the amount of drinking received for a particular amount of lever pressing increases, the amount of time spent lever pressing decreases. Note further that Figure 4.1 indicates that the schedules that introduced the

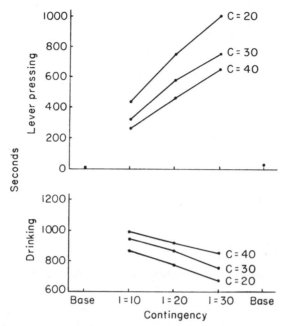

Figure 4.1. *Time spent lever pressing (upper panel) and drinking (lower panel) in 60-minute baseline and contingency sessions. (Precontingency baselines appear at the left, and postcontingency baselines at the right. Each remaining point is for one of the nine schedules formed by combining* I = *10, 20, and 30 second of lever pressing with* C = *20, 30, and 40 second of drinking. Each point represents a four-session mean averaged across the six rats.) (From J. Allison, M. Miller, and M. Wozny, Conservation in behavior.* Journal of Experimental Psychology: General, *1979, 108, 4–40. Copyright 1979 by The American Psychological Association. Reprinted by permission of the publisher and authors.)*

condition of response deprivation for drinking tended to facilitate lever pressing and suppress drinking relative to baseline.

Allison, Miller, and Wozny (1979; see also Timberlake, 1980) presented general mathematical model analyses of reinforcement relationships (see Staddon, 1979, for a suggestion that the model may be limited to certain special cases). Rather than describe the details of the model I will discuss in a rather general way certain features of the analysis that suggest new directions for understanding the influence of reinforcement. The analysis of reinforcement developed by Allison involves comparisons between behavior under free or noncontingent situations, which presumably indicate an organism's preference patterns under unconstrained conditions, and the effects of introducing constraints and limitations on the attainment of what may be conceived of as a desired or optimal pattern of activities. Behavior under constrained conditions may be conceived of as a compromise between the preferred state of responses and the costs to the organism of attaining that preferred state. This way of thinking of reinforcement permits one to draw analogies between economics and psychology. One can think of the instrumental activity as the cost to the organism of attaining a preferred level of the contingent response. As the price of the commodity (the contingent response of drinking in the experiment) increases, the consumption of the commodity decreases. According to the demand law of economics, as the price of the commodity increases, the quantity demanded of the commodity decreases—and this is exactly the result obtained in this experiment.

The analogy with economics may be extended. The study of the demand for commodities under conditions of constraint is a fundamental economic problem. Also, economists deal with what is called the elasticity of demand. The demand law asserts that the total quantity of a commodity sold is inversely related to price. The extent to which the demand for the commodity varies as a function of price is called the elasticity of demand. Unit elasticity is defined as the case in which a constant proportionality of changes in price and the amount of a commodity sold exists. Thus a 1% increase in price would yield a 1% decrease in sales. Inelastic demand would result when a 1% increase in price resulted in a less than 1% decrease in amount of the commodity sold. Such a commodity may be said to be inelastic because the amount of the commodity sold is partially independent of the cost. Elastic demand is defined as a decrease in the amount of a commodity sold which is proportionally larger than the increase in the price. It would result when a 1% increase in cost is accompanied by a larger than 1% decrease in the amount sold. Allison, Miller, and Wozny's model predicts that demand will initially be relatively inelastic. However, the elasticity of demand will increase as the price of the commodity increases. Quite apart from heuristic benefits, the exploration of the analogy with economics principles calls attention to a number of issues in motivational theory. These include the notion that there are constraints to the choice of activities and the allocation of resources in order to attain some compromise between an ideal and an attainable set of affairs.

There are other issues that are suggested by this analogy with economic theory that are of some motivational interest. What we have called the elasticity of demand refers to the extent to which changes in one activity are substitutable for changes in a second activity. It should be obvious that the activities that are in a sense exchanged in this analysis may be the subject of investigation. Rachlin, Green, Kasel, and Battalio (1976) dealt with this issue, and they reported experiments in which the substitutability of one commodity for another was investigated. For example they argued that root beer and Tom Collins mix were relatively substituable for a rat, such that an increase in the price as defined in terms of the ratio of responding required to receive one of the commodities tended to decrease the consumption of the second commodity. Food and water by contrast were far less substituable, hence the demand function was relatively inelastic for these commodities. In this sort of experiment, the selection of pairs of commodities that are relatively elastic or substitutable or not is aided by intuition of biological utilities. However, the exploration of the relationships with respect to substitutability of various commodities might lead to the development of systematic theory.

Opponent Process Theory

Solomon and Corbit (1974) developed a theory of acquired motivation called the opponent process theory. The theory provides an explanation of hedonic contrast effects. Central to the theory is the assumption that any intense emotional state will automatically elicit an emotional state with an opposite sign or quality. Intense pleasure or positive affect is assumed to elicit a strong negative emotional state, and intense pain is assumed to elicit a contrasting positive state.

The theory offers an explanation for three classes of phenomena. First, there is the phenomenon of affective contrast. Solomon (1980b) argued that in a variety of settings the presentation of a stimulus that elicits a powerful affective state will elicit the opposite or contrasting state following its withdrawal. Consider the following examples that he cited. If a newborn baby is given a sucking nipple with a sweet nutrient and the nipple is withdrawn after one minute, the baby will begin to cry for several minutes. The distress resulting from the withdrawal of the nipple probably would not have occurred if the baby had not previously been presented with a nipple that presumably elicited a positively toned affective state. Thus the crying is indicative of a negative state that results from the previous induction of a positive state. Solomon called this an example of hedonic affective contrast.

Affective contrast can also occur when the initial inducing state is negative. In this case the contrasting affective state would be positive. Epstein (1967) performed a number of studies of the affective consequences of parachute jumping. He reported that the initial experience of parachute jumping creates an experience of fright and terror. After the completion of the jump individuals report a feeling of elation. The elation that results is presumed to represent a state of affective contrast that develops as a result of the opposite-toned experience that preceded it.

The presumed occurrence of affective contrasts can be accompanied by corresponding psychophysiological changes. Solomon (1980b) cited data obtained in a study of heart rate changes in response to electrical shock presented to dogs (Church, Lolordo, Overmier, Solomon, & Turner, 1966).

Figure 4.2 presents these data. Note that the presentation of a shock elicits an increase in the heart rate. However, shock termination results in a decrease in heart rate below baseline level.

A second general phenomenon that opponent process theory proposes to explain is the occurrence of affective habituation. Affective habituation occurs when the response to repeated presentations of a stimulus that has the capacity to elicit a powerful affective state indicates a diminished level of affective response to the stimulus. For example, individuals who have an initial dose of an opiate report a highly euphoric state. However, after considerable opiate doses the experience is reported to be less euphoric and less intense. Similarly, repeated presentations of a stimulus that elicits a negative affective state can result in a reduction of the intensity of the state. Parachute jumpers appear to lose the terror associated with their initial jumps. Similarly, dogs who receive repeated shocks demonstrate a reduced level of responsiveness to the shocks. Their heart rate response to repeated shock presentations

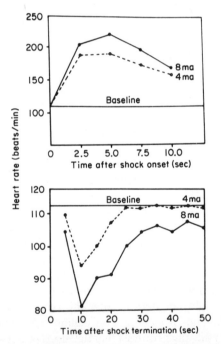

Figure 4.2.   The unconditioned heart rate response in dogs during a 10-second shock (ma = milliampere) to the hind paws (upper panel) and after the shock is terminated (lowel panel). (Note the change in scale for the ordinate in the lower panel.) (From R. L. Solomon. The opponent-process theory of required motivation. American Psychologist, 1980, 35, 691–712. Copyright 1980 by the American Psychological Association. Reprinted by permission of the publisher and author.)

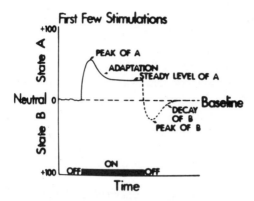

Figure 4.3.   The standard pattern of affective dynamics produced by a relatively novel uncondi-
tioned stimulus. (From R. L. Solomon. The opponent-process theory of required motivation.
American Psychologist, 1980, 35, 691–712. Copyright 1980 by The American Psychological
Association. Reprinted by permission of the publisher and author.)

demonstrates a reduced acceleratory response, and it may be accompanied
by a somewhat exaggerated deceleratory response following shock termination. Figures 4.3 and 4.4 indicate affective contrast and affective habituation
in response to repeated presentations of a stimulus that induces a particular
affective state.

Third, repeated presentations of a stimulus that elicits a strong affective
state results in an increased magnitude of the oppositely toned after effects.
Solomon called the increase in the magnitude of the opposite state, affective
withdrawal. The classic example of such a state with respect to a positively

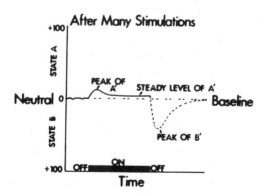

Figure 4.4.   The standard pattern of affective dynamics produced by a familiar, frequently
repeated, unconditioned stimulus. (From R. L. Solomon. The opponent-process theory of required motivation. American Psychologist, 1980, 35, 691–712. Copyright 1980 by The American Psychological Association. Reprinted by permission of the publisher and author.)

toned initial state can be seen in response to opiates. The strength of the negative response called withdrawal increases after repeated experience with opiates. Affective withdrawal is also assumed to occur following repeated presentations of stimuli that initially elicit negative affective states. For example, after repeated experiences with jogging, the initial mild relief presumably accompanying the opportunity to rest from extreme exertion and fatigue, is replaced by a sense of well-being or even euphoria that can be of long duration. Similar changes can be observed in the psychophysiological responses of the dog to electrical shock. Recall that the magnitude of the deceleratory response to termination of the shock increases with repeated exposures to the shock.

The opponent process theory assumes that the induction of a strong affective state leads to the automatic recruitment or induction of an opposite or opponent process. The original state is called the A state, and its opponent process is called the B state. The B state is said to be a slave state, since its occurrence and intensity is defined solely by the characteristics of the A state that induces it. The B state is presumed to be sluggish—that is, to have a long latency, to have a slow buildup in intensity, and to decline slowly after it reaches its asymptote. In addition, the B state is assumed to be conditionable—that is, it is assumed to increase in intensity and duration as a result of repeated induction. The affective state of the organism is defined by the combined effects of the A and B state. The rule for their combination is $|A - B|$. If A is greater than B, the affective state of the organism is defined by the affective sign or direction of the A state. If B is greater than A, the affective state of the individual is defined by the affective sign of the B state. The intensity of affective experience is defined by the absolute value of the $A - B$ difference.

It is easy to see how these simple assumptions serve to explain the three types of phenomena that are assumed to be relevant to the study of affective dynamics. Affective contrast is explained by the automatic induction of the B state. Affective habituation is explained by reference to the conditionability or buildup of the B state over repeated experiences resulting in a situation in which the combined effects of the A and oppositely signed B state result in a dampened or diminished response to the stimulus eliciting the A state. Affective withdrawal is explained by the increase in strength of the B state following repeated induction of the A state.

Solomon discussed the application of opponent process theory to attachment phenomena. Hoffman and Solomon (1974) and Starr (1978) presented an opponent process theory analysis of imprinting in ducklings. Newly hatched ducklings exposed to their mothers, or indeed to any moving object, become excited and proceed to follow the object. The removal of the object is followed by what appears to be an opponent process in which the duckling emits distress crying. Starr attempted to test implications of an opponent process analysis of imprinting. He reasoned that the intensity of the distress and the duration of distress crying would increase with repeated exposure to the imprinting object, which is presumed to elicit the positive affective state that controls the development of an opponent B state. Second, he reasoned that the development of distress crying would be decreased if the intervals between successive exposures to the critical imprinting object would be increased. This implication follows from the assumption that the B process decays over time and that if a sufficiently long interevent time is used between presentations, the B process will dissipate and not be able to develop or increase in strength. Third, he assumed that any change in the character of the imprinting object that would increase its capacity to elicit a powerful affective state would increase its ability to strengthen the B process and distress crying, which is taken as an observable manifestation of the B state.

Starr manipulated the duration of the interwithdrawal period of the imprinting object following successive 30-second exposures to the object. His results are presented in Figure 4.5, which indicates, in agreement with theoretical expectations, that the frequency of distress crying increased following successive withdrawals of the imprinting object. Figure 4.5 also indicates that the development of distress crying was diminished if the interval between successive presentations of the imprinting object were increased. Note that the data indicate that the development of distress crying was diminished if an interval of 2 minutes between presentations was used and that the development of distress crying was virtually eliminated if an interval of 5 minutes was used. Thus under the conditions of this study, a 5-minute interval appears sufficient to permit the decay of the B process and to eliminate its influence on the response to withdrawal of the stimulus that is assumed to elicit the opposing A process.

Starr also found that the increases in the intensity of the stimulus that elicits imprinting (in this case by having the imprinting object emit honking noises) would increase the duration of the decay function for the B state. He reported that distress crying builds up over successive 30-second presentations of an imprinting object that honked using a 5-minute or longer stimulus interval between presentations of the imprinting object. These results suggest that an increase in the intensity of the A process is accompanied by an increase in the intensity of the slave B process and in the time taken for the B process to decay to baseline levels.

Mineka, Suomi, and Delizio (1981) used opponent process theory to analyze the response of adolescent monkeys to mulitple separations from social living conditions. They argued that successive social separations should result in an increase in a distress reaction to the experience. Furthermore, they indicated that social separations in the monkey were usually followed by

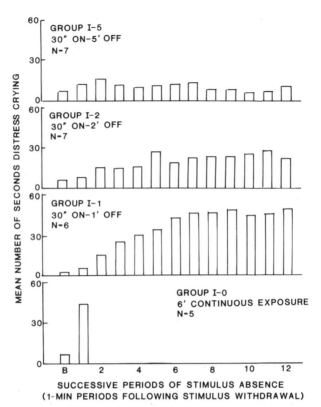

Figure 4.5.   *The growth of the opponent process (indexed by intensity of distress calling) for the action of an imprinting unconditioned stimulus (UCS) as a function of the temporal pattern of presentations and absences of the imprinting UCS. (Note that the total familiarity of all four groups with the UCS was the same [6 minutes], although the groups differed in their time intervals between exposures [see text].) (From R. L. Solomon. The opponent-process theory of required motivation.* American Psychologist, *1980, 35, 691–712. Copyright 1980 by The American Psychological Association. Reprinted by permission of the publisher and author.)*

increases in socially directed behaviors after their termination when the monkeys were reintroduced into social living conditions. However, according to the opponent the process theory analysis, the magnitude of the increase in socially oriented behavior should decrease with successive experiences of separation. This follows from the assumption that successive separations permit the increase in the development of the B opponent process that should detract from the intensity of the response to the situation that elicits the A process. In addition, the opponent process theory implies that the intensity of the distress response to repeated separations should increase over successive separations following the buildup of the B process, which is the presumed basis of the distress reaction. In their studies, they exposed different groups of adolescent monkeys to eight cycles of 4 days of separation in cages that permitted them to see and hear other monkeys, but prevented contact between monkeys. Each separation period was followed by a 3 day reunion period in which the monkeys were returned to group living conditions. Figure 4.6 presents representative results of one of their studies. The data are, in general, supportive of the opponent process theory analysis and indicate that there was an increase in the magnitude of such self-directed behaviors as self-clasping and huddling following successive separation experiences. Also, the magnitude of locomotion decreased over successive experiences with separation. The self-directed behaviors exhibited by these monkeys toward the end of a sequence of separations were taken by Mineka, Suomi, and Delizio to be indicative of a depressive reaction that is quite rare among adolescent monkeys. What is most noteworthy among the behaviors exhibited during

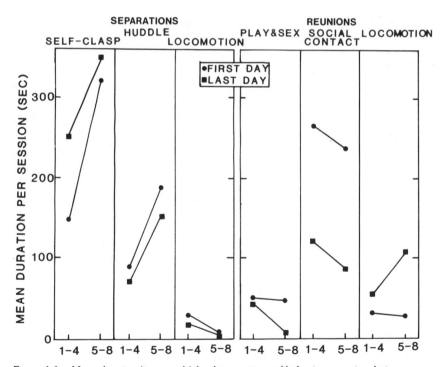

Figure 4.6. *Mean duration (in seconds) for three patterns of behavior occurring during separations (left side) and three patterns of behavior occurring during reunions (right side) for the monkeys in Experiment 1. (First Day and Last Day refer to Days 1 and 4 for separation periods, and to Days 1 and 3 for reunion periods. 1–4 = first four separation–reunion cycles; 5–8 = last 4 separation–reunion cycles.) (From Mineka, Suomi, and Delizio [1981].)*

the reunion periods was the high level of social contact behavior that decreased over repeated separation experiences. Presumably the decrease is attributed to the strengthening of the B state which detracts from the A state, which elicits the social contact behavior.

Although the results of the studies of response to the separation among monkeys extend the opponent process theory to a consideration of attachment behavior that is considerably more complex than that studied in the imprinting experiments, the results of these studies also raise some difficulties and point to some of the uncertainties in the application of the theory. Mineka, Suomi, and Delizio indicated that the response of different groups of monkeys included in their study was somewhat different to the repeated separation experiences. The data presented in Figure 4.6 were obtained from monkeys who had been separated from their mothers at birth. Among monkeys who had not experienced maternal separations, there was comparatively little increase in such self-directed behaviors as clasping over successive separation experiences. These monkeys did, however, exhibit high and increasing levels of stereotypical behavior, defined as repeated identical movements performed in a rhythmic manner. Such behavior may be considered analogous to agitated depressive behavior. Also, the diminution in social contacts following successive reunions did not occur in these monkeys. Thus the pattern of response to successive separation experiences was not invariant among different groups of monkeys having different socialization experiences. These results point to a lacuna in opponent process theory. The precise nature of the responses to B state are not specified. As the complexity of the behavioral repertoire of the organism studied increases, this problem may become more serious. There is a certain vagueness and lack of precision in the definition of the behaviors that will emerge or indeed in the exact nature of the opposing affective state that is presumed to reflect B process.

Mineka, Suomi, and Delizio also indicated that there was some ambiguity in applying the theory to situations in which the event that elicited the A state was not presented for the first time. Monkeys living in cages with other monkeys clearly had had ample opportunities to develop attachment behaviors. However, it may be the case that attachment is not at its maximal level since monkeys clearly do many nonsocial things during periods in which they are living in social situations. The increase in socially directed behaviors following a separation period may provide for the development of an enhanced A process and correspondingly for the development of an enhanced B process. Since the relevant strengths of the A and B processes that have developed as a result of previous experiences are not studied and are unknown, the impact of the experimental treatments occurs against an undefined background. Mineka, Suomi, and Delizio speculated that separation following a period of previous experiences with social living conditions might in fact lead to a stronger B state than one in which the organism has never experienced the A state that elicits the B state. Thus as more complicated behaviors are studied, the precise conditions necessary for the development of opponent processes of high intensity may be more variable. Despite some of the ambiguities surrounding the application of opponent process theory to this setting, it is also the case that the theory was in large measure supported. In particular the changes observed in behaviors exhibited with successive experiences of separation and reunion are strongly supportive of an opponent process theory analysis.

Solomon attempted to explain phenomena associated with parachute jumping in terms of the opponent process theory. He cited data obtained by Epstein (1967) indicating that changes in hedonic responses to the experience of parachute jumping develop as a result of experience with this activity. The initial reaction to the experience of parachute jumping is one of steadily developing anxiety as the time for the jump approaches. The experience of the jump itself is described as one of terror. Following the completion of the jump, there is a positive hedonic state that is euphoric. According to Solomon, the hedonic experiences associated with parachute jumping change with experience. Experienced parachutists exhibit a diminution of fear preceding the jump. In fact the negative emotional state produced by the jump is replaced by one of thrill followed, after the completion of the jump, by a state of euphoria that may be of long duration. Although this sequence of events is perfectly compatible with the sequence postulated by Solomon in opponent process theory, it is not in point of fact identical with the results obtained by Epstein. Figure 4.7 presents the results of a self-rating of fear and avoidance tendencies exhibited by experienced and inexperienced parachutists prior to and after a jump. Note that, in agreement with the opponent process theory analysis, the experienced parachutists did exhibit a decrease in anxiety and avoidance tendencies prior to the jump, at least as measured by self-reports. This finding could be attributable to the development of the B process opposing the initial A process that is hedonically negative. However, in two respects these data do not appear to be compatible with an opponent process theory analysis. Note that following the jump experienced parachutists exhibited an increased feeling of anxiety—not elation—as one would have predicted on an opponent process theory analysis. Once the stimulus of the jump is removed, the A process is removed, and the strengthened B process should be expressed in terms of an oppositely signed hedonic event. The removal of the initially aversive event is paradoxically accompanied by an increase in anxiety. Note further that Figure 4.7 indicates that experienced parachutists exhibited high levels of anxiety at a very early period in the jump sequence. Solomon explicitly assumed that A processes do not change as a result of experience. Changes in hedonic experiences are to be explained solely by the

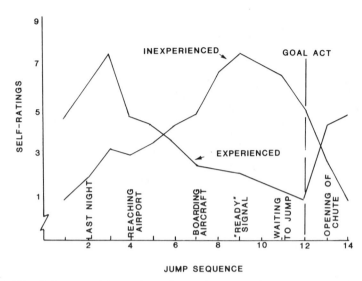

Figure 4.7. *Self-ratings of fear and avoidance of novice and experienced parachutists as a function of the sequence of events leading up to and following a jump. (From Epstein [1967].)*

development of B processes and resultant changes in the magnitude of the absolute value and sign of the difference between the A and B processes. The theory should, therefore, imply that the magnitude of the primary aversive state elicited by the jump experience should remain invariant as a result of experience. The opponent state of elation can be expected to increase in magnitude with experience and to detract from the negative aversive state. However, an increase in the aversive state at times that are temporally remote from the peak effects of the stimulus that elicits the primary affective state is not compatible with this theory. Therefore, the increase in anxiety that occurs prior to the jump and after the jump among experienced parachutists does not appear to be compatible with opponent process theory.

Epstein (1967) also reported data on the response of experienced and inexperienced parachutists to cues that are of differing degrees of relevance to the possibility of receiving bodily harm as a result of parachute jumping. In this study GSR responses were obtained to words judged to be of differing degrees of relevance to parachute jumping as a function of experience. Epstein's results are presented in Figure 4.8. These data are longitudinal results for a single subject. However, the results reported may be considered as representative, since other subjects exhibited a similar tendency toward the development of inverted V curves as a result of experience, with high magnitude responses occurring to stimulus words of low or medium relevance to parachuting. These results may be analogous to the findings with self-reports of anxiety, indicating a displacement of anxiety not only to temporally remote periods, but also to stimuli that are psychologically remote or weakly related to the original fear-inducing stimulus. Even though the GSR does not indicate the direction of the valence of the emotional response, the data contained in Figure 4.8 do not appear to be compatible with opponent process theory. The theory requires one to explain an increase in the magnitude of a combined A and B process as a result of experience that would result in an increase in the magnitude of the GSR response. However, the increase should occur with greatest intensity in response to the stimulus which initially elicits the most intense A response. The development of an intense response to a stimulus that did not initially elicit such a response is not compatible with the opponent process theory.

There are, however, other physiological data collected by Epstein that are compatible with the opponent process theory. Epstein obtained heart rate, respiration, and GSR data from experienced and inexperienced parachutists at different times leading up to a jump. Experienced parachutists exhibited psychophysiological responses of low magnitude in comparison to inexperienced parachutists just prior to a jump. Figure 4.9 presents respiration rate data collected by Epstein. These data may be considered as representative for the other psychophysiological data, which exhibit comparable patterns. Note that experienced parachutists were not more aroused either prior to the jump or after the completion of the jump. These data, on the surface, appear to support an opponent process theory analysis. Superficially, they suggest a disjunction between the psychophysiological measures and the self-report measures. However, the disjunction is more apparent than real. The peaking of the self-report of anxiety presented in Figure 4.7 occurred at a time prior to reaching the airport. The first psychophysiological measurements

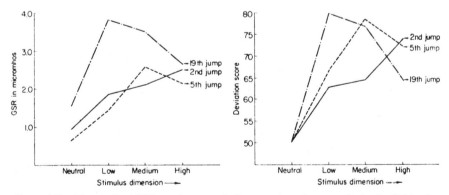

Figure 4.8. *Magnitude of GSR as a function of relevance of words to parachuting for Subject 1. (From Epstein [1967].)*

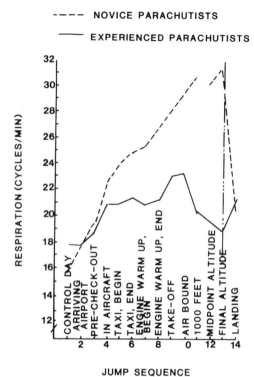

Figure 4.9.   *Respiration rate of experienced and novice parachutists as a function of the sequence of events leading up to and following a jump. (From Epstein [1967].)*

were taken when subjects reached the airport. Thus the psychophysiological measurements were not taken at the early period in which high anxiety and avoidance was reported by subjects. The data for the apparent disjunction of self-report and psychophysiological measurement that occurred after the jump are somewhat more ambiguous. The measurements in this case were taken at approximately the same point in the sequence, and they do indicate high self-reported anxiety after completion of the jump for the experienced parachutists and little or no difference for the psychophysiological measures taken at the same time.

Solomon (1980a) used opponent process theory to explain schedule-induced adjunctive behaviors. Adjunctive behaviors involve a generalization from one motivational system to another. One example is the case of "schedule-induced polydipsia," which occurs when rats are placed on a schedule that permits access to pellets of food at fixed intervals. If rats are provided access to a drinking tube during the interval when they are not given access to the pellets of food, rats will tend to drink water. What is of some interest is the magnitude of the increase in water consumption that occurs under these conditions. Water intake may increase as much as 10 times over baseline intake and is said to become polydipsic (see Falk, 1977). Solomon's analysis of this behavior is based on the assumption that the occurrence of the polydipsic adjunctive behavior is controlled by the development of the B process following the ingestion of food, which engenders an A process. Solomon assumed that the rat experienced distress following eating of food and the ingestion of water served to reduce the distress. Note that on this analysis the water ingestion is not mandated by the previous experience of eating but occurs as a response that removes the vague distress of the rat. Presumably any other activity that has the capacity to eliminate the B distress state would become adjunctive. Solomon's analysis of adjunctive behaviors implies a number of testable consequences. In the case of schedule-induced polydipsia, if access to the water spout is not provided immediately after the pellets are eaten, and a critical period of time elapses, the B state will decay and, therefore, will no longer serve to motivate drinking. Thus, adjunctive polydipsia will not occur if access to the water spout is delayed beyond some undefined period of time. Solomon (1980b) reported the results of an experiment by Rosellini that indicated that adjunctive polydipsia does not develop if access to the water is delayed for 200 seconds. This implies that for the particular reinforcers used in this study, the decay period for the B process was exceeded by the 200-second interval.

Solomon's analysis also implies that the development of adjunctive behaviors would increase over trials as an organism has repeated experiences with the reinforcer that is presumed to initiate an A process and the slave B process. In addition, the theoretical analysis assumes that the development of the B process is dependent on the intensity of the A process which engenders it. Therefore, if the intensity of the A process is manipulated by varying the reward value or satisfying character of the stimulus that elicits it, then the development of adjunctive behaviors should be correspondingly manipulated. In a test of these assumptions, Rosellini and Lashley (as reported in Solomon, 1980a) presented rats with quinine-adulterated pellets of food (such pellets are assumed to have reduced reward value because of their bitter flavor), standard pellets, and sucrose-adulterated pellets (which are assumed to be highly rewarding). The results for their experiment are presented in Figure 4.10. Note that the magnitude of adjunctive drinking increased over repeated sessions, thus supporting the assumption that the increase of the B process with experience is responsible for the development of the adjunctive behavior. In addition, the data indicate that the magnitude of adjunctive behavior was dependent upon the intensity of the reward value associated with the primary reinforcer, or in Solomon's terms, the intensity of the A state.

The research analysis of adjunctive behaviors points to some rather general motivational principles. It is, for example, reminiscent of certain principles

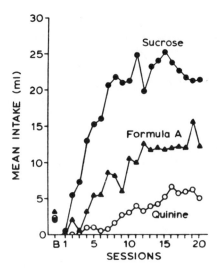

Figure 4.10.   *The growth of adjunctive drinking as a function of the preference value of the food reinforcer. The graphs represent the mean values from five subjects. The greater the preference value, the more rapidly the adjunctive drinking develops and the greater the asymptote of polydipsia is. (From Solomon [1980a].)*

suggested by the theory of action. According to the theory of action, the duration of time spent performing a particular action tendency is determined in part by the magnitude of the consummatory force acting upon it. Also the opportunity for any of a variety of alternative incompatible action tendencies to emerge in behavior is dependent upon the rate of reduction in strength of the action tendency that is being expressed. The rate of reduction of the original action tendency is also determined by the magnitude of the instigatory force acting upon the action tendency. These notions are in some respect analogous to the assumptions contained in opponent process theory. The removal of a stimulus that elicits a powerful motivational state or hedonic state is analogous to the removal of an instigatory force. The reward value of the stimulus that controls the development of the A state is analogous to the magnitude of the consummatory value that determines the rate at which the consummatory force reduces the strength of the original action tendency. The reduction of the strength of the original action tendency increases the probability that some alternative incompatible action tendency will emerge. Since there are assumed to be several possible action tendencies that can emerge following the removal or ending of a particular action tendency, it is the case that both theories assume that there is a diffuse somewhat unpredictable character to the behaviors that may emerge following the cessation of a particular action tendency. For example, Solomon has discussed jogging from the perspective of oppo-

:1ent process theory. In jogging an initially aversive state has as its presumed alternative B state the development of a postjogging elation or high. This high, which may persist for a long period of time, is compatible with any of a variety of behaviors. An individual experiencing this postjogging elated state may report increased interest or satisfaction in sexual activity or in work activity. Although the theory is not able to predict the precise character of the behavior that follows the induction of an intense motivational state, it can predict a heightened readiness to engage in any of a large class of behaviors hedonically compatible with the induced-opponent process. Note further that both Solomon's theory and the theory of action share two rather general symmetries. Both theories focus on time as a critical dimension of behavior. This fact is perhaps a superficial analogy, since the role of duration is rather different in the two theories. In opponent process theory the duration of time expended on an initial activity is irrelevant. Rather, what is of critical importance is the decay functions defining the opponent process. For the theory of action, what is of central importance is the duration of an initial action prior to its being abandoned for a new action. What is possibly of more enduring interest is the common focus in both theories on the aftereffects of engagement in an initial activity. Both theories involve a shift in the focus of motivational study from a single goal-directed action sequence to the relationship between a goal-directed action sequence and its sequelae.

Although the opponent process theory has received impressive research support, and it has demonstrated the capacity to shed light on a diverse and interesting class of phenomena, it should be noted that the theory does exhibit some ambiguities that become manifest especially when dealing with complex organisms. Recall that the theory was not able to deal with the subtleties of the changes in the experience of parachute jumping reported by Epstein in his research. Also there were some ambiguities in the application of the theory to the attachment behavior of monkeys. Perhaps the greatest ambiguity in the theory is the vagueness in the specification of the nature of the opponent process that is induced following any strong affective state and, correspondingly, by the vagueness in the prediction of the precise character of the behavior that is to be expected following the induction of B state. In the case of the development of adjunctive polydipsia, Solomon assumes that the aversive B state is removed by the opportunity to engage in a rewarded behavior. In the case where the B state is induced by separation experiences in monkeys, the aversive B state in different groups of monkeys leads either to a kind of depressive self-directed behavior or to a ritualized or stereotyped display of a behaviors, which are considered as analogous to agitated depressions. The conditions under which behaviors will merely express the B state or behaviors will act to reduce an aversive B state need to be specified. Also the question of the universality of the development of opponent processes needs to be determined. In their original presentation of the theory, Solomon and Corbit (1974) speculated about the possibility that some affective A states might not elicit an opponent B state, and they mentioned in this regard the possibility that aesthetic experiences might not be accompanied by opponent processes. However, relatively little research or discussion has been directed to the question of the universality of opponent processes.

Reinforcement theory, opponent process theory, and the theory of action are each related in diverse ways to an emerging conception of motivation that deals with changes among diverse action tendencies. It is possible to distinguish among three rather general classes of motivational problems. The first class of problems may be considered the problem of induction. It relates to the conditions required to induce an organism to engage in a particular goal-directed action tendency. In the animal literature deprivation of a basic biological substance such as food was the standard method for inducing a goal-directed activity in an organism. For the most part deprivation studies have not been a prominent feature of the human motivational literature. Curiously, the theories that have been considered here do not address the issue of induction of a motivational state in a systematic way. The conditions used to induce a motivational state are often part of the experimental lore associated with different areas of motivational investigation.

Second, is the issue of the distribution of several action tendencies over a particular time period. This issue is of central concern to both contemporary reinforcement theory and to the theory of action. Both theories permit one to derive formal expressions of equilibrium states indicating the relationship between final response distributions and underlying motivational states. Thus in a rather general sense, it impossible to argue that both theories represent the expression of a final set of behavioral tendencies as the result of the expression of a series of latent or hypothetical motivational tendencies. In modern reinforcement theory the latent motivational tendencies may be defined as the preferences exhibited by an organism under totally unconstrained or noncontingent conditions. The distribution of behaviors, or action tendencies, represents a compromise between a psychological ideal and what is possible under constraints imposed by external forces or contingencies, which are arranged by the experimenter. The influence of external constraints or "schedule-induced behavior" is not examined in the theory of action. However, the theory does study the distribution of several action tendencies over a period of time and does in this sense deal with the problem of the relationship between latent motivational tendencies and their ultimate expression in behavior.

Third, is the motivational problem of the effects of the expression of one action tendency upon the subsequent disposition to continue expressing that tendency. The occurrence of satiation effects and the influence that they have on the selection of subsequent action tendencies is dealt with in both the theory of action and in opponent process theory. Both theories assume that the tendency to engage in a goal-directed action tendency leads to a dampening of the action tendency and leads to a corresponding increase in tendency to engage in some alternative action tendency.

All three theories are part of an emerging conception of motivational psychology in which the study of a single goal-directed action tendency is being displaced as the paradigm in the study of motivation by a conception of motivation that emphasizes the waxing and waning of diverse action tendencies and the ultimate distribution of diverse tendencies.

Chapter 5

MOTIVATION AND COGNITION: IN SEARCH OF THE GHOST IN THE MACHINE

Cognitive events may be conceived of, to use Gilbert Ryle's phrase, as "ghosts in the machine [Ryle, 1949]." It is clearly the case that one could have a psychology of motivation that does not involve cognitions. Such a psychology could be nonpurposive as, for example, the motivational theories examined in Chapter 2, or it could be purposive. One can treat motivation as a latent or hypothetical state, and the specific beliefs, cognitions, or even the phenomenal status (i.e., the ability to experience or to be aware) of the motives postulated to influence behavior need not be considered. In fact, the motivational issues have been substantially examined from this perspective. However, human beings clearly have thoughts of which they are aware and these throughts tend to accompany their actions. What is by no means transparent is the specific explanatory role to be assigned to such cognitive states within a complete motivational psychology. Several logical possibilities may be distinguished. One may dismiss the occurrence of such cognitions as a kind of idle chatter that is irrelevant to the control and influence of behavior. Such a posture is analogous to an epiphenomenalist position according to which the occurrence of conscious states is not causal and is outside the chain of causal events. On such a view one could safely ignore a person's thoughts. Alternatively, one might assume that the thoughts and beliefs of subjects are relevant to their actions and thus should be studied in order to develop a complete psychology of motivation. In the latter case one may choose to distinguish among several possibilities with respect to the phenomenal status of the postulated cognitive state of an individual. The phenomenal status of the cognitive states that are assigned a motivational role may be undefined. This is reminiscent of Tolman's use of cognitive language in a strictly behavioristic psychology in which the inquiry into the phenomenal status of constructs was eschewed and even forbidden. Thus the ordinary connotations of awareness that are normally associated with cognitive states could be removed in the development of formal theory. Alternatively, one might assume that the phenomenal status of cognitive states might be affirmed. In this latter case one could inquire whether or not the phenomenal status of the cognition is a necessary condition for its psychological or motivational influence. Such an inquiry directs one's attention to the distinction between conscious and unconscious motivational states. Furthermore, if the cognitions influencing motivation are phenomenal, the issue of the methodology for the determination of their phenomenal status is raised. One might assume that individuals are aware of their states but may be unable to use verbal reports accurately.

In this chapter the role of cognitive processes in motivation will be considered. I will take a historical approach to this issue that will consider changes in the role assigned to cognitive processes in motivation. First, theoretical developments that assigned a central role to cognition in motivation will be considered. Then, I will demonstrate that subsequent research has, in each instance, suggested that the initial belief about the centrality of cognitive processes is questionable and that it is perhaps appropriate to assign a somewhat more circumscribed role to such processes. Then, recent research and theoretical developments that explicitly argue that phenomenal events are to be assigned a central role in the control of motivated behavior will be discussed. Finally, having created a seemingly irreconcilable conflict a possible resolution of the conflict will, tentatively, be considered.

During the 1960s the psychology of motivation appeared to shift in the direction of assigning a central role to cognitive processes in the control of behavior. More recent research has suggested that cognitive influences on motivational processes appear to be somewhat more problematical than earlier research and theory had implied.

The Unconscious

I will begin with a discussion of research on unconscious processes. It is possible to trace a pattern of change in belief with respect to the probity of empirical demonstrations of unconscious processes. Considerable interest was attached to experimental demonstrations of unconscious phenomena.

Subsequently these demonstrations were challenged (see Brody, 1972), and more recent research has again provided evidence in favor of the view that stimuli that are out of awareness may have motivational influences. One of the classic experiments on this problem was reported by McGinnies in 1949. McGinnies presented subjects with a series of taboo words such as "whore" and "Kotex." These stimuli were presented very rapidly with a tachistoscope at "below threshold" levels. The duration of exposure was increased until a subject was able to correctly identify the word. McGinnies recorded the GSR during presentation of the taboo words. The response of subjects to these words was compared to their response to emotionally neutral words. McGinnies reported two findings. First, the threshold for the correct identification of the taboo words was higher than the threshold for the correct identification of the neutral words. Second, the GSR to taboo words was higher than to neutral words prior to correct recognition of the taboo words. McGinnies argued that these findings were to be interpreted as being indicative of a process of perceptual defense in which there was an unconscious recognition of the taboo words and a response (indexed by the GSR) to the emotional meaning of the taboo words. Furthermore, through a process of defense, access to the unconscious was blocked.

McGinnies's interpretation of these results was challenged (see, for example, Howes & Solomon, 1950). An alternative interpretation of this finding is that subjects were reluctant to report the perception of taboo words and simply adopted a higher criterion of confidence before being willing to assert that they had seen such a word. Such a criticism is surely plausible since subjects would appear in an embarrassing light if they had uttered a taboo word when a neutral word was presented.

In order to circumvent these difficulties, Lazarus and McLeary (1951) designed a two-stage experiment. In the first stage of the experiment, subjects were presented with 10 nonsense syllables, 5 of which were paired with electric shock in a conditioning paradigm. In the second phase subjects were presented with the nonsense syllables tachistoscopically, and GSR responses to the stimuli were obtained. The stimuli were presented at below threshold durations, and the duration of exposure was increased until a subject was able to correctly identify the stimulus being presented. Their analysis centered on the GSR responses to neutral and shock stimuli on those trials in which the subject did not correctly identify the stimulus. They found that the average GSR response to stimuli that were not correctly identified was larger when the stimulus that was presented was a shock syllable rather than a nonshock syllable. This difference defined the "subception effect"—which was taken as evidence of discrimination without awareness. This implies that the individual is able to emotionally respond to the stimuli at levels below conscious recognition.

Both Goldiamond (1958) and Eriksen (1957, 1958) criticized the discrimination without awareness interpretation of the subception effect on methodological grounds. Eriksen presented an empirical and theoretical analysis of subception that supports an alternative interpretation of the phenomenon. Eriksen's analysis starts with the observation that the subception effect is defined in terms of a discrepancy between two different response systems that are indices of a subject's perception. The GSR response system is a continuous one that permits the registration of a range of magnitudes of response to the stimulus. The verbal scoring system used in the Lazarus and McLeary study, by contrast, permits only a dichotomous response—correct recognition versus incorrect recognition. This difference raises the possibility that the verbal scoring system may artificially restrict the sensitivity of the verbal response. This possibility could plausibly arise in the following way: On a particular stimulus presentation, the subject is uncertain whether or not the stimulus was one of two stimuli. His or her first response (and the only response permitted the subject in the Lazarus and McLeary study) might be a nonshock syllable that is incorrect. However, the second verbal response, which would have been a shock syllable and the correct response, is never given. The GSR on the other hand registers the subject's uncertainty and possible awareness of the presence of a shock syllable.

Eriksen designed a series of studies to explicate the relationship among various response indicators of perception. In one of these studies, Eriksen presented subjects with 11 different-sized squares. Each square was assigned a number indicative of its size. The stimuli were presented tachistoscopically. Three different response systems were used as indicators of perception, a first verbal response, a second verbal response, and a motor response in which the subject adjusted a continuously varying lever to the point indicative of the magnitude of the stimulus. Eriksen computed the correlation between each response and the stimulus. He found that the magnitude of the correlation of the first verbal response with the stimulus was higher than the correlation of the other responses with the stimulus. This finding supported earlier results in Eriksen's studies indicating that the verbal system is equal to, or more sensitive than, any other response indicator of perception including the GSR. For example, in a repeat of the Lazarus and MacLeary study, Eriksen found that the verbal response correctly identified the nonsense syllable presented on 45% of the trials. The GSR was able to discriminate the presence or absence of a shock syllable (note that the GSR does not indicate which syllable was presented) on 60% of the trials. However, the probability of being correct by change is 50% in the GSR case (that is, on 50% of the trials a shock syllable will be presented) whereas the probability of being correct by change for the verbal response is 10%. If the verbal response is set the same task as the GSR, to discriminate the presence or absence of a shock syllable, a correction for chance responding can be obtained as follows: The verbal response is accurate on 45% of the trials. By chance, the verbal response should be accurate on one-half the remaining trials. Half of 55% is 27.5%, giving a corrected estimate of accuracy for the verbal response of 72.5%, which exceeds the obtained accuracy of the GSR. These results indicate that the verbal response system is a more accurate index of perception than the GSR and question the notion of the GSR as an index of unconscious perception.

Eriksen went on to compute a series of partial correlations to study the relationship between response systems and stimuli in the experiment involving the discrimination of different-sized squares. He found that the partial correlation between the second verbal response and the stimuli, holding constant the first verbal response, was significant. This finding indicates that the second verbal response gives information about the stimulus that is independent of that given by the first response. Put another way, this finding indicates that one would be more accurate in predicting the stimulus actually present on any given trial if one had information about both the first and second verbal response than if one had information about only one of these responses.

The partial correlation between the lever response and the stimuli holding constant the first verbal response was also significant. This indicates that the lever response contains information about the stimulus that is independent of that contained in the first verbal response. The partial correlation between the lever response and the stimulus with the first verbal response held constant is exactly analagous to the subception effect that may be defined as a significant partial correlation between the GSR and the stimuli with the first verbal response held constant. Eriksen's studies indicate that different response indices of perception tend to be correlated imperfectly with each other and to have significant partial correlations with stimuli when one of the other response systems is held constant. The subception effect will occur for any pair of response indices that account for partially independent sources of variance in the stimuli. Such an interpretation of subception contradicts the view that it represents discrimination without awareness.

Eriksen's analysis of subception assigns a central role to experiential states in the determination of behavior. On Eriksen's analysis a subject is really aware of the nature of the stimulus being presented, but that awareness is only imperfectly indexed by the responses by means of which awareness is usually inferred. Thus a line of experimental research that initially attempted to limit and circumscribe the role assigned to conscious processes in the control of behavior was, for a time, interpreted as supporting the notion that individuals would not be influenced by external stimuli that were truly out of awareness. However, more recent research, using different paradigms, and including controls for the problems of response measurement has again supported the view that subjects are influenced by external stimuli that are out of awareness. I will present research approaches that attempt to demonstrate that subjects are influenced by stimuli of which they are not aware.

Kunst-Wilson and Zajonc (1980) attempted to elicit an emotional response to a stimulus that a subject is not able to identify. They relied on the finding that subjects develop a liking for stimuli to which they have been exposed (see Harrison, 1977; Zajonc, 1968)—that is, that there is a positive relationship between familiarity and liking for a stimulus. In their experiment subjects were presented with a series of geometric forms. The stimuli were presented under tachistoscopic viewing conditions (1-msec exposure) that made it difficult for subjects to identify the stimulus being presented to them. The experiment had two phases. In the first phase subjects were exposed to 10 of 20 stimuli five times in random order. In the second phase of the experiment, subjects were presented with stimulus pairs in which one member of the pair was a previously presented stimulus and the other member was a new stimulus. In one condition subjects were asked to indicate which of the two stimuli was previously presented to them. Responses were essentially at chance levels. Thus using a test of discrimination (a test procedure usually considered to be the most accurate index of subjects' awareness of a stimulus), subjects were not able to distinguish between stimuli they had previously encountered and stimuli that they had not encountered. In addition, subjects were asked to express their confidence about their judgments. Confidence judgments were unrelated to the accuracy of judgment. Thus subjects were no more likely to be accurate in their judgment of which of the two stimuli they had encountered when they expressed confidence in their judgments than when they did not express confidence. In a second group subjects were asked which of the two stimuli they preferred. Subjects were significantly more likely to prefer the stimuli they had previously encountered. Also, they were more likely to select a previously encountered stimulus when they were confident of their judgment than when they were not confident of their judgments. This study demonstrates that subjects may develop an emotional response to a stimulus that they are not aware of having seen. There are two somewhat different interpretations of the results of the Kunst-Wilson and Zajonc experiment. On one interpretation subjects were aware of the stimuli on initial contact but the immediate recognition of the stimulus is not retained or transferred from short-term memory. Thus, on being asked to recall which of the stimuli they had encountered, subjects are not able to perform this task with better than chance accuracy. However, they are able to redintegrate or reexperience an emotional response to the stimuli they had encountered. On the second interpretation subjects were never aware of the stimuli they had been presented and would not have been able to discriminate them from other similar stimuli even if the recognition task had occurred immediately after stimulus presentation. On either interpretation the Kunst-Wilson and Zajonc experiment appears to demonstrate that subjects are capable of developing an emotional response to a stimulus that they are not capable of recognizing. Presumably such an emotional response would color and effect subjects' actions with respect to such a stimulus.

Seamon, Brody, and Kauff (in press, 1983) replicated and extended the Kunst-Wilson and Zajonc findings. Their first experiment was essentially an attempt to replicate the Kunst-Wilson and Zajonc experiment. They compared recognition and preference responses obtained from subjects who had seen 5 of 10 geometric stimuli five times at rapid exposure. The results for their experiment are presented in Table 5.1 which indicates that subjects were more likely to choose the previously presented stimuli if they were asked which of the stimuli they preferred than if they were asked which of the two stimuli they had encountered. Thus the results of this experiment replicate those reported by Kunst-Wilson and Zajonc. However, under the conditions of viewing used by Seamon, Brody, and Kauff, recognition responses of subjects were above chance.

In a follow-up investigation, Seamon, Brody, and Kauff attempted to make the recognition task more difficult by adding a distractor. They used a shadowing condition in which subjects were required to listen to a tape of a list of words and repeat them as they heard them. The results for this study are also presented in Table 5.1. Note that under shadowing conditions subjects' recognition responses are reduced to chance levels. However, preference responses for old stimuli are above chance. Thus these results suggest, in agreement with Kunst-Wilson and Zajonc, that subjects will develop preferences for stimuli that they cannot recall observing.

W. R. Wilson (1979) used a distractor paradigm to demonstrate the development of a positive affective response to a stimulus in the absence of accu-

TABLE 5.1
Percentage of Target Stimulus Selection for Previously Presented Stimuli

	Experiment 1		Experiment 2	
	Affect	Recognition	Affect	Recognition
Nonshadowed	64.5	66.0	66.0	59.0
Shadowed	65.5	59.1	56.5	47.5

Source: Seamon, Brody, and Kauff, 1983.
Note: Chance = 50%.

rate recognition of the stimulus. In his study subjects were presented with a series of tone sequences to the left ear. They listened to a tape in which words they were required to shadow were presented to the right ear. After listening to the sequences, subjects were presented with the tones they had heard and a set of tones that they had not previously heard; they were required to state whether they liked the tones they heard or, in a different condition, if the tone was one they had heard before. Wilson was able to demonstrate that subjects' recognition responses in this shadowing paradigm were essentially at chance level. Given Zajonc's theorizing about the effects of familiarity on liking, one would expect that subjects would develop a liking or preference for those tone sequences they had previously heard. Table 5.2 presents the results of Wilson's experiments and indicates that subjects did in fact develop a preference for those tone sequences that they had previously encountered even though they were not able to recognize them at better than chance levels of accuracy. These results thus buttress the findings of Kunst-Wilson and Zajonc and indicate that the development of a preference for a stimulus can occur even though the subject is not aware of having encountered the stimulus.

Corteen and Wood (1972) used this type of paradigm in a frequently cited study. In their experiment subjects were presented with an initial conditioning task in which words were associated with electric shock. After the initial conditioning phase of the experiment, subjects were presented with a shadowing task in which the previously shocked words were presented to one ear while they were instructed to shadow words presented to the other ear. They found that words presented to the unattended ear, which the subject claimed to be unaware of, produced electrodermal responses, indicating some sort of emotional response to the stimuli.

Corteen and Wood's results, although frequently cited as providing evidence for some sort of semantic processing that exists outside of awareness

TABLE 5.2
Recognition and Affect Judgments for Tones

Affect judgments		Recognition
Old stimuli	3.51	3.17
New stimuli	3.03	—

Source: W. R. Wilson. Feeling more than we can know. Exposure effects without learning. *Journal of Personality and Social Psychology,* 1979, *31,* 811–821. Copyright 1979 by the American Psychological Association. Reprinted by permission of the publisher and author.
Note: Chance accuracy = 3.00.

(see Posner, 1978), are controversial. Wardlaw and Kroll (1976) reported that they were unable to replicate these findings (see also Corteen & Dunn, 1974). Dawson and Schell (1982) have reported a replication and extension of the Corteen and Wood results that clarifies the conditions under which the original phenomena is likely to appear and provides some tentative evidence for a neurophysiological model of the phenomena. In their experiment somewhat more stringent procedures were employed to control for awareness of stimuli being presented to the unattended ear. They indicate that, in the original Corteen and Wood study, evidence for the absence of awareness of stimuli being presented to the unattended ear was obtained by the use of a postexperimental questionnaire. It is possible that brief shifts of attention to the unattended ear occurred and that subjects were unable to recall these shifts. Dawson and Schell presented single words to be shadowed and noted the occurrence of any errors in shadowing. They also included postexperimental questionnaires and provided subjects in one of their groups with a key to press if they believed that they heard a previously shocked word in the unattended ear.

The results of the Dawson and Schell study indicate that the phenomenon previously reported by Corteen and Wood may in part be mediated by the failure to adequately control for attentional shifts. They found that if the analysis was restricted to just those trials in which there was no evidence for an attentional shift, the phenomenon was not clearly present—that is, that the probability and magnitude of electrodermal responses to words that had previously been associated with shock was not significant different from the responses to words that had not been previously associated with shock. This aspect of the results would lead to the suggestion that the Corteen and Wood phenomenon is essentially artifactual and is to be explained not in terms of the influence of stimuli that are out of awareness but rather in terms of momentary shifts in attention that the subject does not subsequently recall. However, Dawson and Schell also found that significant results could be demonstrated on trials in which there was no evidence of shifts in attention provided the stimuli that were not being attended to were presented to the left ear rather than to the right ear. Table 5.3 presents these results and indicates that for both measures of electrodermal response, probability and magnitude, there is evidence of a conditioned electrodermal response to the critical stimuli if the previously conditioned stimulus is presented to the left ear.

This finding is buttressed by other results in the literature. For example, investigators who had found positive results using this paradigm had used left ear presentation for the unattended words (Corteen & Wood, 1972; Corteen & Dunn, 1974), and those investigators who had reported negative results had used counterbalanced presentations (Wardlaw & Kroll, 1976). Why

TABLE 5.3
Electrodermal Probability and Magnitude on the Nonshift Test Trials for the Left Ear and Right Ear Subgroups

Group	EDR probability			EDR magnitude		
	S+	S−	p	S+	S−	p
Right ear (N = 18)	.14	.12	NS	.08	.09	NS
Left ear (N = 17)	.27	.14	p < .05	.16	.09	p < .01

Source: Dawson and Schell, 1982.

should the ear of presentation be related to the occurrence of conditioning to a stimulus that is out of awareness? In order to explain this phenomenon, it is necessary to indicate something of the literature surrounding laterality effects. Such effects are attributable to the fact that the human brain has two separate hemispheres, and there is considerable evidence that the hemispheres are differentially specialized. The left hemisphere, particularly among right-handed individuals, is specialized for language comprehension and production. The right hemisphere is specialized for spatial perception. In a dichotic listening experiment, it is known that the principal pathways from the ears to the brain are contralateral. Thus stimuli entering the left ear are principally sent to the right hemisphere, and stimuli presented to the right ear are initially sent to the left hemisphere. If a subject is shadowing a message presented to the right ear, the material to be attended to and verbally described enters directly into the left hemisphere. The subject is thus able to describe the shadowed material, and the right hemisphere is "free" to process material being presented to the unattended channel without the necessity of involving the left hemisphere. Thus the right hemisphere could be responsible for the occurrence of an electrodermal response that is not mediated by a verbal response mechanism. When the shadowed stimulus is presented to the left ear, it would initially be presented to the right hemisphere and would presumably have to be transferred across the corpus callosum for the performance of the appropriate verbal response since the right hemisphere is not capable of controlling the production of speech. The left hemisphere would be preoccupied as it were with processing the shadowed stimulus and would not be free to mediate the occurrence of an electrodermal response to a stimulus that were not in awareness. Figure 5.1 presents a model of the neurophysiological explanation of the results of the Dawson and Schell experiment.

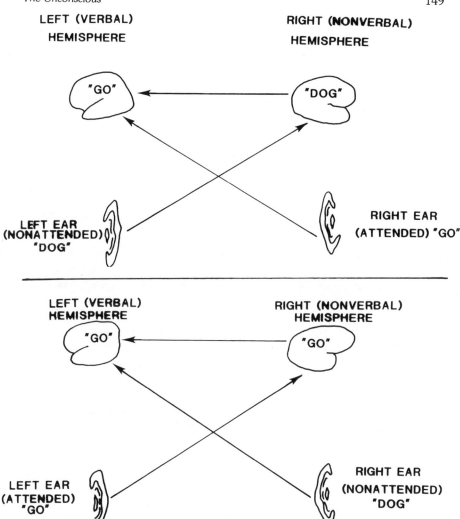

Figure 5.1.   *Model of hemispheric asymmetry for dichotic listening experiment. (From Dawson and Schell [in press].)*

Dawson and Schell's results must be accepted cautiously. They are based on a post hoc analysis. What is interesting about these results is that they provide a tentative model or mechanism for circumventing a difficulty surrounding the earlier work on unconscious perception. Namely, how is it possible to respond to a stimulus of which one is not aware. The reasonably well-established evidence for hemispheric specialization provides a plausible anatomical and physiological mechanism for dissociation between the processing of stimulus information and the inability to provide an appropriate verbal label indexing awareness of the stimulus. Dawson and Schell are not the only researchers who have attempted to relate unconscious processing of information to hemispheric specialization.

Seamon, Brody, and Kauff (in press, 1983) attempted to use the Dawson and Schell theoretical model as a basis for understanding the phenomenon reported by Kunst-Wilson and Zajonc. They reasoned that the development of affect in the absence of a verbally indicated recognition response might in part be due to the partial dissociation of hemispheric functioning in which the right hemisphere is likely to register the emotional significance of a stimulus in the absence of a clear-cut verbal response labeling the stimulus that is derived from the activity of the left hemisphere. Following Dawson and Schell they reasoned that the positive emotional response to a stimulus in the absence of the ability to recognize the stimulus as an old stimulus, would be enhanced by presenting the stimuli to the right hemisphere while the left hemisphere is occupied with the task of verbal production. In their study subjects were presented with geometric stimuli several times to either the right or left visual field. Stimuli presented rapidly to the right visual field are projected initially to the left hemisphere, and stimuli presented initially to the left visual field are projected initially to the right hemisphere. In one condition subjects were required to listen to a tape of a series of words and repeat the words they heard while viewing the tachistoscopically presented stimuli. If this experiment is conceived of as an analogue of the Dawson and Schell study using visual stimuli rather than auditory stimuli, we should expect that the clearest development of preference for previously encountered stimuli would be present for stimuli presented to the left visual field (projected initially to the right hemisphere) under conditions in which the subject is shadowing. Table 5.4 presents the results of the Seamon, Brody, and Kauff experiment. An examination of the results indicates that the findings of this experiment were not in accord with theoretical expectations. Note that subjects developed a preference for previously encountered stimuli. Thus these results again replicate the Kunst-Wilson and Zajonc findings. Where these results most dramatically depart from theoretical expectations is in the direction of the hemispheric effect. Stronger preferences for previously presented stimuli occurred for those stimuli that were presented to the right visual field and were thus projected initially to the left hemisphere. Thus these results are exactly opposite of those reported by Dawson and Schell. There is, however, a possible basis for reconciliation of these disparate results. There is some evidence that the hemispheres are differentially specialized for positive and negative effect. Although this is a relatively speculative notion, there is data available that suggests that the left hemisphere is associated with positive affective states

TABLE 5.4
Percentage of Recognition and Affect Judgments for Previously Presented Stimuli

	Affect		Recognition	
	Left hemisphere	Right hemisphere	Left hemisphere	Right hemisphere
Nonshadowed	65	52	47	57
Shadowed	66	59	47	47

Note: Chance = 50%.

	Within subject comparison		
	Affect > recognition	Recognition > affect	No diff.
Nonshadowed			
Left hemisphere	55	15	30
Right hemisphere	30	40	30
Shadowed			
Left hemisphere	60	25	15
Right hemisphere	55	25	20

Source: Seamon, Brody, and Kauff, 1983.

and the right hemisphere is associated with negative affective states. Clinical studies of brain-damaged individuals provide some evidence for the hypothesis of differential lateralization of positive and negative affective states. Gainotti (1979) suggested that patients with left hemisphere lesions are likely to exhibit depressive responses and patients with right hemisphere lesions are likely to exhibit euphoric responses. G. E. Schwartz, Ahern, and Brown (1979) reported greater activity in the left side of the face in the region of the corrugator facial muscle in response to questions designed to elicit negative affect and greater activity on the right side of the face in the region of the corrugator muscle in response to questions designed to elicit positive affective states. Since the facial musculature is thought to be controlled by the contralateral hemisphere, these results are compatible with the view that positive affective states are related to left hemisphere activity and negative emotional states are related to the activity of the right hemisphere.

Direct evidence for the lateralization of positive and negative affect is contained in a study reported by Reuter-Lorenz and Davidson (1981). In their study subjects were presented simultaneously with two pictures of the same individual. The pictures were projected to the left and right visual field thus lateralizing their presentation. One picture presented the individual in an emotionally neutral state and the second picture represented the individual in either a happy or a sad pose. The subject was required to indicate which of the two pictures presented the individual in an emotional state, and the reaction times for this response were noted. Figure 5.2 presents the results of the study, and the pattern of results supports the hypothesis of lateralization of affect. Note that subjects responded more rapidly when a happy face was presented to the right visual field and thus projected to the left hemisphere and when the sad face was presented to the left visual field and thus initially projected to the right hemisphere. These results suggest that the right hemisphere is specialized for the perception of negative affect and the left hemisphere is specialized for the perception of positive effect.

If the hypothesis of specialization of affective states in different hemispheres is accepted, it is possible to reconcile the findings of both the Dawson and Schell and the Seamon, Brody, and Kauff studies. Dawson and Schell were dealing with negative emotional states (the stimuli they dealt with developed a negative state by virtue of an aversive conditioning procedure). Thus

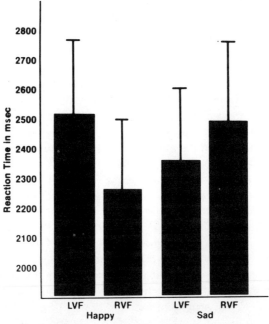

Figure 5.2. *Mean reaction time for happy and sad stimulus presentations, separately for each visual field (bars indicate standard errors). (From P. Reuter-Lorenz and R. J. Davidson. Differential contributions of the two cerebral hemispheres to the perception of happy and sad faces.* Neuropsychologia, *1981, 19, 609–613.)*

they obtained stronger results when stimuli were initially presented to the right hemisphere. Note that on this interpretation their results are not attributable to the distracting effects of the verbal production activity required of the left hemisphere. Seamon, Brody, and Kauff obtained stronger results when stimuli were initially projected to the left hemisphere because they were dealing with positive emotional states.

An additional method for studying the influence of stimuli on behavior that individuals are not aware of involves the use of masking procedures (see Turvey, 1973). If a stimulus is followed shortly after its onset by the presentation of a second stimulus the second stimulus may serve to obliterate the awareness of the initial stimulus. Two types of masking stimuli have been used in the studies to be described here. The first type is called a noise, and it consists of very noisy, complex, and detailed forms that fill the visual field. A second type, pattern mask, consists of randomly arranged elements of the original stimulus that creates a visual pattern. Either type of mask is capable of removing awareness of the initial stimulus. In the studies of Marcel (1980) and Fowler, Wolford, Slade, and Tassinary (1981), the stimulus onset asynchrony was individually adjusted such that the subject could not discriminate between the presence of a masked stimulus or its absence. Thus he or she was not only not capable of informing the experimenter about the nature of the stimulus he or she had seen, but also the subject was not even capable of informing the experimenter with better than chance accuracy whether or not he or she had even seen a stimulus. These researchers attempted to demonstrate that appropriately masked stimuli may, despite subjects' lack of awareness of their presence, nevertheless influence subsequent responses. Both Marcel and Fowler *et al.* used a lexical decision task in which the subject was required to indicate whether or not a particular string of letters constituted a word in English. The reaction time for this lexical decision was noted. In their experiments an initial stimulus was presented prior to the stimulus requiring the lexical decision. The initial stimulus may have influenced in complex ways the time taken to reach the lexical decision. If the original stimulus was semantically related to the second stimulus, the time taken to reach a decision about the second stimulus would be decreased. Thus, for example, the word *ocean* would serve to decrease the time taken to reach a decision about the word *water* in comparison to a condition in which the word *water* was preceded by the word *start*. However, if the initial or prime stimulus were either graphically or phonemically similar to the second stimulus, the reaction time for the lexical decision would be increased. Fowler *et al.* compared lexical decision times for prime stimuli that were either pattern masked or were not masked. Under conditions in which the prime stimulus was masked, the subject was not aware of the presence or absence of the stimulus. Table 5.5 presents the results of their study and shows quite clearly that the priming

TABLE 5.5
Priming Effects for No-Mask and Mask Conditions in Experiment 5

	Priming effect	
Condition	Graphemic/phonemic	Semantic
No mask	32	−38
Mask	30	−29

Source: C. A. Fowler, A. Wolford, R. Slade, and L. Tassinary. Lexical access with and without awareness. *Journal of Experimental Psychology: General,* 1981, *110,* 341–362. Copyright 1981 by the American Psychological Association. Reprinted by permission of the publisher and authors.

Note: Each cell represents the mean reaction time (in milliseconds) for a test condition minus the mean reaction time for a corresponding control condition.

effects of the initial stimulus is unrelated to the presence of the mask. Thus the effects of the prime stimulus are the same whether or not the subject is aware of it. The results also indicate that the semantic content of the prime stimulus was cognitively processed and influenced the subject since the lexical decision occurred 38 msec more rapidly under conditions in which the prime was semantically related as opposed to conditions under which the prime stimulus was not semantically related. In addition, the error rate for semantically related words was lower than the error rate for unrelated word pairs.

Marcel (1980) reported the results of an experiment that suggested a somewhat different effect of masked stimuli. In the Fowler *et al.* study, which was essentially a replication of a study by Marcel (in press), the influence of the masked stimulus was essentially identical to the influence of the same stimulus when it was not masked and when the subject was aware of the stimulus. In a study employing a different design Marcel (1980) was able to show that the influence of a masked stimulus was different from its influence when it was not masked and was in awareness. Marcel contrasted pattern masking, noise masking, and no-mask conditions in a study in which the subject was provided with three stimuli. The task was a lexical decision task in which the subject was required to indicate whether a particular string of letters constituted an English word or not. The principal dependent variable was the time taken to reach this decision. The task involved the presentation of an initial word followed by a second word that was either masked or not followed by the third letter string that was the stimulus to which the subject was required to respond. The second word was semantically ambiguous. For example, the word *palm* could be either a part of the hand or a type of tree. In one set of conditions, the third word was related to one of the two meanings of the second word. Thus, for example, the word *palm* might be followed by the word *wrist*. The initial word in the series was either unrelated to the first word or was, in certain conditions, related to one of the meanings of the second word. I will describe the results obtained under each masking condition.

When the second word was noise masked, it was as if the second word had never been presented. The time taken to reach a lexical decision about the third word was dependent upon the relationship between the first and the third words. If the first word was semantically related to the third word, the decision about the third word was more rapid than if the first word was unrelated to the third word. Under noise masking conditions the character of the second word was irrelevant. Marcel argued that noise masking removed all cognitive representations of the stimulus. It was as if the second word had never been presented.

Under conditions in which the second word was not masked and was clearly in awareness, the influence of the second word on the third word depended upon the relationship between the first and second words. If the first word primed one of the two meanings of the second word *not* related to the third word, it retarded the time required to reach a decision about the third word. Thus, the triad "tree, palm, and wrist" led to slower reaction times than the triads "hand, palm, and wrist" and "clock, palm, and wrist" if the second stimulus were not masked. This finding may be explained by assuming that the first word primes or selects one of the two meanings of the second word and if this meaning is not semantically related to the third word or is in semantic disagreement with the third word the second word retards the processing of the third word.

If the second word were pattern masked rather than noise masked, the effects were different. Under pattern masking conditions the facilitative effects of the word *palm* occurred irrespective of the nature of the word that preceded it. Thus the triad "tree, palm, and wrist" was as facilitative as the triad "hand, palm, and wrist" as well as "clock, palm, and wrist." These results may be explained by assuming that, under conditions of pattern masking in which the subject was not aware of the second word, it influenced the third word irrespective of the influence of the first word on the second word. Since its influence was not dependent on the nature of the first word, as it was when it was not masked, it was apparently the multiple meanings of the word that continued to coexist and to be cognitively present.

If we consider the results of the experiments using masking procedures that have just been described collectively, they appear to support the suggestion that stimuli that are out of awareness are capable of influencing the processing of other stimuli and are in a sense still cognitively present and significant.

Moreover, the results of the distinctive effects of pattern masking in the Marcel experiment with triads suggests that consciousness serves to restrict and specify one of several possible potential meanings of a stimulus.

I have examined studies that demonstrate that stimuli an individual is not aware of having seen can nevertheless influence subsequent cognitive processes and affective reactions. The masking studies demonstrated that the semantic content of stimuli whose presence cannot be ascertained is cognitively available at a preconscious level. These studies do not establish that the semantic content of allegedly preconscious stimuli can have consequences for goal-directed actions. Perhaps the most dramatic demonstration of this type of unconscious influence is contained in an extensive set of studies published by Silverman and his associates that were designed to test hypotheses derived from psychoanalytic theory (see Silverman, 1976). It is beyond the scope of this book to review what is a rather extensive body of research. However, I will describe several of these studies in order to indicate the scope of this research effort. Silverman, relying on psychoanalytic theory, argued that stimuli presented under viewing conditions that are sufficiently degraded as to prevent accurate or above chance discrimination of their presence or absence, or of distinctions among the stimuli, will nevertheless be processed at an unconscious level. Such stimuli are capable of influencing unconscious processes leading either to the creation of unconscious conflicts or to the amelioration of unconscious conflicts. On this view the effects of the subliminal stimulus are precisely contingent upon the fact that the stimulus is subliminal. If the stimulus was supraliminal, it would not have a direct effect on unconscious processes and its capacity to modify unconscious processes would be decreased. Moreover, the precise influence of the subliminal stimulus is contingent upon the particular content of the stimulus. Psychoanalytic theory is relied upon in these investigations to provide hypotheses about the specific effects of the unconscious subliminal stimuli that are investigated. Furthermore, theoretical predictions are derived from psychoanalytic theory about the specific behavioral consequences that are to be expected from an attempt to ameliorate or intensify unconscious conflicts. Thus, this research program can be understood as a simultaneous attempt to test hypotheses derived from psychoanalytic theory and to provide evidence for the view that behavior is controlled by unconscious processes.

Silverman, Ross, Adler, and Lustig (1978) reported the results of a series of experiments using college students in which the dependent variable measured was the performance in a dart-throwing task. In this series of studies, subjects were presented with a series of messages designed to be subliminal. The most critical comparisons involved the effects of differences in the effects of the messages "Beating Dad is OK" and "Beating Dad is wrong." In order to demonstrate that the stimuli they used were subliminal, subjects were presented with these stimuli postexperimentally under the conditions of viewing used in the experiment proper and were required to judge whether a second stimulus set of the same type was the same or different from the first stimulus set present. Each subject was given 20 discrimination trials. Not one of 20 subjects was able to make this judgment at better than chance levels, and for the set of judgments considered in total, subjects were as likely to be correct as incorrect in their judgments of similarity. Thus, by the usual criterion of discriminability, the stimuli appear to be subliminal.

Silverman, Ross, Adler, and Lustig assumed that many college students would have unconscious conflicts about competition with their fathers. Accordingly, they reasoned that the subliminal message "Beating Dad is OK" would serve to ameliorate an unconscious conflict and as a result would tend to improve the quality of subjects' performances. The message "Beating Dad is wrong," by contrast, was assumed to intensify this unconscious conflict and on this hypothesis should impede the quality of performance. In order to create and intensify the conditions under which these allegedly subliminal messages would be maximally effective, Silverman *et al.* attempted to induce or prime the underlying conflict that they were attempting to subliminally influence by presenting their subjects with Rorschach cards and TAT cards that were assumed to activate potential oedipal conflicts. In addition, subjects were primed by being asked to listen to a story that contained oedipal elements.

The principal findings in this series of studies concerned the differences between dart-playing accuracy following the two different subliminal messages. Silverman *et al.* reported the results of four experiments. In three of the four studies, they found that subjects who were given the subliminal message "Beating Dad is OK" improved their performance in dart playing relative to an initial baseline measure of performance, and subjects given the subliminal message "Beating Dad is wrong" exhibited a decrease in the quality of their performance relative to a baseline measure. In one of the studies reported (Study 3), these results were not obtained. However, in this study they used a high level of illumination in their tachistoscope, and they were able to show in the last study reported that the subliminal influences, for reasons that are somewhat obscure, occurred only under conditions of low illumination. The experiments considered collectively provide evidence for the influence of subliminal contents on action tendencies.

Silverman also used the technique of subliminal stimulation as an adjunct to behavioral treatment. A study reported by Silverman, Martin, Ungaro, and Mendelsohn (1978) is indicative of this use of subliminal stimulation. They reported two studies using obese women as subjects in which the therapeutic intervention used was designed to promote weight reduction. All of the subjects in these studies were given a behavioral modification treatment program designed to promote weight loss. In addition, they were randomly assigned to two groups. Subjects in one group received the subliminal stimulus "Mommy and I are one"; subjects in the second group received a control subliminal stimulus "People walking," or, in the second study, the stimulus "People are walking." Table 5.6 presents the results of both studies and indicates that subjects given the message designed to ameliorate unconscious conflicts exhibited greater weight loss than those given the control stimulus. The differences in weight loss were not statistically significant at the termination of therapy but became significant on follow-up measurements. The differences between the two groups were due to the continued weight loss for the women assigned to the relevant subliminal stimulation group.

Silverman argued that the impact of a subliminal stimulus is dependent upon the relationship between the contents of the stimulus and the particular unconscious conflicts present in an individual. Silverman, Bronstein, and Mendelsohn (1976) reported a series of studies with different groups of individuals designed to test the notion that the impact of a subliminal stimulus is contingent upon its relationship to the presumed unconscious conflicts present in an individual. They studied four groups of individuals—schizophrenics, depressives, stutterers, and homosexuals. On the basis of psychoanalytic theory they assumed that each of these groups of individuals would be responsive to particular subliminal material designed to elicit unconscious con-

TABLE 5.6
Mean Weight Loss (in Pounds)

Time	Experiment 1	
	Subliminal group	Control group
Pretreatment	181.8	183.8
Posttreatment	173.8	178.5
Follow-up (12th week)	170.9	179.4
Experiment 2		
Pretreatment	168.6	171.8
Posttreatment (12th week)	156.8	164.7
Follow-up 1 (16th week)	154.6	165.1
Follow-up 2 (24th week)	153.5	165.9

Source: L. H. Silverman, A. Martin, R. Ungaro, and E. Mendelsohn. Effect of subliminal stimulation of symbiotic fantasies on behavior modification treatment of obesity. *Journal of Consulting and Clinical Psychology,* 1978, *46,* 432–441. Copyright 1978 by the American Psychological Association. Reprinted by permission of the publisher and authors.

flicts. They assumed that schizophrenics and depressives would be responsive to material designed to elicit conflicts concerning aggression, that homosexuals would be particularly responsive to material designed to elicit oedipal conflicts dealing with incest, and that stutterers were assumed to be particularly responsive to anal messages. The stimuli they presented to their subjects were as follows: A picture of an angry-looking man about to stab a woman accompanied by the message "Destroy Mother" as an aggressive stimulus; a picture of a nude woman and man in a sexually suggestive pose accompanied by the verbal message "Fuck Mommy" used as an incest stimulus; and a picture of a person crouched and defecating accompanied by the message "Go shit" used as a stimulus designed to elicit anal conflicts. Silverman, Bronstein, and Mendelsohn noted any behavioral indices of pathology following the presentation of various subliminal stimuli and also obtained specific indices relevant to the particular type of subject they studied. For schizophrenics they noted the presence of disordered or pathological thought in a story recall task and in response to an inkblot test. They obtained a measure of homosexual preference from their homosexual subjects by asking them to rate the sexual attractiveness of pictures of males and females. They noted the presence of stuttering in their sample of stutterers. Finally, they obtained a measure of depression based on self-reports from their depressive subjects. In each of the studies using a different clinical sample of subjects, they compared responses to a subliminal stimulus assumed to be particularly relevant to the unconscious conflicts of that sample with a subliminal stimulus designed to be irrelevant for that sample of subjects. Table 5.7 presents a summary of the findings of these four studies. Considered collectively, the data present clear-cut support for Silverman's theoretical assumptions. Table 5.7 indicates that, for the majority of measures used, the relevant subliminal stimulus elicited an intensification of the behavior characteristic of each clinical group, and the presentation of an irrelevant stimulus had no effect on behavioral characteristics of these clinical groups.

Silverman argued that the results of his studies are contingent upon the fact that the stimuli are subliminal. He argued that supraliminal stimuli will not have the same impact on the amelioration or intensification of unconscious conflicts. One of the studies he cited in support of this assertion is a study by Silverman and Spiro (1968). In this study schizophrenic subjects were presented with a subliminal picture or a supraliminal picture that was designed to elicit aggressive impulses assumed to intensify psychopathology in schizophrenics. The picture presented was of a charging lion with bared teeth. This stimulus was contrasted with a picture of a bird used as a neutral or control stimulus. After the presentation of these stimuli, subjects were presented with a variety of tests designed to demonstrate pathological thought processes. These included a measure of the ability to recall the contents of stories, a

TABLE 5.7
Summary of Results of Subliminal Activation Studies

Subject group	Chief symptom	Relevant stimulus	p values for differences between relevant stimulus condition and control condition		Irrelevant stimulus	p values for differences between irrelevant stimulus condition and control condition	
			Chief symptom	Pathological nonverbal behavior		Chief symptom	Pathological nonverbal behavior
Schizophrenics	Thought disorder	Aggression	.004	.002	Incest	n.s.	n.s.
Homosexuals	Homosexual orientation	Incest	.04	.02	Aggression	n.s.	n.s.
Stutterers	Stuttering	Anality	.04	n.s.	Incest	n.s.	.08
Depressives	Depressive feelings	Aggression	.04 (original analysis) n.s. .06 (post-hoc analysis)	.04	Anality	n.s. (original analysis) n.s. (post-hoc analysis)	n.s.

Source: Silverman, Bronstein, and Mendelsohn, 1976.

word association test, a questionnaire measure of pathological body experiences, such as "I feel as if I am melting or merging with the things around me," and a measure of pathological overt behavior including such indices as the presence of inappropriate laughter. Table 5.8 presents the results of the comparison between the supraliminal and the subliminal presentations of the aggressive stimulus presumed to intensify psychopathology in these subjects. The data indicate that the subliminal stimuli intensified psychopathology more than the supraliminal stimuli for three of the four psychopathological indices. These results do indicate that the effects of a visual stimulus designed to intensify unconscious conflicts were contingent upon the fact that the stimulus was subliminal, as indexed by the inability of subjects to discriminate between two of the stimuli presented with better than chance accuracy. However, these results are anamolous in one respect. In the Silverman and Spiro study, there was a third condition of stimulus presentation. In this condition subjects were presented with these stimuli supraliminally and then asked to verbally describe the contents of the picture. In this condition the intensification of psychopathology relative to a baseline condition was comparable to that attained under conditions of subliminal presentation. Table 5.9 presents the results for this condition. Silverman and Spiro did not report the results of statistical analyses of the differences between the subliminal stimulus presentations and the presentations of the same stimuli supraliminally with vocal descriptions of the contents of the stimuli. However, they did assert that there were no significant differences between the supraliminal stimulus presentation with vocalization and the subliminal stimulus presentation. An examination of the data presented in Table 5.9 supports this assertion since the differences between these two conditions are clearly trivial.

These data suggest a somewhat different interpretation of the findings with respect to the subliminality of the stimuli designed to intensify unconscious conflicts. They suggest that subliminal stimuli have involuntary cognitive consequences that permit them to exert cognitive influences with respect to multidimensional representations. In this respect these data are reminiscent of Marcel's demonstration of the restricting effects of consciousness in his study of priming in triadic stimulus sets. The addition of the vocalization of the stimuli may be interpreted as forcing subjects to more completely notice the dimensions of the stimuli that they would perhaps normally be inclined to process in a restrictive manner. Thus these results suggest that, paradoxically, stimuli that are presented subliminally may have more impact than stimuli presented supraliminally but that the impact of the supraliminal stimulus may be intensified by forcing subjects to notice and to respond extensively to it. I will subsequently discuss studies purporting to demonstrate the existence of a phenomenal enhancement effect that may suggest a comparable effect.

Silverman's research program suggests that there may be unconscious

TABLE 5.8
Mean Change Scores for the Subliminal and Supraliminal Aggressive Sessions

	·Subliminal aggressive session change score	Supraliminal aggressive session change score	Difference between change scores	Standard deviation of differences	t	p^*
Word association pathology (total sample; N = 32)	+2.09	−.28	+2.37	4.95	+2.70	.01
Story recall pathology (total sample; N = 32)	+1.47	−1.00	+2.47	6.94	+2.01	.03
Pathological body-affective experience (total sample; N = 32)	+2.15	+2.38	−.23	5.55	<1	NS
Pathological overt behavior (total sample; N = 32)	+2.90	+1.41	+1.49	4.47	+1.88	.04
Faces test projection of aggression (chronic paranoid; N = 7)	+.57	+1.28	−.71	4.16	<1	NS
Story recall accuracy† (chronic non-paranoid; N = 14)	−1.14	−.21	−.93	5.90	<1	NS

Source: L. H. Silverman and R. H. Spira. The effects of subliminal, supraliminal and vocalized aggression on the ego functioning of schizophrenics. Journal of Nervous and Mental Disease, 1968, 146, 50–61.

*p values are for a one-tailed test. NS = not significant.

†For this variable only, the *lower* the score, the *greater* the ego impairment.

TABLE 5.9
Mean Change Score for the Vocalization of Aggression and Supraliminal Aggressive Sessions

	Supraliminal aggressive change score	Vocalization of aggression change score	Differences between change scores	Standard deviation of differences	t	p*
Word association paology (total sample; N = 32)	-.28	+2.12	-2.40	4.60	-2.95	.01
Story recall pathology (total sample N = 32)	-1.00	+.47	-1.47	7.68	-1.08	NS
Pathological body-affective experi- ence (total sample; N = 32)	+2.38	+1.88	+.50	3.20	<1	NS
Pathological overt behavior (total sample; N = 32)	+1.41	+2.94	-1.53	5.92	-1.46	NS
Faces test projection of aggression (chronic paranoid; N = 7)	+1.28	+1.57	-.29	5.93	<1	NS
Story recall accuracy† (chronic non- paranoid; N = 14)	-.21	-5.43	+5.22	9.83	+1.99	.08

Source: L. H. Silverman and R. H. Spiro. The effects of subliminal, supraliminal and vocalized aggression on the ego functioning of schizophrenics. *Journal of Nervous and Mental Disease,* 1968, *146,* 50–61.

*p values are for a two-tailed test. NS = not significant.
†For this variable only, the *lower* the score, the greater the ego impairment.

influences on goal-directed actions. A somewhat different demonstration of the possibility of unconscious (or perhaps, more aptly, noncognitive) influences on goal-directed action is contained in a study reported by Langer, Blank, and Chanowitz (1978).

They studied the willingness of persons using a photocopier to permit someone else to interrupt them and use the machine. Subjects in the experiment were not aware that they were serving as subjects, and the request for interruption and use of the machine occurred in an actual setting in which subjects were copying materials. They studied requests that were made in three different ways. In one condition a request was made without the addition of any particular reason for the request. The request was: "Excuse me, I have 5(20) pages. May I use the Xerox machine?" Note that in this condition no reason is provided for the request to interrupt the activities of the person using the copier. Also note that the person using the copy machine is requested to relinquish it for a relatively brief period (5 pages) or a relatively extended period (20 pages). In another condition, called the real information condition, the request to use the copier is accompanied by a reason for the requested interruption—"I'm in a rush." In the third condition, called the placebic information condition, the request to use the machine is accompanied by a reason that on examination is not a reason at all. "May I use the Xerox machine because I have to make copies?" It is apparent that this request provides the subject with the form of a reason for the requested interruption without the substance of the reason. An examination of the results of the experiment presented in Table 5.10 indicates that, when they did not involve an extended interruption, requests that provided a reason for the interruption were more likely to be honored than requests without the inclusion of a reason for the interruption. However, it does not appear to

TABLE 5.10

The Proportion of Subjects Who Agreed to Let the Experimenter Use the Copier

Favor	Reason		
	No info	Placebic info	Real info
Small	.60	.93	.94
Big	.24	.24	.42

Source: E. J. Langer, A. Blank, and B. Chanowitz. The mindlessness of ostensibly thoughtful action: The role of placebic information in interpersonal interaction. *Journal of Personality and Social Psychology,* 1978, *36,* 635–642. Copyright 1978 by the American Psychological Association. Reprinted by permission of the publisher and authors.

matter whether the reason provided was actually a reason or was merely in the form of a reason. These results suggest that the behavior of the subjects in this situation is indicative of a kind of mindless failure to process information. It is probably the case that subjects attended to and were aware of the original part of the request and were aware that, if the request were honored, they would have to relinquish their use of the machine for either a short or a relatively long period. If the requested interruption were likely to involve a minimal interruption, attention was not clearly focused upon the subsequent part of the request, and any request that conformed to the usual practice of providing a reason was likely to be acceded to. This type of experiment provides us with the suggestion that consciousness is a rather fitful or lazy event. Many action sequences may proceed with relatively little involvement of conscious processes and may in fact unfold as if conforming to a pre-defined script. Note that this study does not imply that the occurrence of such an automatic unfolding process is the norm. The results also indicate that consciousness may be invoked and that it may exert an influence on our behavior. Although the results obtained in this experiment under conditions where the agent of the experimenter requests a small favor are dramatic and tend to capture our attention, the results for the conditions in which the favor requested is relatively large also serve to illuminate the role of conscious processes. When the requested favor is large, it is apparently the case that the subject is likely to focus more closely on the actual request made and is less likely to behave in a mindless fashion. Note that, under these conditions, a request without a real reason is no more effective than a request without any reason provided at all. Thus in a sense one may view the Langer, Blank, and Chanowitz experiment as simultaneously providing information about the role of conscious and nonconscious processes in the control of behavior. Although some social behavior may proceed mindlessly, when situations pose larger motivational demands, consciousness is likely to be mobilized, and one is likely to attend to the demands made in the external world, and this attentional focus may change the nature of one's response to the world.

The Rise and Fall of Cognitive Explanations of Motivated Behavior

This section will discuss a number of theoretical developments that date from the 1960s during which cognitive processes were assigned a central role in the control and modification of goal-directed action sequences. For each of the theoretical developments discussed I will indicate that more recent research has tended to assign a somewhat more circumscribed role to the cognitive events that were assumed to explain behavior. In this respect the review of this body of research will parallel the review of studies of the unconscious.

In 1962 Schachter and Singer presented a two-factor theory of emotion (see also, Schachter, 1964). They viewed emotions as resulting from the interplay of a state of physiological arousal and cognitions about the reasons for that arousal that served to define and interpret the arousal. Thus physiological arousals on this theory were viewed as relatively undifferentiated states that did not serve to determine and define the nature of an individual's emotional experience. In order to have an emotion, individuals would be required to assign a cognitive label to the experience. Schachter and Singer cited research reported by Maranon in which injections of epinephrin, a sympathomimetic drug that leads to physiological arousal of the sympathetic nervous system—not to an experience of an emotion, but rather to a kind of psuedoemotional experience described as an "as if" experience. In order to develop a true or complete emotional experience, Maranon was forced to provide subjects with a cognition. For example, if he asked them to think about an emotional topic, subjects might be calm prior to the injection, but the combination of a cognition and the physiological arousal caused by an injection of adrenalin served to create an emotional state. Schachter and Singer reasoned that individuals who were physiologically aroused but did not have an appropriate explanation for their state of arousal would develop any emotional experience for which an appropriate cognition was provided. In their study subjects were assigned to one of four treatment groups. All were given an injection. One group received a placebo injection, and the subjects in the other three groups received an injection of epinephrin. All subjects were told that the injection experiment involved the effects of drugs on visions. Subjects who received epinephrin were provided with different kinds of information about the effects of the drug. One group was given rather accurate information about the physiological effects of the drug; a second group was not given any information about the effects of the drug, and a third group was given information about the drug's effects that was not correct. According to the theory motivating this research, subjects given a drug that leads to physiological arousal for which they do not have an appropriate explanation should be emotionally manipulable, and if they are provided with a possible rationale for their experience, they should embrace the cognition provided and experience an appropriate emotional state.

In order to manipulate possible cognitions about the reasons for the physiological states that the subjects were experiencing, Schachter and Singer attempted to introduce an experience of euphoria and one experience of anger. To induce euphoria they used an agent who was described to the subjects as another subject in the experiment. The agent performed, in a standardized sequence, a series of foolish acts. Subjects assigned to an anger-

TABLE 5.11
Self-report and Behavioral Outcomes for Subjects Assigned to the Euphoria Condition

Condition		Self-report scales	Comparison p	Behavior activity	Comparison
Epi inf	(1)	.98	1 vs. 3 < .01	12.72	1 vs. 3 < .05
Epi ign	(2)	1.78	1 vs. 2 < .02	18.28	1 vs. 2 n.s.
Epi mis	(3)	1.90	4 vs. 3, 2, or 1 n.s.	22.56	4 vs. 3, 2 n.s. or 1
Placebo	(4)	1.60		16.00	

Source: S. Schacter and J. E. Singer. Cognitive, social and physiological determinants of emotional state. *Psychological Review,* 1962, *69,* 379–399. Copyright 1962 by the American Psychological Association. Reprinted by permission of the publisher and authors.

inducing condition were also exposed to an agent. In this condition the agent expressed anger and hostility towards a questionnaire presented to the subjects that asked for information of a personal nature and was phrased in a provocative and insulting manner. Schachter and Singer used both self-report and behavioral data to assess the emotional state of their subjects.

Tables 5.11 and 5.12 present the results of their study, and the data show a pattern of results that only partially support the theory. For both self-report and behavioral measures of euphoria, subjects assigned to the epinephrin-informed conditions were less likely to exhibit euphoria than those in the misinformed condition. These results suggest that subjects who experienced a state of physiological arousal for which they did not have an adequate explanation tended to attribute their arousal to an externally available cue and, once having embraced a particular explanation for their arousal, would in effect behave as if the state that they attributed to themselves were present. Thus on this view the cognition determines the behavior. Note, however, that Table 5.11 also indicates that subjects assigned to the placebo group were not significantly less likely to be euphoric than subjects assigned to the groups not

TABLE 5.12
Self-report and Behavioral Outcomes for Subjects Assigned to the Anger Condition

Condition		Self-report scales	Comparison p	Behavior anger units	Comparison p
Epi inf	(1)	1.91	1 vs. 2 < .08	−.18	1 vs. 2 < .01
Epi ign	(2)	1.39	3 vs. 1 or 2 n.s.	2.28	1 vs. 3 < .05
Placebo	(3)	1.63		.79	3 vs. 1 n.s.

Source: S. Schacter and J. E. Singer. Cognitive, social and physiological determinants of emotional state. *Psychological Review,* 1962, *69,* 379–399. Copyright 1962 by the American Psychological Association. Reprinted by permission of the publisher and authors.

provided with an appropriate explanation for their state of physiological arousal. These results suggest, contrary to theory, that the state of physiological arousal is not a necessary condition for the experience of the emotion.

The data for subjects assigned to the anger-arousal conditions is presented in Table 5.12. The pattern is somewhat different from that obtained for the condition of euphoria. First, there are no significant differences for self-report measures of anger. However, for a behavioral measure of anger, the results are in agreement with theoretical expectations. Subjects assigned to the group given epinephrin who were not informed of the drugs' effects behaved significantly angrier than those assigned to the informed group, and they were also angrier than those assigned to the placebo group. These results indicate that, at least for the behavioral measure, a state of arousal for which no adequate explanation is present leads to the induction of an emotional state when some external basis for the cognitive interpretation of the state is present.

Schachter and Wheeler (1962) reported a follow-up investigation that used a film presenting slapstick humor to induce a state of amusement. In this experiment subjects were assigned either to a placebo condition, a condition in which they were given epinephrin, or a condition in which they were given chloropromazine (a drug that is assumed to act as a sympathetic depressant). Subjects were misinformed with respect to the physiological effects of the drugs. There were no significant differences among the groups with respect to their evaluation of the humor of the film. However, subjects assigned to the epinephrin condition were more likely to laugh in response to the film than those assigned to the placebo or to the chloropromazine conditions. There was no epinephrin-informed group in this study, so the effects of misinformation with respect to the influence of the drug that acted as a source of arousal was not investigated.

If all of the results obtained in these two studies are considered, certain tentative conclusions can be suggested. First, it is apparent that the induction of a physiological state for which an individual does not have an adequate explanation tends to lead the individual to respond to an externally presented attempt to induce an emotional state. Presumably the emotional behavior is attributable to a cognitive interpretation or attribution assigned by the individual as an explanation of the emotional state of arousal. However, when providing a self-report about the emotional state that has been induced the subject is not as consistently likely to report the emotion. It is as if the individual behaves emotionally but does not actually know, at least as determined by verbal reports, that the emotional state that has been induced is present. I will return to this peculiar disjunction between the behavioral indices of emotion and the self-report of emotions.

The Schachter and Singer study is one of the most influential studies in psychology. Despite its theoretical importance no attempts at replication were reported until 1979—perhaps because of the elaborate nature of the experiments involving the use of experimenters' agents and deception, as well as the use of drugs (see Marshall & Zimbardo, 1979; Maslach, 1979; and Schachter & Singer, 1979). Marshall and Zimbardo compared subjects assigned to a placebo condition with those assigned to an epinephrin group that was misinformed about the influence of the physiological effects of the drug. They did not include an anger-induction procedure, but they did include a euphoria-induction procedure. They found no evidence of increased euphoria among subjects in the epinephrin group as compared to those in the placebo conditions. This failure to find significant results extended to both the behavioral and self-report measure of euphoria. Marshall and Zimbardo indicated that if anything their results suggested that subjects provided with epinephrin for which they are not given an adequate explanation were likely to develop a somewhat negative affective state and were likely to be resistant to the development of a state of euphoria. In a criticism of this study, Schachter and Singer indicated that some of the alleged symptoms that subjects were informed would occur as a result of the injection that they received were actual symptoms of the drug. Hence subjects assigned to the epinephrin condition in the Marshall and Zimbardo experiment may in fact have been comparable to subjects in the epinephrin-informed condition in the Schachter and Singer study. It should also be noted that the symptoms that were provided were minor symptoms, and the subjects were not really accurately informed of the effects of the drug in the Marshall and Zimbardo study. Thus the issue is not readily resolvable on the basis of the available data.

In the Schachter and Singer studies, subjects were in a condition in which they were misinformed about the physiological effects of a drug and were induced into labeling the state of arousal they experienced as being attributable to an external cue. This line of research was followed by other research in which subjects were induced to attribute an externally caused arousal to the action of a pill that was actually chemically inert. Nisbett and Schachter (1966) reported such a study. In their study subjects were given painful electric shocks following the receipt of a pill placebo whose psychophysiological effects were described to them as being congruent with the usual effects of shock or as leading to consequences that were not those usually induced by electric shock. They reasoned that subjects in a condition in which they were able to attribute their physiological reactions to shock to the effects of the pill would find the shock less aversive than those who would not be able to attribute the effects of the shock to the pill. They found that subjects in the condition in which they were able to attribute their reactions to the shock to the influences of a pill had a higher tolerance for pain than those who were told that the drug would lead to symptoms that were unlike those induced by shock. In other words, the former subjects were willing to take higher levels of shock before reaching the upper limit of tolerance at which the shocks ended. In addition, these subjects reported that the highest level of shock that they were willing to tolerate was not as painful as the highest level of shock that the subjects in the latter group were willing to tolerate, despite the fact that the former subjects were rating a significantly more intense shock. The Nisbett and Schachter study again suggests that the cognitive process that serves to interpret and to label an internal state defines the character and influence of that state. In this study the label that subjects have been induced to assign to the state may be considered as a misattribution in that it clearly involves a change of meaning of the naturally occurring state and is clearly incorrect with respect to the cause of the state.

Schachter's theory was not the only theory to assign a central role to a process of cognitive reappraisal in the control of motivational states. Zimbardo (1969) and his associates reported a number of studies based on the theory of cognitive dissonance that attempted to demonstrate cognitive influences on motivational states.

Dissonance theory has as its central premise the notion that contradictory beliefs held by an individual create a state of psychological tension and that individuals will initiate efforts to remove that tension (see Brehm & Cohen, 1962; Festinger, 1957). For example, if an individual believes that smoking leads to cancer and if that individual is aware that he or she smokes, then the former belief is psychologcially contradictory to the second cognition—the knowledge that he or she smokes. The psychological tension created by the contradictory beliefs may be eliminated in any of several ways. The individual might change one of the beliefs. Perhaps he or she might come to doubt the probity of the evidence in favor of the view that smoking leads to cancer or might come to believe that he or she is immune from the disease by not smoking enough or by having a constitution that renders the individual insusceptible to the disease. Or, the person might stop smoking. Any of these activities would serve to remove the conflict created by the contradictory beliefs and would as a result remove the state of cognitive dissonance.

Zimbardo (1969) reported the results of a number of studies based on dissonance theory that attempted to demonstrate cognitive influences on motivational states. Most of these studies attempted to create a state of cognitive dissonance by inducing individuals to endure some unpleasant state without providing them sufficient justification for agreeing to endure the state. The behavior of subjects assumed to be in a high dissonance condition was contrasted with the behavior of subjects in a low dissonance condition who were given adequate justification for their decision to endure the unpleasant state. Those in the high dissonance condition could eliminate dissonance by changing the unpleasant state—that is, if a person had cognitive dissonance created by the knowledge that he or she has agreed to endure something unpleasant and if he or she had not been provided with adequate reasons to endure the unpleasant event, the dissonance would be removed if the person redefined the event as pleasant. In applications of this paradigm to motivational states, hungry subjects might be induced to go without eating for an additional period of time. Subjects given insufficient justifications for continuing to go without eating who nevertheless agree to continue in the experiment abstaining from eating can eliminate their dissonance by eliminating their hunger. Zimbardo attempted to demonstrate that the reduction in the motive state induced by the induction of a state of cognitive dissonance involves more than a simple cognitive relabeling of the state. In other words, he attempted to demonstrate that the motive state itself is reduced and thus the change that occurs is reflected in both direct and indirect indices of the several manifestations of the central motive state-including behavioral and physiological indices.

One of the best controlled studies reported in the Zimbardo volume deals with pain. Zimbardo, Cohen, Weisenberg, Dworkin, and Firestone (1969) exposed subjects to painful electric shocks. They were then assigned to groups in which they were either given a choice to continue with a second phase of the experiment in which they would receive additional electric shocks or they were assigned to a no choice condition. Subjects in the no choice condition were either given moderate levels of shock that were marginally painful or the same high levels of shock they had received earlier. Subjects in the choice condition were assigned to a high or a low dissonance group. Those in the high dissonance group were informed that the experiment was exploratory, and they were not given any particularly persuasive reasons for participating in the experiment. Subjects in the low dissonance group were given ample justifications to continue in the experiment. All of the subjects in the choice conditions received high levels of electric shock that were painful. Zimbardo *et al.* assumed that the subjects in the high dissonance condition would attempt to eliminate their state of dissonance by reducing the state of pain normally experienced in response to the shocks—that is, the knowledge that one agreed to endure painful shocks for no particular reason would not create a state of dissonance if the shocks were not particularly painful. Among the measures used by Zimbardo *et al.* to assess the effects of intensity of pain response experienced by the subjects in this study was a verbal report of the pain experienced, a learning task for which previous research had demonstrated that pain would interfere with adequate performance on the task, and a GSR response. Table 5.13 presents the results for the level of pain reported by the subjects assigned to the various experimental groups. Subjects assigned to the no choice control group who were given moderate levels of shock exhibited a clear-cut decrease in their rating of the pain of the shocks they endured relative to subjects who continued to receive

TABLE 5.13
Mean Perceived Pain and Physical Shock Level of Sample Shocks

Group	N	Mean shock (volts)	Precommitment	Postcommitment	Difference
			Perceived pain		
Control:					
High-moderate	15	42–22	46	20	−26
High-high	15	44	50	47	−3
Dissonance:					
Low	20	38	49	47	−2
High	20	49	46	37	−9

high levels of shocks during the second phase of the experiment. Subjects in the high dissonance group had a slightly larger decrease in the magnitude of pain they reported than those in the low dissonance group. However, the difference between the magnitude in reduction in reported pain experienced by subjects assigned to the low and high dissonance groups was not significantly different. Although there was only marginal evidence for a reduction of the state of pain in the verbal reports of subjects assigned to the two different dissonance conditions, there was definite evidence for significantly different response to pain between the two dissonance groups on the nonverbal indices of the pain state. Figure 5.3 presents data for the results of performance on the learning task used in this experiment. The pattern of results suggests that subjects assigned to the high dissonance group were less responsive to the pain stimulus. Subjects in the control condition who performed the task under conditions of low or moderate shock tended to learn the list more rapidly than those assigned to the low dissonance condition. Thus their responses on the learning task resemble the responses of subjects who performed the task under moderate rather than intense levels of shock.

Similar results are obtained for the GSR measure of responsiveness to shock. Figure 5.4 presents the data for this measure. An examination of the data indicates that subjects assigned to the high dissonance group decreased their GSR responsivenesses to the shocks in a manner analagous to those subjects in the control group who received moderate rather than intense levels of shock. Subjects in the low dissonance group exhibited GSR responses comparable to the responses exhibited by subjects assigned to the control group who continued to receive intense shocks.

Recent research has changed our understanding of the influence of cognitive processes on motivational states. Subjects may not be aware of the cognitive processes whose putative influences are manipulated in these ex-periments. Second, it may be possible for induced motivational states to continue to exert an influence on a person even though the person has been induced into misattributing the state to a different source of arousal. Third, I will argue that the process of cognitive control of motivation through misat-tribution may be dependent upon individual differences among subjects.

Both attributional manipulations of motivational states and dissonance manipulations of motivated states share in common a demonstration that the induction of a cognitive state serves to change an individual's motivational state resulting in a change in the behavioral manifestations of that state. It was generally supposed, although the matter was not explicitly discussed, that the cognitive process initiated by the elaborate experimental inductions and de-ceptions used in much of this research were phenomenally present—that is, that in order to explain the behavior of subjects in these experiments the psychologist postulated the existence of an elaborate process of reasoning on the part of the subjects in which they attributed the states they were experi-encing to particular causes and these attributions then influenced their moti-

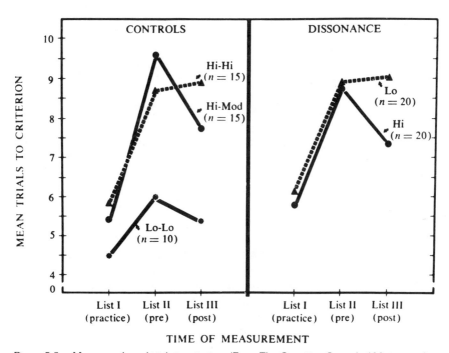

Figure 5.3.   *Mean number of trials to criterion. (From* The Cognitive Control of Motivation *by Philip G. Zimbardo. Copyright © 1969 Scott, Foresman and Company. Reprinted by permission.)*

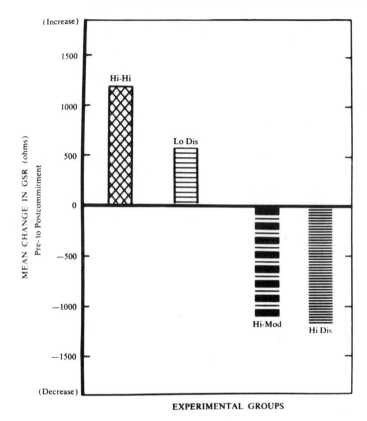

Figure 5.4.   *Mean differences in galvanic skin response (ohms) between the first three shocks in List II (precommitment) and the first three shocks in List III (postcommitment). Negative values indicate reductions in GSR, whereas positive ones indicate increases. (From* The Cognitive Control of Motivation *by Philip G. Zimbardo. Copyright © 1969 Scott, Foresman and Company. Reprinted by permission.)*

vational states. Presumably, subjects were aware of the processes of reasoning in which they had engaged and were in addition aware of the changes in the motivational states induced by these cognitive processes, although it was assumed that subjects were not aware of the deceptions practiced upon them that induced them to undergo the cognitive change processes. In a seminal article, Nisbett and Wilson (1977) analyzed the literature dealing with attributional and dissonance induced changes in motivational states and argued that subjects have, in several senses, rather limited knowledge of the cognitive processes that the psychologist assumes to have occurred and that serve as the putative explanations of the behavior of subjects in these experiments. They indicated that, in the experiments in this tradition in which both verbal reports and behavioral indices of the motivational state are obtained, subjects' behavior may change in the absence of a change in the verbal report about the motivational state. Evidence has been seen for this disjunction between changes in the behavioral and verbal manifestations of a motivational state in the original Schachter and Singer study that was largely responsible for the initiation of the attributional research tradition. Recall that in their study subjects in the anger-induction conditions who were misinformed with respect to the physiological effects of a sympathomimetic drug behaved in a way that was indicative of anger in the absence of evidence of a change in their verbal reports about anger. Similar findings are contained in the dissonance study reported by Zimbardo *et al.* (1969). Recall that in their study subjects in whom a state of cognitive dissonance was assumed to be induced by virtue of being provided with inadequate justification for exposing themselves to electric shocks were assumed to have eliminated that state of dissonance by a change in the state of pain induced by the shock. Behavioral and physiological indices of pain did in fact support the inference that the state of pain of these subjects had in fact been reduced. However, verbal reports about the state of pain did not exhibit a comparable reduction.

Nisbett and Wilson reported that in a number of these studies both the verbal reports and the behavioral indicants of a central motivational state may have been significantly altered by the presumed cognitive reappraisal of that state. However, in these cases the nonverbal indices of the state usually undergo more profound and clear-cut changes than the verbal indices. Furthermore, they indicated that there was a subset of these studies in which the data permitted the calculation of a correlation between the magnitude of changes in the verbal reports and the magnitude of changes in the nonverbal indices of change in motivational states. These correlations were usually close to zero.

Nisbett and Wilson argued that subjects were not only unlikely to be able to provide accurate reports about the presumed motivational changes that were alleged to occur in these experiments but that they were also unaware of the cognitive events and processes of reasoning whose occurrence provided the putative explanation of their behavior. When asked about their behavior in these experiments, the subjects invariably failed to report the occurrence of the cognitive processes that were alleged to have occurred, and, moreover, when the explanation of their behavior was provided to them by the psychologist, they explicitly denied that such processes occurred and serves as an adequate explanation of their behavior in the experiment.

The Nisbett and Wilson analysis of these studies provides us with a new understanding of the role of cognitive processes in these experiments. Although it appears to be reasonably clear that some type of reappraisal must be postulated to explain the behavior of subjects in these studies, it is apparently the case that the cognitive events are ones that subjects are either unaware of or at least unable to recall postexperimentally. Thus the quality of phenomenal representation usually taken to be the hallmark of cognitive events is apparently not present for the particular cognitive processes that are assumed to have occurred in these experiments. One may assume that these experiments provide evidence for a kind of unconscious cognition. Alternatively, one may choose to think of the cognitive processes that are alleged to have occurred in these experiments in a manner analagous to Tolman's use of cognitive language in strictly behavioristic sense in which the ordinary phenomenal connotations of the terms were purged in their technical usage. Thus they may be assumed to be on the one hand either nonphenomenal or neither phenomenal nor nonphenomenal. In this latter case the term a phenomenal might be coined to describe their status.

Berkowitz (1978) reported the results of an experiment designed to demonstrate that the cognitive labels assigned to a state do not invariably change the character of the state and that a mislabeled state can continue to exert an influence on behavior that is consonant with its original character. In his experiment subjects were required to peddle a stationary bicycle at either high or low levels of speed. Half of the subjects assigned to each of these peddling conditions were assigned to a frustration condition. Frustration was induced by informing subjects that they would receive a prize if they were able to match the peddling speed of a fictitious partner whose peddling speed was indicated to them by signal lights. Subjects were frustrated by the introduction of a sudden change in the signaled peddling speed towards the end of the experimental session thus depriving subjects of an opportunity to receive the prize. They were provided with a plausible explanation for the arousal that they might have experienced. They were led to believe that their arousal was a result of exercise. Subjects were shown a computer printout that they were told indicated that they were physiologically aroused as a result of the exercise.

In a second phase of this experiment subjects were permitted to deliver rewards or punishments to their fictitious partner in the first phase of the experiment while the partner worked on a game. Berkowitz obtained self-reports from the subjects about their mood states. He reported that subjects who were frustrated and those who were not frustrated reported comparable moods. There were no differences between these groups with respect to their reported frustration, anger, or irritation. Presumably the information about the exercise-induced arousal led subjects to attribute any frustration-induced arousal to the influence of the exercise. However, frustrated and nonfrustrated subjects differed with respect to their behavior in the second phase of the experiment. Berkowitz reports that those assigned to the frustration condition were more likely to be punitive to their partners and were less likely to reward the partner. In addition those subjects who were most aroused physiologically by virtue of having been assigned to the groups required to peddle rapidly were more likely to deliver punishments to the partner if they had been frustrated.

Berkowitz argued that this experiment suggested that subjects need not have labeled their psychological state of as one of anger in order to have behaved in an angry manner following frustration. In effect Berkowtiz's experiment may be viewed as a kind of mirror image of the typical attributional study in which the behavior of an individual is changed because a new cognitive interpretation has been assigned to a motivational state. In the typical study subjects' behavior is determined by the new cognitive interpretation assigned to the state rather than the original or prior condition of the motivational state. In Berkowitz's experiment a state of frustration-induced anger continued to determine the behavior of an individual even though the individual had been induced into relabeling and reinterpretating the motivational state as one of exercise-induced physiological arousal.

The tendency of subjects to misattribute the source of motivational arousal may be related to individual differences in the characteristics of subjects. Gibbons and Wright (1981) attempted to demonstrate that the tendency of subjects to attribute their arousal to a placebo rather than to a sexually explicit film related to individual differences in the tendency to feel guilty about sexual arousal. They selected subjects with extreme scores on the Mosher Inventory of Sex Guilt (see Mosher, 1968). Subjects whose scores were very high or low on the inventory were assigned to groups that observed a nonarousing movie about biological topics or a sexually explicit movie. All of the subjects were given a pill placebo that they were told would have some of the side effects of sexual arousal such as increases in breathing and heart rates, and sweaty palms. Those who scored high on the inventory of sex guilt reported the drug more arousing under conditions in which they were exposed to the erotic film than under conditions in which they were exposed to the biological film. Subjects who scored low on the inventory of sex guilt reported the drug as being more arousing under conditions in which they were exposed to a movie about biological topics than under conditions in which they were exposed to an erotic movie. These results indicate that the tendency to misattribute a state of arousal to a placebo drug may be determined by the extent to which the subject found the true source of the arousal state acceptable or congenial (that is, the misattribution of arousal states may be influenced by a defensive process).

Duncan and Laird (1980) also reported a study providing evidence for individual differences in the tendency to misattribute the source of arousal. In studies of misattribution processes, subjects were induced to attribute their arousal to a pill rather than to some experimental manipulation, and thus the effect of the manipulation was decreased. It should be noted that in many such situations the results obtained in these studies are opposite of the effects that are typically reported in clinical investigations of the effects of placebos. For example in a study reported by Storms and Nisbett (1970), a drug placebo that was presumed to lead to relaxation actually increased the probability of insomnia, and a placebo that the subject was informed was an arouser actually decreases the insomnia. The usual placebo influence of a drug that the subject is informed is a relaxer would be to decrease insomnia. In point of fact there is empirical evidence in favor of the usual clinical influence of placebos on insomnia (see Bootzin, Herman & Nicassio, 1976). Duncan and Laird (1980) termed the usual result in a misattribution study a reverse placebo effect and reported the results of an experiment that provided evidence with respect to the conditions under which a reverse as opposed to an ordinary placebo effect would be obtained. They suggested that, in the typical misattribution experiment, there is a conflict between the information provided by the experimenter and the information available to the subject by an examination of the subject's own internal states. Consider an experimental situation in which the subject is exposed to a fear-inducing situation such as electric shock. If provided with a placebo pill that he or she is informed should serve as a relaxer and he or she is inclined to accept the information provided by the psychologist, then the pill should have the usual placebo effect and serve to reduce the subject's fear. Similarly, if informed that the pill should serve to intensify arousal, he or she would presumably experience an intensification of affect in the presence of a fear-inducing object. Subjects inclined to attend to their inner physiological states rather than to blithely accept the assertions of the psychologist should have a different pattern of response to the information about the physiological effects of the placebo. If informed that a particular placebo will act as a relaxer and the subject attends to the internal responses of fear, he or she is likely to infer that he or she is in fact experiencing an intense fear since the placebo was ineffective. Similarly, if informed that a placebo acts as a physiological arouser and the subject attends to his or her inner state, then the experience of inner arousal caused by a feared stimulus object is likely to be attributable to the placebo, and the subject should report a reduction in fear. Thus on this analysis the operation of the reverse placebo effect is dependent upon the mediation of attentional processes in which the subject monitors his or her internal responses.

Duncan and Laird assumed that subjects differ in their tendency to attend to their inner physiological states. In order to classify subjects with respect to their tendency to be responsive to their physiological states, they presented subjects with a task previously used by Laird (1974) to demonstrate the effects of feedback from physical states on emotional experiences (see also Duncan & Laird, 1977). In this procedure subjects were asked to place their facial musculature in the shape of a smile and a frown, and their emotional state was assessed. They were not informed that their facial musculature was placed in the shape of a smile or a frown but were induced to do so by colorless mechanical instructions. The act of placing the facial musculature in these positions influenced subjects' reported mood states.

In the Duncan and Laird study, subjects were classified with respect to the extent to which they were influenced by the facial musculature manipulation of mood states. Those who were responsive to this manipulation were called self-produced cue attenders, and subjects who were not responsive to this manipulation were called situational cue attenders. All of the subjects chosen to participate in this study were somewhat afraid of electric shocks. Both of these groups of subjects were assigned to different conditions in which they were told that the placebos were arousers, neutral, or relaxers. They were then asked to rate their degree of fearfulness in response to receiving electric shocks. Table 5.14 presents the fear ratings obtained in this study for both groups of subjects given different information about placebo effects. The data indicate that self-produced cue attenders exhibited decreases in fear when they were informed that the placebo was an arouser and exhibited relatively small decreases in fearfulness when informed that the placebo was a relaxer. Thus they exhibited the reverse placebo effect. Those who were assumed to be situationally responsive exhibited the usual placebo effect.

This review of research related to the Schachter and Singer experiment has suggested a number of qualifications with respect to the phenomena they reported. Zimbardo and Marshall suggested that the phenomena are not replicable. Nisbett and Wilson suggested that the cognitive processes that they

TABLE 5.14

Mean Change in Electric Shock Fearfulness Scores of Self-produced and Situational Cue Attenders for Relaxer, Arouser, and No-Drug Conditions

	Relaxer		No drug		Arouser	
Cuers	*M*	*N*	*M*	*N*	*M*	*N*
Situational	−5.5	7	1.0	7	1.6	9
Self-produced	−1.0	12	−3.0	11	−5.5	13

Source: J. W. Duncan and J. D. Laird. Positive and reverse placebo effects as a function of differences in cues used in self-perception. *Journal of Personality and Social Psychology*, 1980, *39*, 1024–1036. Copyright 1980 by the American Psychological Association. Reprinted by permission of the publisher and authors.

Note: Negative scores indicate reduced fear.

used to explain the phenomena are not phenomenal. Berkowitz suggested that the misattribution process need not necessarily interfere with or eliminate the influence of the motivational state that has been misattributed, and Gibbons and Wright and Duncan and Laird suggested that the occurrence of a misattribution process may be influenced by individual differences among subjects. Collectively these more recent developments cast doubt on the generality of the phenomena reported by Schachter and Singer. They also serve to assign a somewhat circumscribed role to the influence of cognitive processes on motivational states.

It is possible to argue that a similar state of affairs exists with respect to the efforts of Weiner (see especially, 1980) to reinterpret research on achievement motivation from a cognitive point of view. Weiner (1972; 1974; 1980) attempted to develop an attributional theory of behavior with particular applications to achievement phenomena. Weiner's theory is concerned with the set of cognitions developed by an individual that explain his or her reasons for success or failure at a task. Weiner distinguished between attributions that were stable—that is, relatively unlikely to change—and those that were unstable and vacillate over time. He also distinguished between attributions that were internal to the individual or external to the individual. An example of this two-dimensional scheme for the classification of attributions for success or failure is presented in Table 5.15. Weiner also complicated this scheme by consideration of a third dimension of success or failure at a task called controllability. Table 5.16 presents this three-dimensional scheme. Weiner and his associates performed several studies that examined the variables that influence the development of these various attributions for success and failure. These studies will not be reviewed here (see Weiner, 1980 for a relatively comprehensive review), but rather a core assumption of Weiner's approach to motivation will be discussed. Weiner assumed that the attributions developed by the individual determine his or her motivational response. Thus, for Weiner, cognitions about the world would serve to guide and control behav-

TABLE 5.15

A Two-Dimensional Classification Scheme for the Perceived Determinants of Achievement Behavior

	Locus of control	
Stability	Internal	External
Stable	Ability	Task difficulty
Unstable	Effort, mood, fatigue, illness	Luck

Source: Weiner, 1980.

TABLE 5.16
A Three-Dimensional Taxonomy of the Perceived Causes of Success and Failure

	Controllable		Uncontrollable	
	Stable	Unstable	Stable	Unstable
Internal	Stable effort of self	Unstable effort of self	Ability of self	Fatigue, mood, and fluctuations in skill of self
External	Stable effort of others	Unstable effort of others	Ability of others, task difficulty	Fatigue, mood, and fluctuations in skill of others, luck

Source: Weiner, 1980.

ior. On this analysis if an individual believes that failure at a task is attributable to stable factors that cannot be controlled, such as task difficulty and ability, the individual will not attempt to work harder to succeed at subsequent encounters with the task. If for example I believe that I have failed to solve a puzzle because the puzzle is either inherently insoluble or because I do not have the requisite knowledge or skill to permit me to solve such a puzzle, on Weiner's analysis, I should not continue to try to solve such a puzzle. In other words my beliefs are rather directly causally related to my actions and are in fact conceived as the principal determinants of action.

There are several studies that appear to demonstrate that action is determined by beliefs about the reasons for success or failure at a task. Weiner and Sierad (1975) studied performance on a digit–symbol substitution task as a function of individual differences in achievement motivation measured by the Mehrabian tests in an experiment in which they introduced a misattribution condition. They assigned individuals differing in achievement motivation to a pill condition or a no-pill control condition. Subjects assigned to the pill condition were told that the pill would interfere with hand–eye coordination—a skill necessary for performance on the digit–symbol substitution task. Subjects failed the task repeatedly, and their performance changes over trials were noted. It was assumed that subjects who were high in achievement motivation who attributed their poor performance to the pill would lose interest in the task and would not work hard to improve performance. However, subjects high in achievement motivation in the control group would be expected to attribute poor performance on the task to low effort and would therefore work harder following failure. Accordingly it was expected that those who were high in achievement motivation would show greater improvement in the control condition than in the pill condition. The opposite pattern of relationships was expected for subjects who were low in achievement-related motives. In the control condition it was expected that they would attribute their failure to low ability and would experience negative affect as a result of failure and would also assume that their performance could not be improved by extra effort expenditure. However, in the pill condition they would be able to attribute their failure to the effects of the pill and would as a result not experience the negative affect of shame as a result of their failure. The performance consequences of the differences in attributions and the consequent affective experiences that followed from the different attributions in the pill and the control conditions are not as clear-cut for the subjects who were low in achievement motivation. From a rational point of view, failure attributed to one's ability or to a pill represented stable causes of performance that were outside the volitional control of the individual. Weiner (1980) assumed that the negative effect of shame caused by the attribution of failure to ability served to depress performance. Therefore, subjects low in achievement motivation were expected to exhibit better performance in the pill condition than in the control condition. Figure 5.5 presents the results of the Weiner and Seirad study. Note that the results were exactly as expected. Subjects who were assumed to be high in need achievement exhibited the largest performance gains under circumstances in which they were presumably free to attribute the outcome of performance to their own efforts rather than to a pill. Subjects who were presumably low in need achievement exhibited the best performance gains under circumstances in which they were presumed to attribute failure to an external agent outside their own control. The Weiner and Seirad study clearly demonstrates that the relationship between individual differences in achievement motivation and performance may be mediated by attributions held by subjects about the reasons for their performance. It should be noted that the attributions that are assumed to mediate performance differences are inferred in this study and are not measured directly. Similarly the affective consequences of the hypothetical differences in attribution are also inferred. Thus the study provides at best indirect evidence for the cognitive events that are assumed to mediate between individual differences in motivation and performance. A somewhat simpler interpretation of these results could be derived from the traditional view of achievement motivation as reflecting pride of accomplishment due to personal effort. One might argue that achievement related motivation is not engaged in a task in which the outcome of performance is attributable to effects that are outside of one's control, such as the influence of a pill. Under these conditions the task is no longer relevant to the expression of achievement-related motives. The induction of achievement-related motivation tends to improve performance among subjects high in achievement motivation and

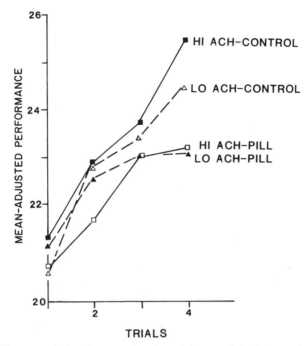

Figure 5.5. *Mean speed of performance (number of digit–symbol substitutions), adjusted for pretest performance, for the test trials as a function of level of achievement needs (high versus low) and the experimental condition (control versus pill attribution). (Abbreviations are as follows: Hi Ach = high achievement; Lo Ach = low achievement.) (From B. Weiner and J. Sierad. Misattribution for failure and enhancement of achievement strivings.* Journal of Personality and Social Psychology, *1975, 31, 415–421. Copyright 1975 by the American Psychological Association. Reprinted by permission of the publisher and authors.)*

decreases performance among those low in achievement motivation. These results can be explained somewhat more parsimoniously by stating that the differences between the pill and the control conditions are to be theoretically understood as involving a task that acts to induce and arouse achievement-related needs on the one hand as opposed to a task in which achievement-related needs are not involved.

Meyer (1970, as cited in Weiner, 1980) reported a study providing somewhat more direct evidence of the influence of attributions for success and failure on behavior. Meyer had high school students perform a digit–symbol substitution task. The experiment was arranged in such a way that subjects experienced failure after each trial. They were not able to attain the goal set for them. Following each failure experience subjects were required to attribute the reasons for their failure to their ability, task difficulty, effort, or luck. In addition, they were asked to state their subjective probabilities of success on the next trial. Figure 5.6 presents the subjective probabilities of success for subjects who were either high or low in their attributions to each of these four possible responses. Note that subjects who tended to attribute their failure to their ability or to task difficulty—stable causes of failure—tended to have lower subjective probabilities of success than those who attributed their failure to luck or to effort—the unstable causes of failure.

Attributions about performance were not only related to subjective proba-

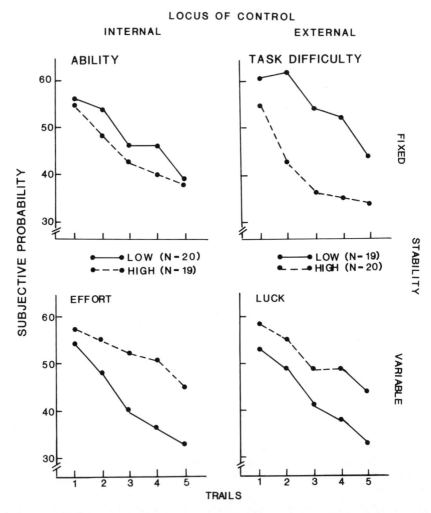

Figure 5.6. *Expectancy of success as a function of above- or below-median ascription to the four causal elements. High ascription indicates lack of ability, a difficult task, lack of effort, and bad luck. (From Weiner [1980].)*

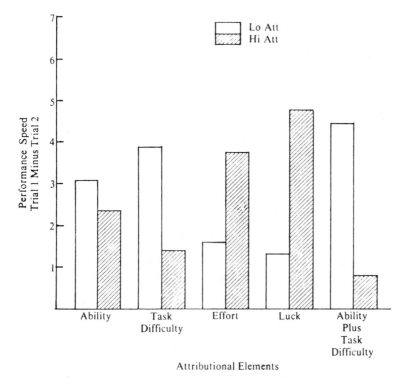

Figure 5.7.   *Intensity of performance in seconds (Trail 1 minus Trial 2) as a function of attribution to the four causal elements and to the combined stable factors. High numbers indicate greater improvement in speed. (From Weiner [1980].)*

bilities of success, but they were also related to the actual level of performance. Meyer obtained as a measure of performance, speed in digit–symbol substitution, for the first and second trials. The difference between these measures reflects changes in performance. Meyer related improvement in performance to the attributions for failure developed by subjects after the first trial. Figure 5.7 presents these data. Subjects who attributed their failure to the stable causes of task difficulty and ability tended to show relatively little improvement in performance. Those who attributed their failure to unstable reasons such as effort and luck demonstrated relatively high levels of improvement. These data provide evidence for a direct relationship between what a person asserts are the reasons for an action and the person's subsequent efforts.

Covington and Omelich (1979) reported the results of a study analogous to Meyer's in a nonlaboratory setting. Subjects in their study were students in an introductory psychology class. The testing procedures used in the class permitted students to retake examinations. At the completion of a particular unit, subjects were given a multiple choice examination and were given feedback of the results of their examination. Those who were dissatisfied with their grades were given an opportunity to retake the examination. Approximately half the students chose to retake an alternative form of the examination 2 days later. Covington and Omelich obtained achievement motivation scores for the subjects in their study using the Mehrabian measures as well as expectancy and attributional information about the reasons for their inadequate performance on the original test prior to the time when subjects could retake the examination. These data permit an examination of the role of motivation and attributions for failure in determining performance in a situation in which the outcome is of some relevance to the subjects. Weiner's position implies that the influence of achievement motivation is mediated by the attributions that subjects differing in motivation are likely to give for the outcome of their efforts and that these attributions influence the effort expended by subjects and thus ultimately the level of performance attained. Those who are low in achievement motivation are assumed to attribute failure to such influences as poor ability and hence are not assumed to work harder following failure since they cannot change their ability level.

The results of Covington and Omelich's study provide little or no support for Weiner's attributional analysis. Their analysis indicates that achievement motivation does relate to performance. There was a small but significant positive relationship between performance and achievement motivation (r = .145). They used path analysis techniques to decompose this influence into a direct and indirect influence. Indirect influences would be represented by motivational influence on attributions that in turn would influence performance. Direct influences would be represented by the influence of achievement motivation that is statistically independent of the effects of differences in attributions. The results indicate that the major portion of the influence of motivation on performance is a direct influence (the path coefficient is .087) and the total indirect influence has a path value of .058. Approximately 75% of the indirect path value is attributable to variations in the expectancy for success on the second examination held by subjects. This influence of expectancy on performance is compatible with the general model of the influence of motivation on performance developed by Atkinson. The influence of various attributions for success on performance is vanishingly small in this analysis. The total path value for attributions to effort, luck, ability, and task difficulty is .014. Covington and Omelich indicate that the attributions given by subjects for failure does not add significantly to our ability to predict performance. Covington and Omelich's results are in direct contradiction to the results reported by Meyer. Perhaps the different outcomes of these two studies is related to the settings in which they occur. Meyer's study was a laboratory investigation in which attributions for failure were immediately followed by the presentation of a task that was probably of little relevance or interest to subjects. Also in this setting there was a very short time period intervening between the collection of attribution data and performance of the task. By contrast the measure of performance in the Covington and Omelich study was obtained 2 days after subjects provided attributional information. Also the performance measure determined a course grade and was of some importance to subjects. An additional difference in the studies that may be of significance derives from the nature of the performance measures obtained. Performance on a digit–symbol substitution test may be more clearly determined by effort. Performance on an examination may be less clearly indicative of motivational effort and may be related to the ability of subjects to study effectively. Thus it might in fact be the case that the effort expended in preparation for the examination was determined by the attributions for failure but that effort was only weakly related to performance outcomes. Irrespective of the validity of these speculations, the Covington and Omelich study does indicate that performance influences of achievement motivation are not necessarily mediated by cognitive attributional variables. These results tend to cast doubt on the attributional analysis of performance developed by Weiner.

T. D. Wilson and Linville (1982) provided evidence that also casts doubt on the attributional analysis of motivational influences on performance developed by Weiner. They studied attributional influences on college grades. They assumed that freshmen who encountered academic difficulties in their first semester in college might attribute their performance to inadequate ability. Such a stable internal cause for attribution would lead, on Weiner's analysis, to a reduction in effort and subsequent academic difficulties. Accordingly, Wilson and Linville attempted to induce their subjects to develop an attribution of their performance that was external and unstable. In order to accomplish this they informed a group of college freshmen that many who experience academic difficulties in their first semester in college, exhibit improvements later on and thus their academic problems might be temporary. They found that those who were provided with this information were less likely to drop out of college at the end of the second semester of their sophomore year and increased their grade-point average, whereas subjects in a no-information condition had a slight decline in grade-point average. On the surface these results appear to support Weiner's analysis, since a one-time experimental manipulation designed to change subjects' attributions of the reasons for poor performance in a significant real life setting had a definite effect on performance a year later. However, although subjects' behavior changed, the changes did not appear to be clearly related to changes in subjects verbal reports about the psychological states that are presumed to mediate the consequences of changes in the attributions of subjects. Wilson and Linville did report that subjects' expectancies for future success did increase if they were assigned to the attributional information condition. However, the correlation between these expectancies and actual behavior was not different from zero. The correlation between expectancy of improvement in grades and the probability of remaining in college was .21, and the correlation between the expectancy measure and actual improvements in grade-point average was $-.31$. Although this latter correlation is not significant, it is of some interest to note that the correlation is in the opposite direction of what one would expect on the assumption that the behavioral effects of the attribution are mediated by a cognitive belief that is phenomenally present. In addition, Wilson and Linville reported that various measures of moods that on Weiner's analysis might be expected to mediate the influence of attributional states were unrelated to behavior change. Wilson and Linville argued that their results were compatible with the theoretical position advanced by Nisbett and Wilson that assumes that the variables determining verbal reports about the cognitive reasons for human action are distinct from the variables determining the behavior of subjects. Thus, this study generalizes the notion that the cognitive processes that influence behavior are not phenomenal to a study that demonstrates a successful attributional intervention based on Weiner's theory.

Prophenomenological Research

This section will consider prophenomenological research and theory, which assigns a central role to phenomenal events in the control of motivated behavior. In particular I will consider Bandura's theory of self-efficacy and Carver and Scheier's research on self-focused attentional processes.

Bandura (1977a; 1977b; 1982) attempted to explain the results of studies dealing with the effectiveness of various methods of behavior therapy by appeal to a phenomenological mediating variable. Bandura argued that therapeutically desirable change is mediated and influenced by the development of changes in beliefs held by an individual about ability to accomplish various behavioral activities. Bandura called this variable self- or personal efficacy. He defined this term as a belief held by an individual that he or she would be able to perform or execute behaviors that would produce some desired outcome. One may believe that a particular course of action will produce some desired result while at the same time doubting his or her own capability of executing the required actions. For example, an obese person might believe that following a particular diet would result in weight loss while doubting his or her ability to follow the diet. Bandura assumed that the effectiveness of a variety of therapeutic interventions is contingent, in at least a stochastic or probabalistic sense, on the development of suitable efficacy beliefs. If a person does not believe that he or she is capable of performing a given action, that individual, in Bandura's view, is unlikely to be able to perform the actions. Similarly, if a person has developed a strong sense of self-efficacy and believes that he or she is capable of performing some action, then it is likely that the person will be capable of performing the action.

Bandura and his colleagues reported the results of several studies designed to test the theory of self-efficacy. In addition, he attempted to interpret several existing findings in the literature in terms of efficacy theory. Bandura reported the results of a number of studies of modeling (see Bandura 1977b, for a general review; see also Bandura, Blanchard, & Ritter, 1969), in which subjects who were phobic were exposed to models who engaged in a variety of behaviors with the objects of their phobia. Usually the observation of a model who was able to exhibit relatively fearless behavior would enable a phobic subject to engage in behaviors with the phobic object that the individual was not previously able to perform. The effectiveness of observation of the model depended on a variety of characteristics of the model and of the behavior of the model. For example, if the phobic subject were a child, then a child model would be more effective than an adult model. Bandura attempted to explain this by assuming that the observation of a child performing actions that the subject was not able to perform, might lead the child subject to develop a belief in his or her efficacy. The observation of an adult behaving fearlessly would not be as likely to convince a child that he or she was capable of emulating the behavior of the model. Thus the effectiveness of observations of the model was mediated by the kind of inferences that the observer of the model was likely to make from his or her observations.

Bandura provided a similar analysis for the finding that the observation of models who performed actions that an individual was not capable of performing in a facile manner was likely to be less effective in enabling individuals to perform actions that they were not previously capable of performing than the observation of models who appeared to be capable of performing the actions only after the exertion of some effort. Bandura explained this phenomena by arguing that an individual who was phobic was not likely to develop a sense of personal efficacy from the observation of facile models. The model's performance was simply discounted, and phobics might have tended to view such performances as being accomplished by individuals whose abilities were sufficiently different from their own as to provide little indication of what they themselves could accomplish. On the other hand, the observation of a model who appeared to be struggling to perform an action that the observer might not have been able to perform might have led the observer to infer that he or she was also capable of overcoming adversity and performing the action. Note that Bandura's theory implies that an individual is largely capable of doing what he or she believes he or she is capable of doing and is largely incapable of doing that which he or she believes himself or herself incapable of doing. Thus the task of inducing desirable forms of behavioral change is in part reducible to the task of inducing an individual to change his or her beliefs about his or her capabilities. In addition, Bandura implied that the beliefs about personal efficacy were phenomenally present and could readily be inferred from verbal reports.

Bandura and his associates performed several studies designed to specifically test the assumptions of self-efficacy theory. Bandura, Adams, and Beyer (1977) assigned adult subjects who were snake phobic to one of three groups: a no treatment control; a participant modeling group in which subjects were assisted to actually perform actions with snakes; and a modeling group in which subjects observed models performing various actions with snakes. (Subjects in this latter group were mere observers.) Previous research has suggested that participant modeling is a more effective method of inducing behavior change than modeling (see for example, Bandura, Blanchard, & Ritter, 1969). Accordingly, Bandura, Adams, and Beyer (1977) assumed that subjects assigned to this condition could exhibit greater improvement than subjects in the other conditions, and in addition they would develop a stronger sense of personal or self-efficacy. Figure 5.8 presents the results of this experiment. An examination of the data indicates that there was a close relationship between the magnitude of changes in verbal reports about a subject's ability to perform a variety of actions and the actual magnitudes of

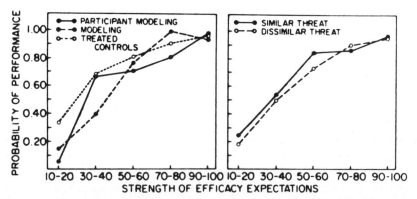

Figure 5.8.   Probability of successful performance of any given task as a function of strength of self-efficacy. (The left panel shows the relationship for vicarious and performance-based treatments; the right panel shows the relationship between strength of self-efficacy and successful approach responses toward similar and dissimilar threats combined across treatments.) (From A. Bandura, N. E. Adams, and J. Beyer. Cognitive processes mediating behavioral change. Journal of Personality and Social Psychology, 1977, 35, 125–139. Copyright 1977 by the American Psychological Association. Reprinted by permission of the publisher and authors.)

behavioral change that occurred as a result of treatment. Also the verbal reports about subjects' efficacy beliefs were predictive of behavior in a generalization task. In this phase of the study, subjects were presented with a snake of a discernably different appearance and were asked to perform a variety of behaviors with that snake. One could attempt to predict subjects' ability to perform these various actions by generalizing from the actual terminal behaviors performed by subjects with the first snake. Alternatively, one could attempt to predict the ability of the subject to perform terminal behaviors with new snakes by using a measure of subjects' self-efficacy reports. Bandura, Adams, and Beyer found that predictions of the ability of subjects to perform all of the assigned actions with a new snake were more accurate when they were based on efficacy assertions rather than on the actual behaviors performed with the original snake. In 52% of the cases, those who were able to perform all of the required actions with the original snake were not able to perform all of the required actions with the new snake. Of the subjects who had maximal efficacy assertions about their ability to perform the required actions with the original snake, 24% were able to perform all of the required activities with a new snake.

Bandura and Schunk (1981) attempted to influence the development of self-efficacy by providing subjects with what they called "proximal goals." In this technique a subject was instructed to focus upon the attainment of a limited set of goals that would lead eventually to the attainment of an ultimate goal. Proximal goals may be distinguished from distal goals, which are remote in time and involve the accomplishment of a rather more extended sequence of instrumental acts for ultimate goal attainment. They studied elementary school children who had difficulty in mathematics and who were unable to successfully perform subtraction problems. They were randomly assigned to one of four groups. Three of the groups were provided with a special instructional program, and the fourth group served as a control group. The three experimental groups differed among themselves with respect to the kinds of goals provided for them. One group was not given any specific goal to accomplish. A second group, the proximal goal group, was given the goal of completing six pages of instructional material each day. A third group, the distal goal group, was given the goal of completing the entire set of instructional materials (42 pages) by the end of the seventh session.

Bandura and Schunk assumed that subjects provided with proximal goals would develop a greater sense of self-efficacy and would as a result perform at a higher level of competence than those assigned to the other groups. They reasoned that the process of subgoal, or proximal goal, attainment would develop a sense of personal efficacy and self-satisfaction. This, in turn, might foster a sense of intrinsic interest in the activity. The assignment of distal goals would prevent an individual from experiencing goal attainments, and in addition the awareness of the disparities between attainments and ultimate goals might serve to attenuate the development of self-satisfaction and a sense of personal efficacy.

Figures 5.9 and 5.10 present some of the results of the Bandura and Schunk study. Children assigned to the proximal goal-setting condition developed a greater sense of self-efficacy as judged by their beliefs about their capability of solving math problems, attained a higher level of competence on a test of their acquisition of the skills presented in the instructional materials, and, when given a choice of working on substraction problems or on some other nonmathematical problems, spontaneously chose to work on subtraction problems. In addition, children assigned to the proximal goal-setting group were more accurate in their self-appraisals (that is, their judgments of their ability to solve specific types of subtraction problems presented to them briefly were more predictive of their actual ability to solve similar problems).

These results suggest that phenomenal events interact with a temporally extended goal-directed behavior sequence and influence ongoing behavior.

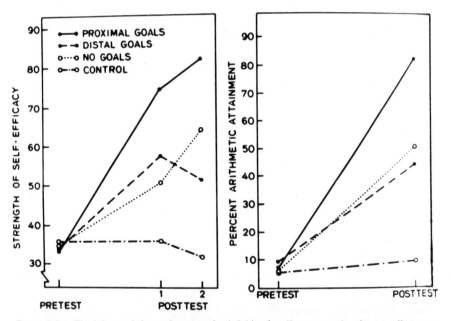

Figure 5.9.   The left panel shows the strength of children's self-percepts of arithmetic efficacy at the beginning of the study (pretest), and before (Post₁) and after (Post₂) they took the subtraction posttest. The right panel displays the children's level of achievement on the subtraction tests before and after the self-directed learning. (From A. Bandura and D. H. Schunk. Cultivating competence, self-efficacy, and intrinsic interest through proximal self-motivation. Journal of Personality and Social Psychology, 1981, 41, 586–598. Copyright 1981 by the American Psychological Association. Reprinted by permission of the publisher and authors.)

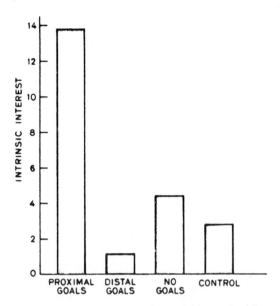

Figure 5.10. *Average number of subtraction problems children in the different conditions chose to solve when given free choice of activities. (From A. Bandura and D. H. Schunk. Cultivating competence, self-efficacy, and intrinsic interest through proximal self-motivation. Journal of Personality and Social Psychology, 1981, 41, 586–598. Copyright 1981 by the American Psychological Association. Reprinted by permission of the publisher and authors.)*

The successful attainment of a proximal goal may lead a subject to experience a sense of success, to revise beliefs about self-efficacy, and to develop intrinsic interest in instrumental activities that will serve to accomplish additional proximal goals, and will in turn increase the likelihood of accomplishment of an ultimate goal. Thus, Bandura's theoretical analysis suggests that phenomenal events can influence an emerging behavior sequence and alter its ultimate outcome.

The most extensive body of evidence bearing on the influence of the phenomenal character of cognitions for motivated behavior is contained in a program of research summarized in a book-length manuscript by Carver and Scheier (1981). Their research was based on the investigation of the influence of self-directed attentional processes. They made use of two different procedures to study the effects of self-directed attentional processes. In one procedure they attempted to manipulate the direction of attentional processes by using a mirror and contrasting the behavior of their subjects under conditions in which a mirror was present with behavior under conditions in which a mirror was not present. The mirror was placed in a location that was designed to permit subjects to observe themselves and to be at the same time relatively unobtrusive. The mirror was usually described as being part of the equipment of another experiment. Thus, subjects were not assumed to be aware of the influence of the mirror or of its central role as an experimental variable in these studies. Carver and Scheier argued that the presence of a mirror led subjects to become more self-reflective and to become more aware of their inner psychological states. The mirror was not presumed to create a state that was not actually present in the individual, nor was it assumed to enhance the perceptual capabilities of an individual. Rather it was assumed merely to change the focus of an individual's attention to the inner psychological state of the individual.

Carver and Scheier also assumed that individuals differ in their tendency to focus upon their inner states as a matter of personal disposition. In order to measure this tendency, they used a paper-and-pencil test called The Self-Consciousness Scale developed by Fenigstein, Scheier, and Buss (1975). This scale is assumed to measure both a disposition to be aware of the private as well as the public aspects of the self. It is the former component of the scale that is assumed to represent the disposition to be aware of one's inner psychological states. Among the items that define the private self-consciousness scale are the following: I reflect about myself a lot; I am generally attentive to my inner feelings; I'm always trying to figure myself out.

The research strategy used in these studies usually involved a comparison of the behavioral influence of the presence or absence of the mirror with the effects of individual differences in the disposition to be privately self-conscious. If the effects of these two variables were parallel, the inference that the outcomes of a particular experiment were attributable to the hypothetical state variable "self-focused attention" would be buttressed. Several studies that follow this general paradigm will be reviewed.

Scheier and Carver (1977) reported the results of a series of studies purporting to demonstrate a phenomenal enhancement effect attributable to the influence of self-focused attention. In the first experiment in this series, subjects were assigned to a mirror-present or a mirror-absent condition, and they were asked to view a series of slides of nude females. Subjects were then asked to rate the attractiveness of the slides. They found that subjects assigned to the mirror-present condition rated the slides as more attractive than subjects assigned to a mirror-absent condition. In the second experiment reported in this series, subjects were asked to view the same type of slides as a method of inducing a positive affective state and were also asked to view slides that were designed to elicit states of aversion and disgust. Individual differences in self-focus were studied by using the private self-consciousness scale. The results for this investigation are presented in Table 5.17. An examination of the data clearly indicates that individual differences in private self-consciousness were related to an intensification of the affective experience

TABLE 5.17
Mean Pleasantness Ratings for Each Treatment Group of Experiment 2

Stimulus	Private self-consciousness		
	Low	High	Row *M*s
Positive slides	22.6	24.6	23.6
N	18	14	
Negative slides	12.5	10.0	11.3
N	10	15	
Column *M*s	17.6	17.3	17.5

Source: M. F. Scheier and C. S. Carver. Self-focused attention and the experience of emotion: Attraction, repulsion, elation and depression. *Journal of Personality and Social Psychology,* 1977, *35*, 625–636. Copyright 1977 by the American Psychological Association. Reprinted by permission of the publisher and authors.
Note: The higher the number, the higher the pleasantness rating.

induced by viewing the slides. Subjects who scored high on the scale tended to rate positive slides more positively and negative slides more negatively than those who scored low on the scale.

In the third experiment in this series, subjects were subjected to either positive or a negative mood induction procedure (see Velten, 1968). Self-awareness was manipulated by the use of the mirror. The results for this experiment are presented in Table 5.18. An examination of the data indicates

TABLE 5.18
Mean Mood Ratings for Each Treatment Group of Experiment 3

Stimulus	No mirror	Mirror	Row *M*s
Positive statements	8.1	8.9	8.5
Negative statements	6.0	4.4	5.2
Column *M*s	7.0	6.6	6.8

Source: M. F. Scheier and C. S. Carver. Self-focused attention and the experience of emotion: Attraction, repulsion, elation and depression. *Journal of Personality and Social Psychology,* 1977, *35*, 625–636. Copyright 1977 by the American Psychological Association. Reprinted by permission of the publisher and authors.
Note: The higher the number, the more positive the mood.

that subjects assigned to the mirror-present condition reported feeling more positively following a positive mood induction and more negatively following a negative mood induction than those assigned to the mirror-absent condition. The final experiment in this series was a conceptual replication of the third experiment except that the self-focusing variable was defined in terms of scores on the private self-consciousness scale. The results were essentially similar to those obtained when self-consciousness was manipulated using the mirror.

The studies reviewed have suggested that changes in self-focusing behavior can influence verbal reports about phenomenal states. Carver, Blaney, and Scheier (1979a, 1979b) studied the interaction between changes in phenomenal states and beliefs about the likelihood of successful completion of a behavioral sequence on the performance of that sequence. In the first of these studies Carver, Blaney, and Scheier (1979a) studied the influence of a mirror-present and a mirror-absent condition on responses to a moderately fearful stimulus. In this experiment subjects were presented with the task of reaching into a cage and picking up a boa constrictor. All of the subjects chosen for this study were moderately fearful of snakes. On the basis of their responses to a pretest questionnaire, subjects were classified as belonging to a group that was doubtful of their capability of performing the act and a group who were at least moderately confident of their ability to perform this task. The experimenters assumed that these differences in outcome expectancy would interact with self-focusing manipulations to determine the performances of subjects on the assigned task. Specifically, they reasoned that a self-focusing condition would lead subjects who had feelings of inadequacy and anxiety, to become aware of these feelings and as a result would lead them to withdraw from the task and to have more difficulty completing the task than subjects who were doubtful but who had not been assigned to the self-focusing condition. The effects of a self-focusing condition were expected to be different for subjects who were relatively confident about their ability to complete the assigned task. Although they might be expected to experience a phenomenal enhancement of their anxiety states in the presence of the mirror, they would also experience in an enhanced way their awareness of the goal and perhaps as well of their belief in their ability to attain the goal. Presumably the mirror would lead these subjects to focus upon whatever cognitive influences were present that led them to believe that they would attain the goal in the first place. Tables 5.19 and 5.20 present the results of this study. An examination of the data indicates that the initial confidence in the ability to complete the assigned task interacted with the presence of the mirror to influence actual goal attainment. Confident subjects exhibited a slight but insignificant increase in their approach behavior in the presence of the mirror. Doubtful subjects exhibited a significant decrease in their approach behavior in the

TABLE 5.19
Self-reported Anxiety Experienced in the Presence of the Snake, Self-reported Momentary Sense of Inadequacy and Fearfulness during the Approach Task, and Actual Level of Approach toward the Snake

	Condition	
Group	Mirror present	Mirror absent
Self-reported anxiety[a]		
Confident	4.33	3.46
Doubtful	5.25	3.56
Self-reported sense of inadequacy[a]		
Confident	4.20	3.85
Doubtful	5.38	3.63
Approach behavior[b]		
Confident	8.47	8.23
Doubtful	6.38	8.31

Source: C. S. Carver, P. H. Blaney, and M. F. Scheier. Focus of attention, chronic expectancy, and responses to a feared stimulus. *Journal of Personality and Social Psychology,* 1979, *37,* 1186–1195. Copyright 1979 by the American Psychological Association. Reprinted by permission of the publisher and authors.
[a]Larger numbers indicate greater anxiety and felt inadequacy.
[b]Larger numbers indicate greater approach.

presence of the mirror. An analysis of the postexperimental questionnaire data indicates that the presence of the mirror changed retrospective reports about the phenomenal events that transpired during the experiment in a way that is comprehensible and congruent with the outcomes of the experiment. Doubtful subjects reported increases in anxiety, a sense of inadequacy, an awareness of chronic levels of fearfulness, their state of physiological arousal, and a decrease in their awareness of the discrepancy between their behavioral attainments and the attainment of the goal. Subjects who expressed confidence also reported an increase in their awareness of their fear and anxiety in the presence of the mirror, but the level of increase was less extreme for these subjects. In addition this increase was also accompanied by an increase in the awareness of the goal state. It is as if the presence of the mirror led doubtful subjects to focus upon the factors that determined their inability to complete the task and confident subjects to counterbalance this increase in their doubts and anxieties with a renewed focus on the goals of their behavior.

Carver, Blaney, and Scheier (1979b) reported the results of another set of

TABLE 5.20
Self-reports of Attention Paid to Chronic Level of Fearfulness, Self-assessment of Bodily Arousal and Behavior–Goal Comparison

	Condition	
Group	Mirror present	Mirror absent
Chronic level of fearfulness		
Confident	4.67	4.23
Doubtful	4.81	3.56
Assessing degree of bodily arousal		
Confident	3.60	4.69
Doubtful	4.31	3.13
Behavior–goal comparison		
Confident	5.93	5.62
Doubtful	5.06	6.06

Source: C. S. Carver, P. H. Blaney, and M. F. Scheier. Focus of attention, chronic expectancy, and responses to a feared stimulus. *Journal of Personality and Social Psychology,* 1979, *37,* 1186–1195. Copyright 1979 by the American Psychological Association. Reprinted by permission of the publisher and authors.
Note: Larger numbers indicate greater attention.

experiments dealing with self-focusing variables and differences in beliefs held about the successful attainment of a goal. In the first of these experiments, subjects were presented with an anagrams task and were told that they had failed to achieve a satisfactory level of performance on this task. Subjects were then given a design problem to solve. One group of subjects was told that poor performance on the anagrams task was predictive of poor performance on the design problem, and the other group was told that poor performance on the anagrams task was related to superior performance on the design problem. Subjects were also assigned to groups that performed the design task in the presence of a mirror or with the mirror absent. The results of this study are reported in Table 5.21 and indicate that those subjects who had negative expectations about the outcome of their efforts tended to withdraw from the task at an earlier stage in the presence of the mirror. Those given positive expectations about the outcome of their efforts did not persist longer on the task. These results provide clear evidence for a phenomenal enhancement effect for subjects given negative expectations about the outcomes of their performance but provide little or no evidence for such an effect for subjects in whom positive expectations were induced. In a follow-up investigation (Experiment 2) an attempt was made to provide somewhat stronger expectations about the likelihood of success on the design task following failure on the anagrams task, and subjects were given somewhat more time to work on the anagrams task in order to eliminate possible ceiling effects. Under these conditions subjects in whom positive expectations were induced did in fact persist longer on the task in the presence of the mirror than in its absence. These results combined with the earlier results reported by these experimenters on the influence of a mirror on behavior in fear-inducing situations provide evidence for the view that a focused awareness on the psychological states that are presumed to determine behavior can actually influence goal-directed actions.

Scheier (1976) reported the results of a study in which subjects who were either low or high in the measure of private self-consciousness were assigned to either a mirror-present or a mirror-absent condition. In addition some of the subjects in each of these four groups were assigned to a condition designed to elicit anger. Anger was manipulated by presenting the subject with a quite difficult problem that he or she had to solve alone in the presence of a second person who was actually an agent of the experimenter. In the anger condition the agent insulted the subject and criticized his or her problem-solving ability. In the anger-absent condition, the agent remained silent. After subjects had worked on the problem-solving task, they were given an opportunity to act as a teacher in an experimental situation in which the subject was instructed to deliver a shock whenever an incorrect response was made by a learner or "victim," who was the experimental agent present during the first phase of the experiment. The subject could choose the level of shock that he wished to deliver to the victim by choosing buttons clearly labeled to indicate that they delivered different intensities of shock. The principal dependent variable was the level of shock intensity chosen by the subject.

Scheier had relatively clear-cut theoretical expectations for the outcome of

TABLE 5.21

Persistence (in Minutes) at an Insoluble Task, as a Function of Outcome Expectancy and Self-attention, Experiment 1

Expectancy	Mirror absent			Mirror present		
	Persistence	SD	N	Persistence	SD	N
Positive	8.15	2.38	17	8.43	2.20	19
Negative	8.51	1.88	17	6.55	2.21	21

Source: C. S. Carver, P. H. Blaney, and M. F. Scheier. Reassertion and giving up: The interactive role of self-directed attention and outcome expectancy. *Journal of Personality and Social Psychology,* 1979, *37,* 1859–1870. Copyright 1979 by the American Psychological Association. Reprinted by permission of the publisher and authors.

this experiment. First, he assumed that the effects of private self-consciousness would parallel the effects of the mirror manipulation. Second, he assumed that both of these variables would enhance the influence of the anger manipulation. Third, he assumed that the intensification of the awareness of the state of anger would result in an increase in the expression of aggression as indexed by the level of shock intensity chosen by the subject. (Incidentally, no actual shocks are delivered in this type of study since the shock condition in deceptive.) Table 5.22 presents the principal results of this experiment, and an examination of the data presents a pattern of results that is completely in accord with theoretical expectations. Note that the intensity of shock selected increases following an anger-induction experience. Subjects who scored high on the dispositional measure of self-consciousness delivered higher levels of shock to their victims if they had been angered. No such difference was present among the nonangered subjects. Similarly, those who were angered and who performed the task in the presence of the mirror gave higher intensities of shock than subjects who did not perform the task in the presence of the mirror. This effect of the mirror was not present in the group of subjects who had not been angered—if anything the difference in this group was in the opposite direction.

Scheier explained these results by assuming that subjects who were high in dispositional self-consciousness or who performed the task in the presence of a mirror became more aware of their anger and this in turn, led them to respond more aggressively in the experimental situation. The analysis of data collected in a postexperimental questionnaire provides support for these associations. Table 5.23 presents an analysis of self-reports of the level of anger experienced during the experimental task for subjects assigned to the anger and nonanger conditions and the mirror and nonmirror conditions. An examination of the data indicates that subjects assigned to the mirror condition who

TABLE 5.22
Mean Shock Intensities Delivered by Subjects in Each Treatment Group

	No anger		Anger	
	No mirror	Mirror	No mirror	Mirror
High self-conscious	2.9	2.7	4.1	4.9
	(11)	(10)	(11)	(11)
Low self-conscious	3.0	2.5	3.3	3.9
	(12)	(12)	(12)	(12)

Source: Scheier, 1976.

Note: The higher the number, the higher the shock intensity. Parentheses contain the number of subjects per group. Main effect means: high self-conscious (3.6), low self-conscious (3.2); anger (4.1), no anger (2.8); mirror (3.5), no mirror (3.3).

TABLE 5.23
Mean Anger Ratings Collapsed across Levels of Self-consciousness

	No anger	Anger	M
Mirror	2.0	4.1	3.1
	(22)	(23)	
No mirror	2.5	2.6	2.6
	(23)	(23)	
M	2.3	3.4	2.8

Source: Scheier, 1976.
Note: The higher the number, the higher the anger rating.
Parentheses contain the number of subjects per group.

were angered rated themselves post-experimentally as being more angry during the experiment than those who were not angered or were angered but were not assigned to the mirror present condition.

I have discussed the results of an experiment by Berkowitz that suggests that the awareness of anger may not be a necessary condition for the psychological state of anger to exert an influence on aggression. Scheier's results suggest that the awareness of the state may enhance its influence. However, his results do not imply that the awareness of influence of the state of anger is a necessary condition for the state to exert an influence on behavior. This assertion is buttressed by a comparison of the data in Tables 5.22 and 5.23. Note that when the mirror was not present, there was no difference in the level of anger reported postexperimentally among subjects who were angered and who were not angered. However, subjects who were angered behaved more aggressively than did those who were not angered. If the veridicality of these reports is accepted, it is clear that the phenomenal enhancement effect coexists with evidence that the effect of the state of anger is not contingent upon the awareness of changes in the state.

There is an additional respect in which the results of Scheier's experiment should be conceived of in a somewhat circumscribed way with respect to their demonstration of the centrality of phenomenal events in the control of motivation. Scheier did not claim (indeed one suspects that he would specifically eschew the claim) that subjects were aware of the influence of the mirror on their behavior. Subjects were assumed to be made aware of anger. They were probably not aware that the mirror acted to enhance their anger, and they may not have been aware that the anger they were aware of may have influenced them to respond aggressively to the victim. Thus it is well to distinguish between the influence of a state of which one is aware and the processes by means of which the awareness of the state is manipulated and the processes by means of which the state made aware influences behavior. Thus, with respect to several aspects of the assertions made by Nisbett and Wilson (1977) about the limitations of subjects' awareness of their own psychological processes the results of the Scheier experiment, while providing evidence for a nonepiphenomenalist position, are nevertheless not in complete contradiction to a theoretical view that ascribes a somewhat limited view to phenomenal events in the control of behavior.

In this chapter research has been reviewed that suggests that phenomenal events play a central role in the control of motivated action sequences and that suggests that such events play a minimal or epiphenomenal role. These apparently centrifugal tendencies may be viewed as being only apparently in conflict (see Brody, 1980). In fact, it should be apparent to the discerning reader that at several places in the review of this research I have indicated that the very same studies that establish either the primacy of phenomenal events or the primacy of nonphenomenal events often provide evidence for the opposite conclusion. In this concluding section, I will attempt to dissolve the apparent conflict between pro- and antiphenomenological approaches to human motivation.

Virtually all of the studies demonstrating unconscious influences on behavior do not necessarily imply that unawareness or unconscious influence of the alleged state putatively assumed to influence behavior is a necessary condition for its motivational influence. Zajonc and his associates have attempted to demonstrate that recognition of a familiar stimulus is not a necessary condition for the development of positive affective responses to that stimulus. Zajonc does not claim and would presumably deny that the development of a positive affective response to a stimulus would be precluded or in some way diminished if a person were aware that the stimulus to which a positive affective response had developed as a result of familiarity was one that was in fact familiar. His claim is merely that knowledge that the stimulus had been previously encountered was not a necessary condition for the affective enhancement of its value. Similarly, studies using dichotic listening tasks to demonstrate the presence of an aversively conditioned emotional response to a stimulus that the subject is not attending to do not imply that the conditioned emotional response to the stimulus would not occur if the subject were not aware of the stimulus. The studies reported by Fowler et al. demonstrating the influence of stimuli that were, as a result of masking, out of awareness appear to parallel the influence of the same stimuli in awareness.

There are of course studies in the literature that, at least on superficial examination, appear to suggest that certain influences of stimuli that are not in awareness are contingent precisely on the unconscious status of the states. Consider two examples. Marcel's studies of lexical decisions using words that have two different meanings as primes suggest that the influence of a prime word is different when the prime word is in awareness than when the awareness of the stimulus is blocked by the use of a mask. Marcel argued that the influence of the prime word was restricted to one of its two meanings when the subject was aware of the stimulus, whereas when he or she was not aware of the stimulus both meanings of the prime word were cognitively present as it were and continued to exert influence on the lexical decision (see also Fowler *et al.,* 1981). Thus, it is argued that consciousness serves to restrict and define the range of possible meanings of a stimulus and serves to focus and make cognitively present a restricted subset of the multiple dimensions and meanings of the stimulus that are processed at a preconscious level. However, the restricting effects of a state of awareness on consciousness occurs under conditions of rapid information processing. Surely the minimal processing of the prime stimulus could be overcome by having the subject note all of the relevant meanings of the prime stimulus. This could be trivially accomplished for example by having him or her read the statement, "A palm is part of the body and is also the name of a tree." I wish to call attention to what I take to be trivially true assertions in order to indicate that the experiments with lexical decisions do not demonstrate any special properties of masked stimuli, which are not in principle at least, capable of being duplicated by events that are phenomenally present. This type of analysis may, albeit somewhat more problematically, extend to the dramatic demonstrations of unconscious influences on behavior reported by Silverman and his associates. Silverman (1976) of course asserted unequivocally that the influence of the stimuli he used to initiate or to ameliorate unconscious conflicts are contingent precisely on their unconscious status and that the influence of these stimuli would be quite different if a subject were aware of them. Recall the results of the Silverman and Spiro study that demonstrated that the influences of unconscious stimuli designed to intensify aggressive feeling in schizophrenics were dependent on the presentation of the stimuli subliminally rather than supraliminally. However, in the same experimental situation, effects virtually duplicating those obtained with subliminal presentations could be obtained with supraliminal presentations combined with a requirement of extensive verbal description of the supraliminally presented stimuli. Silverman and Spiro in fact argued that, because of the conflict created by the contents of the stimulus under the usual conditions of stimulus presentations, subjects are not inclined to consider the elaborated meanings of the stimulus. They also asserted that this inclination is itself motivated. Such results add to the interpretation of the notion of a kind of economy of information processing associated with consciousness the notion of a motivated unwillingness to deal with certain kinds of material. However, it should be noted that these studies do not imply that the cognitive blocking that apparently occurs cannot be overcome. Indeed, in many instances it may be that the blocking can be overcome by the mere expedient of calling the attention of the person to meanings implicit in a stimulus that the person has overlooked. One could argue that there is the phenomenon of resistance. Certain uncongenial interpretations of unconscious material might be also resisted and dismissed. It seems to me that, apart from the observations and speculations on this matter derived from psychoanalytic theory and clinical observations, there are relatively little hard data obtained in sufficiently controlled conditions to permit an empirical resolution of this issue (that is, one could entertain the notion that any subliminal or unconscious influence of a psychological state can, at least in principle, be duplicated by a conscious influence of the same state, if one can get an individual to entertain and to focus consciousness upon that state). If this general principle were in fact correct, the difference between sub- and supraliminal influences of psychological states would essentially evaporate and be reducible to a set of quasi-technological questions about the conditions under which different degrees and kinds of elaborations of meanings of states were likely to occur for states that were preconscious as opposed to conscious. On such a view the differences between pre- and postconscious processing are stochastic rather than fundamental—differences in degree perhaps rather than in kind.

A similar rapprochement is suggested by studies that have attempted to demonstrate the influence of phenomenal events on motivation. Consider in this connection the following research efforts: Bandura's studies of efficacy appear to provide evidence that behavior change is mediated by the phenomenal state of efficacy. However, the relationship reported is essentially stochastic. It is possible that individuals who believe they are capable of performing some action may nevertheless be unable to perform the action. Similarly, an individual may doubt that he or she is capable of performing an action and find to his or her surprise that he or she is able to do it. Bandura's findings indicate that a phenomenal set of events may influence actions and change the likelihood of certain behavioral outcomes, but they do not indicate that such events are invariably necessary. Perhaps more critical for our present purpose are the findings reported by Scheier that indicate that the occurrence of a phenomenal enhancement effect for a state of anger can coexist with evidence that the influence of an induced anger state occurs even if the subject is not aware of the anger. Recall that Scheier found that subjects who were angered behaved more aggressively than those who were not angered even under conditions in which there were no differences in the level of anger that they reported.

Another study that permits a simultaneous view of the effects of a phenomenal state and a demonstration of the impact of an alleged cognitive mediator that is nonphenomenal was reported by Pittmann, Cooper, and Smith (1977). They studied the familiar overjustification effect in which subjects who had been exposed to an extrinsic reward for performing a task were presumed to lose interest in performing the task (see Deci, 1975). This phenomenon is usually explained by reference to a change in cognition. Subjects who are rewarded for engaging in a particular task are assumed to form a cognition that indicates to them that their interest in the task was extrinsic rather than intrinsic. When subjects who have received tangible rewards for performing the task are subsequently given an opportunity to perform the task on their own, they usually choose not to engage in the previously rewarded activity. Pittman, Cooper, and Smith attempted to manipulate the cognitions of intrinsic and extrinsic interest in the task directly. In addition to the usual reward and no-reward conditions included in these studies, subjects were also assigned to conditions in which they received false physiological feedback in which they were informed that their physiological responses indicated a pattern of response characteristic of intrinsic interest in the task or extrinsic interest in the task. Table 5.24 presents subjects' self-reports about their interest in the game that they played and indicates that the manipulations were effective. Note that subjects led to believe that their physiological patterns were indicative of intrinsic interest in the game did indeed express the highest reported intrinsic interest. Note further that subjects who have been given a tangible reward for performance on the task express a decreased intrinsic interest in the task relative to those who have not received extrinsic rewards.

A reduction in intrinsic interest was measured by a reduced tendency to engage in the task during a free-choice period in which the experimenter is out of the room. Table 5.25 presents the results of the measure of the tendency to engage in the task under free-choice conditions. Note that manipulations of cognitions, as indexed by the verbal reports, did influence the behavior of subjects in this experimental situation. Those who had been led to

TABLE 5.24
Mean Amount of Arousal Attributed to Interest in the Game

No reward, no cue	Reward, no cue	Reward, extrinsic cue	Reward, intrinsic cue
47.30_{ab}	40.15_{ab}	35.95_{b}	55.25_{a}

Source: T. S. Pittman, E. E. Cooper, and T. W. Smith. Attribution of causality and the overjustification effect. *Personality and Social Psychology Bulletin*, 1977, 3, 280–283. Copyright 1977 by the American Psychological Association. Reprinted by permission of the publisher and authors.

Note: Subjects responded on a 91-point scale, with 0 indicating no arousal attributed to interest in the game and 90 indicating all arousal due to interest in the game. Cells not sharing a common subscript are significantly different from each other, $p < .05$, Newman–Keuls analysis. $N = .20$.

TABLE 5.25
Mean Number of Trials on the Task during the 5-Minute Free Choice Period

No reward, no cue	Reward, no cue	Reward, extrinsic cue	Reward, intrinsic cue
18.15_a	4.15_c	2.40_c	10.45_b

Source: T. S. Pittman, E. E. Cooper, and T. W. Smith. Attribution of causality and the overjustification effect. *Personality and Social Psychology Bulletin,* 1977, *3,* 280–283. Copyright 1977 by the American Psychological Association. Reprinted by permission of the publisher and authors.
Note: Cells not sharing a common subscript are significantly different from each other; $p < .05$, Newman–Keuls analysis.

believe that they were intrinsically interested in the task did choose to play the game in the absence of the experimenter more than subjects who were led to believe that they had only an extrinsic interest in the game. However, what is of some interest, and is not discussed by Pittman, Cooper, and Smith, is the difference between subjects assigned to the "intrinsic cue" condition and those in the traditional no-reward, no-cue condition. Subjects who had not received a reward for task performance during the first phase of the experiment exhibited the largest behavioral interest in the task during the second phase of the experiment. They were more likely to play the game than those given a reward who were led to believe that their pattern of physiological response was indicative of intrinsic interest in the game. However, these "reward intrinsic cue" subjects had slightly but nonsignificantly higher self-reported intrinsic interest in the game. This pattern of results permits us to suggest some tentative resolution of the apparent paradoxical results suggesting that phenomenal states do and do not mediate cognitive influences on motivation. The use of direct manipulations that change subjects' beliefs about the reasons for their actions can result in a change in their verbal reports about their phenomenal states and, also one may assume, in the underlying phenomenal state that is indexed by the report. However, the change in the phenomenal state does not account for the total motivational influence. There are two possibilities: The reduction in intrinsic interest in a task that follows from receiving a reward for the performance of the task may be mediated by noncognitive events or by cognitions other than those assessed in this experiment. Alternatively, the cognitions that constitute the usual and perhaps even the optimal explanation of the behavior of subjects in these experiments are not phenomenal. Thus evidence of a phenomenal mediation of behavior does not indicate necessarily that the phenomenal mediation is necessary for the occurrence of the particular motivational influence.

This overview of research on attempts to demonstrate the role of conscious and unconscious influences on motivation suggests an emerging conception of the role of conscious experience in goal-directed behavior. It does not appear to be the case that the hallmark of a goal-directed action sequence is one in which the individual is aware of the goals of his behavior and is able to describe with transparent clarity the relationship between actions and goals. At the same time the literature does not support a completely epi-phenomenalist position in which the unquestioned presence of conscious states and beliefs about goals and motives exists as a kind of idle chatter in the mind—safely ignored as being substantially incorrect and irrelevant in any case to the occurrence of goal-directed actions. The focusing of attention on relevant phenomenal states can indeed change and enhance the influence of those states on behavior. Not only can they magnify a particular goal-directed action, but also such results as those reported by Bandura and Schunck on the role of proximal goal-setting conditions suggest that the presence of a phenomenal intervention may disrupt the normal waxing and waning of goal-directed actions. Such a state of awareness may intrude upon the actions of an individual and continue to focus behavioral activity in a particular direction.

EPILOGUE

This book may be read as a commentary on a theory of goal-directed action that is implicit in the layman's conception of purposive behavior. The layman is content with an analysis of action that provides an account of an instrumental action in terms of the goal toward which it is directed. The goal is assumed to be transparent and phenomenally present. Thus, if a person were to answer the question "Why did you walk across the street?" by asserting that she wished to purchase a pack of cigarettes, a satisfactory explanation of the behavior of walking across the street, construed as an instrumental act, would have been rendered and any further inquiry into the reasons for the action would be unnecessary or perhaps even perverse. However, this conception of goal-directed action does not serve as an adequate model for the psychology of motivation. Chapter 2 presented data and theory that supports the notion that there is an important class of motivational problems that is best conceived in purposive terms. In Chapters 3 and 4 theory and research was reviewed that suggests that, in order to understand a particular goal-directed action sequence, one must understand its relation to other sequences that could potentially be expressed at the same time as the original sequence is dominant. Chapter 5 addressed the issue of the relationship between phenomenal and nonphenomenal influences and reviewed theory and research that suggests that the goals of human action are not always transparent and clearly understood by the actor.

Considered collectively, the chapters in this book in diverse ways suggest that the psychology of motivation cannot be built on the foundation of a simple model of goal-directed action in which each particular action sequence is considered in isolation of other action sequences and in which the goal of the action is known to the actor.

REFERENCES

Allison, J., Miller, M., & Wozny, M. Conservation in behavior. *Journal of Experimental Psychology: General*, 1979, *108*, 4–40.

Allport, F. H. *Social psychology.* Boston: Houghton Mifflin, 1924.

Andersson, K. G., & Hockey, G. R. J. Effects of cigarette smoking on incidental memory. *Psychopharmacology*, 1977, *52*, 223–226.

Aronson, E. The need for achievement as measured by graphic expression. In J. W. Atkinson (Ed.), *Motives in fantasy, action, and society.* Princeton, N. J.: Van Nostrand-Reinhold, 1958.

Atkinson, J. W. *Studies in projective measurement of achievement motivation.* Unpublished doctoral dissertation, University of Michigan, 1950.

Atkinson, J. W. Motivational determinants of risk-taking behavior. *Psychological Review*, 1957, *64*, 359–372.

Atkinson, J. W. (Ed.). *Motives in fantasy, action, and society.* Princeton, N. J.: Van Nostrand-Reinhold, 1958.

Atkinson, J. W. *An introduction to motivation.* Princeton, N. J.: Van Nostrand-Reinhold, 1964.

Atkinson, J. W., & Birch, D. *The dynamics of action.* New York: Wiley, 1970.

Atkinson, J. W., & Birch, D. *An introduction to motivation.* New York: Van Nostrand-Reinhold, 1978.

Atkinson, J. W., Bongort, K., & Price, L. H. Explorations using computer simulation to comprehend thematic apperceptive measurement of motivation. *Motivation and Emotion*, 1977, *1*, 1–27.

Atkinson, J. W., & Cartwright, D. Some neglected variables in contemporary conceptions of decision and performance. *Psychological Reports*, 1964, *14*, 575–590.

Atkinson, J. W., & Feather, N. T. (Eds.). *A theory of achievement motivation.* New York: Wiley, 1966.

Atkinson, J. W., & Litwin, G. H. Achievement motive and test anxiety conceived as motive to approach success and motive to avoid failure. *Journal of Abnormal and Social Psychology*, 1960, *60*, 52–63.

Bacon, S. J. Arousal and the range of cue utilization. *Journal of Experimental Psychology*, 1974, *102*, 81–87.

Bandura, A. Self-efficacy: Toward a unifying theory of behavioral change. *Psychological Review*, 1977, *84*, 191–215. (a)

Bandura, A. *Social learning theory.* Englewood Cliffs, N. J.: Prentice-Hall, 1977. (b)

Bandura, A. Self-efficacy mechanism in human agency. *American Psychologist*, 1982, *37*, 122–147.

Bandura, A., Adams, N. E., & Beyer, J. Cognitive processes mediating behavioral change. *Journal of Personality and Social Psychology*, 1977, *35*, 125–139.

Bandura, A., Blanchard, E. A., & Ritter, B. Relative efficacy of desensitization and modeling approaches for inducing behavioral, affective, and attitudinal changes. *Journal of Personality and Social Psychology*, 1969, *13*, 173–199.

Bandura, A., & Schunk, D. H. Cultivating competence, self-efficacy, and intrinsic interest through proximal self-motivation. *Journal of Personality and Social Psychology*, 1981, *41*, 586–598.

Beit-Hallahmi, B. Achievement motivation and economic growth. *Personality and Social Psychology Bulletin*, 1980, *6*, 210–215.

Berkowitz, L. Whatever happened to the frustration–aggression hypothesis? *American Behavioral Scientist*, 1978, *21*, 691–708.

Bindra, D., Paterson, A. L., & Strzelecki, J. On the relation between anxiety and conditioning. *Canadian Journal of Psychology*, 1955, *9*, 1–6.

Blank, T. O., Staff, I., & Shaver, P. Social facilitation of word associations: Further questions. *Journal of Personality and Social Psychology*, 1976, *34*, 725–733.

Blankenship, V. *Substitution·in achievement behavior.* Unpublished manuscript, Indiana University, undated.

Blankenship, V. *The relationship between consummatory value of success and achievement task difficulty.* Unpublished manuscript, Indiana University, undated.

Boden, M. A. *Purposive explanation in psychology.* Cambridge, Mass.: Harvard University Press, 1972.

Bolles, R. C. *Theory of motivation* (2nd ed.). New York: Harper & Row, 1975.

Bootzin, R. T., Herman, C. P., & Nicassio, P. The power of suggestion: Another examination of misattribution and insomnia. *Journal of Personality and Social Psychology*, 1976, *34*, 673–679.

Brehm, J. W., & Cohen, A. R. *Explorations in cognitive dissonance.* New York: Wiley, 1962.

Broadbent, D. E. *Decision and stress.* London: Academic Press, 1971.

Broadbent, D. E. The current status of noise research: A reply to Pulton. *Psychological Bulletin*, 1978, *85*, 1052–1067.

Broadhurst, P. L. The interaction of task difficulty and motivation: The Yerkes–Dodson Law revived. *Acta Psychologica*, 1959, *16*, 321–338.

Brody, N. Anxiety and the variability of word associates. *Journal of Abnormal and Social Psychology*, 1964, *68*, 331–334. (a)

Brody, N. Anxiety, induced muscular tension, and the statistical structure of binary response sequences. *Journal of Abnormal and Social Psychology*, 1964, *68*, 540–543. (b)

Brody, N. Information theory, motivation, and personality. In H. M. Schroder and P. Suedfeld (Eds.), *Personality theory and information processing.* New York: Ronald Press, 1971.

Brody, N. *Personality: Research and theory.* New York: Academic Press, 1972.

Brody, N. Social motivation. *Annual Review of Psychology*, 1980, *31*, 143–168.

Brody, N., Petersen, E., Upton, M., & Stabile, R. Anxiety, d-amphetamine, meprobamate, and the variability of word associates. *Psychological Reports*, 1967, *21*, 113–120.

Brown, J. S. *The motivation of behavior*. New York: McGraw-Hill, 1961.

Buckert, U., Meyer, W. U., & Schmalt, H.-D. Effects of difficulty and diagnosticity on choice among tasks in relation to achievement motivation and perceived ability. *Journal of Personality and Social Psychology*, 1979, *37*, 1172–1178.

Bunge, M. *Causality: The place of the causal principle in modern science*. Cambridge, Mass.: Harvard University Press, 1959.

Bursill, A. E. The restriction of peripheral vision during exposure to hot and humid conditions. *Quarterly Journal of Experimental Psychology*, 1958, *10*, 113–119.

Carver, C. S., Blaney, P. H., & Scheier, M. F. Focus of attention, chronic expectancy, and responses to a feared stimulus. *Journal of Personality and Social Psychology*, 1979, *37*, 1186–1195. (a)

Carver, C. S., Blaney, P. H., & Scheier, M. F. Reassertion and giving up: The interactive role of self-directed attention and outcome expectancy. *Journal of Personality and Social Psychology*, 1979, *37*, 1859–1870. (b)

Carver, C. S., & Scheier, M. F. *Attention and self-regulation: A control theory approach to human behavior*. New York: Springer-Verlag, 1981.

Child, I. L. Personality. *Annual Review of Psychology*, 1954, *2*, 149–170.

Church, R. M., Lolordo, V., Overmier, J. B., Solomon, R. L., & Turner, L. H. Cardiac responses to shock in curarized dogs: Effects of shock intensity and duration, warning signal, and prior experience with shock. *Journal of Comparative and Physiological Psychology*, 1966, *62*, 1–7.

Clark, C. *The conditions of economic progress* (3rd ed.). London: Macmillan, 1957.

Corcoran, D. W. J. Changes in heart rate and performance as a result of loss of sleep. *British Journal of Psychology*, 1964, *55*, 307–314.

Corteen, R. J., & Dunn, D. Shock-associated words in a nonattended message: A test for momentary awareness. *Journal of Experimental Psychology*, 1974, *102*, 1143–1144.

Corteen, R. J., & Wood, B. Autonomic responses to shock-associated words in an unattended channel. *Journal of Experimental Psychology*, 1972, *94*, 308–313.

Cottrell, N. B. Performance in the presence of other human beings: Mere presence, audience, and affiliation effects. In E. C. Simmel, R. A. Hoppe, & G. A. Milton (Eds.), *Social facilitation and imitative behavior*. Boston: Allyn & Bacon, 1968.

Cottrell, N. B. Social facilitation. In G. McClintock (Ed.), *Experimental social psychology*. New York: Holt, Rinehart & Winston, 1972.

Cottrell, N. B., Wack, D. L., Sekarak, G. J., & Rittle, R. H. Social facilitation of dominant responses by the presence of an audience and the mere presence of others. *Journal of Personality and Social Psychology*, 1968, *9*, 245–250.

Covington, M. V., & Omelich, C. L. Are causal attributions causal? A path analysis of the cognitive model of achievement motivation. *Journal of Personality and Social Psychology*, 1979, *37*, 1487–1504.

Craig, M. J., Humphreys, M. S., Rocklin, T., & Revelle, W. Impulsivity, neuroticism, and caffeine: Do they have additive effects on arousal? *Journal of Research in Personality*, 1979, *13*, 404–419.

Crockett, H. J., Jr. The achievement motive and differential occupational mobility in the United States. *American Sociological Review*, 1962, *27*, 191–204.

Crockett, H. J., Jr. Social class, education, and motive to achieve in differential occupational mobility. *The Sociological Quarterly*, 1964, *5*, 231–242.

Daee, S., & Wilding, J. M. Effects of high intensity white noise on short-term memory for position in a list and sequence. *British Journal of Psychology*, 1977, *68*, 335–349.

Danto, A. C. *Analytical philosophy of action*. London: Cambridge University Press, 1973.

Davies, D. R., & Jones, D. M. The effects of noise and incentives upon attention in short-term memory. *British Journal of Psychology,* 1975, *66,* 61–68.

Dawson, M. E., & Schell, A. M. Electrodermal responses to attended and nonattended significant stimuli during dichotic listening. *Journal of Experimental Psychology: Human Perception and Performance,* 1982, *8,* 315–324.

Day, U. Contemporary behaviorism and the concept of intention. In M. R. Jones (Ed.), *Nebraska Symposium on Motivation* (Vol. 23). Lincoln: University of Nebraska Press, 1975.

deCharms, R., & Moeller, G. H. Values expressed in American children's readers: 1800–1950 *Journal of Abnormal and Social Psychology,* 1962, *64,* 136–142.

Deci, E. L. *Intrinsic motivation.* New York: Plenum, 1975.

Duffy, E. *Activation and behavior.* New York: Wiley, 1962.

Duncan, J. W., & Laird, J. D. Cross-modality consistencies in individual differences in self-attribution. *Journal of Personality,* 1977, *45,* 191–206.

Duncan, J. W., & Laird, J. D. Positive and reverse placebo effects as a function of differences in cues used in self-perception. *Journal of Personality and Social Psychology,* 1980, *39,* 1024–1036.

Easterbrook, J. A. The effect of emotion on cue utilization and the organization of behavior. *Psychological Review,* 1959, *66,* 183–201.

Eisenberger, R., Karpman, M., & Trattner, J. What is the necessary and sufficient condition for reinforcement in the contingency situation? *Journal of Experimental Psychology,* 1967, *74,* 342–350.

Entwisle, D. R. To dispel fantasies about fantasy-based measures of achievement motivation. *Psychological Bulletin,* 1972, *77,* 377–391.

Epstein, S. Toward a unified theory of anxiety. In B. A. Maher (Ed.), *Progress in experimental personality research* (Vol. 4). New York: Academic Press, 1967.

Eriksen, C. W. Prediction from and interaction among multiple concurrent discriminative responses. *Journal of Experimental Psychology,* 1957, *53,* 353–359.

Eriksen, C. W. Unconscious processes. In M. R. Jones (Ed.), *Nebraska Symposium on Motivation* (Vol. 6). Lincoln: University of Nebraska Press, 1958.

Eriksen, C. W., & Wechsler, H. Some effects of experimentally induced anxiety upon discrimination. *Journal of Abnormal and Social Psychology,* 1955, *51,* 458–463.

Eysenck, M. W., & Folkard, S. Personality, time of day, and caffeine: Some theoretical and conceptual problems in Revelle et al. *Journal of Experimental Psychology: General,* 1980, *109,* 32–41.

Falk, J. L. The origin and function of adjunctive behavior. *Animal Learning and Behavior,* 1977, *5,* 325–335.

Feather, N. T. Subjective probability and decision under uncertainty. *Psychological Review,* 1959, *66,* 150–164.

Feather, N. T. The relationship of persistence at a task to expectation of success and achievement-related motives. *Journal of Abnormal and Social Psychology,* 1961, *63,* 552–561.

Fenigstein, A., Scheier, M. F., & Buss, A. H. Public and private self-consciousness: Assessment and theory. *Journal of Consulting and Clinical Psychology,* 1975, *43,* 522–527.

Festinger, L. *A theory of cognitive dissonance.* Stanford, Calif.: Stanford University Press, 1957.

Flew, A. *A rational animal.* Oxford, England: Oxford University Press, 1978.

Fowler, C. A., Wolford, A., Slade, R., & Tassinary, L. Lexical access with and without awareness. *Journal of Experimental Psychology: General,* 1981, *110,* 341–362.

Franks, C. M. Effects of food, drink, and tobacco deprivation on the conditioning of the eyeblink response. *Journal of Experimental Psychology,* 1957, *53,* 117–120.

Gainotti, G. The relationship between emotions and cerebral dominance: A review of the clinical and experimental evidence. In J. Gruzelier & P. Flor-Henry (Eds.), *Hemispheric asymmetries of function in psychopathology.* New York: Elsevier/North Holland Biomedical Press, 1979.

Geen, R. G., & Gange, J. J. Drive theory of social facilitation: Twelve years of theory and research. *Psychological Bulletin,* 1977, *84,* 1267–1288.

Gibbons, F. X., & Wright, R. A. Motivational biases in causal attributions of arousal. *Journal of Personality and Social Psychology,* 1981, *40,* 508–600.

Glucksberg, S. The influence of strength of drive on functional fixedness and perceptual recognition. *Journal of Experimental Psychology,* 1962, *63,* 36–41.

Goldiamond, I. Indicators of perception: Subliminal perception, subception, unconscious perception: An analysis in terms of psychophysical indicator methodology. *Psychological Bulletin,* 1958, *55,* 373–411.

Goulet, L. R. Anxiety (drive) and verbal learning: Implication for research and some methodological considerations. *Psychological Bulletin,* 1968, *69,* 235–247.

Hamilton, P., Hockey, B., & Rejman, M. The place of the concept of activation in human information processing. In S. Dornic (Ed.), *Attention and performance VI.* New York: Wiley, 1977.

Harrison, A. A. Mere exposure. *Advances in Experimental Social Psychology,*1977, *10,* 39–83.

Hartley, L. Noise does not impair by masking: A reply to Poulton's *Composite model for human performance in continuous noise. Psychological Review,* 1981, *88,* 86–89.

Hebb, D. O. Drives and the C.N.S. (conceptual nervous system). *Psychological Review,* 1955, *62,* 243–254.

Hempel, C. G., & Oppenheim, P. Studies in the logic of explanation. *Philosophy of Science,* 1948, *15,* 135–178.

Hilgard, E. R., Jones, L. V., & Kaplan, S. J. Conditioned discrimination as related to anxiety. *Journal of Experimental Psychology,* 1951, *42,* 94–99.

Hockey, G. R. J. Changes in attention allocation in a multi-component task under loss of sleep. *British Journal of Psychology,* 1970, *61,* 473–480. (a)

Hockey, G. R. J. Effect of loud noise on attentional selectivity. *Quarterly Journal of Experimental Psychology,* 1970, *22,* 28–36. (b)

Hockey, G. R. J. Signal probability and spatial location as possible bases for increased selectivity in noise. *Quarterly Journal of Experimental Psychology,* 1970, *22,* 37–42. (c)

Hockey, R. Stress and the cognitive components of skilled performance. In V. Hamilton & D. M. Warburton (Eds.), *Human stress and cognition.* Chichester, England: Wiley, 1979.

Hoffman, H. S., & Solomon, R. L. An opponent process theory of motivation: III. Some affective dynamics in imprinting. *Learning and Motivation,* 1974, *5,* 149–164.

Hörmann, H., & Osterkamp, U. Über den Einfluss von kontinuierlichem Lärm auf die Organisation von Gedachnisinhalten. *Zeitschrift für Experimentelle und Angewandte Psychologie,* 1966, *13,* 31–38.

Howes, D. H., & Solomon, R. L. A note on McGinnes' *Emotionality and Perceptual Defense. Psychological Review,* 1950, *57,* 229–240.

Hull, C. L. Knowledge and purpose as habit mechanisms. *Psychological Review,* 1930, *37,* 511–525.

Hull, C. L. Goal attraction and directing ideas conceived as habit phenomena. *Psychological Review,* 1931, *38,* 487–506.

Hull, C. L. *Principles of behavior.* New York: Appleton-Century-Crofts, 1943.

Hull, C. L. *A behavior system.* New Haven, Conn.: Yale University Press, 1952.

Humphreys, M. S., Revelle, W., Simon, L., & Gilliland, K. Individual differences in diurnal rhythms and multiple activation states: A reply to M. W. Eysenck and Folkard. *Journal of Experimental Psychology: General,* 1980, *109,* 42–48.

Kahneman, D. *Attention and effort.* Englewood Cliffs, N. J.: Prentice–Hall, 1973.

Kamin, L. J., & Fedorchak, O. The Taylor scale, hunger and verbal learning. *Canadian Journal of Psychology,* 1957, *11,* 212–218.

Kausler, D. H., & Trapp, E. P. Methodological considerations in the construct validation of drive-oriented scales. *Psychological Bulletin,* 1959, *56,* 152–157.

Koch, S. Clark L. Hull. In W. K. Estes, S. Koch, K. MacCorquodale, P. E. Meehl, C. G. Mueller, Jr., W. H. Schoenfeld, & W. S. Verplanck (Eds.), *Modern learning theory: A critical analysis of five examples.* New York: Appleton-Century-Crofts, 1954.

Koch, S. Epilogue. In S. Koch (Ed.), *Psychology: A study of a science* (Vol. 3). New York: McGraw-Hill, 1959.

Kolb, D. Achievement motivation training for underachieving high-school boys. *Journal of Personality and Social Psychology,* 1965, *2,* 783–792.

Kuethe, J. L., & Eriksen, C. W. Personality, anxiety and muscle tension as determinants of response stereotypy. *Journal of Abnormal and Social Psychology,* 1957, *54,* 400–404.

Kuhl, J., & Blankenship, V. Behavioral change in a constant environment: Shift to more difficult tasks with constant probability of success. *Journal of Personality and Social Psychology,* 1979, *37,* 549–561. (a)

Kuhl, J., & Blankenship, V. The dynamic theory of achievement motivation: From episodic to dynamic thinking. *Psychological Review,* 1979, *86,* 141–151. (b)

Kunst-Wilson, W. R., & Zajonc, R. B. Affective discrimination of stimuli that cannot be recognized. *Science,* 1980, *207,* 557–558.

Lacey, J. L. Somatic response patterning and stress: Some revisions of activation theory. In M. H. Appley & R. Trumbull (Eds.), *Psychological stress.* New York: Appleton-Century-Crofts, 1967.

Laird, J. D. Self-attribution of emotion: The effects of expressive behavior on the quality of emotional experience. *Journal of Personality and Social Psychology,* 1974, *29,* 475–486.

Langer, E. J., Blank, A., & Chanowitz, B. The mindlessness of ostensibly thoughtful action: The role of placebic information in interpersonal interaction. *Journal of Personality and Social Psychology,* 1978, *36,* 635–642.

Lazarus, R. A substitutive-defensive conception of apperceptive fantasy. In J. Kagan & G. S. Lesser (Eds.), *Contemporary issues in thematic apperceptive methods.* Springfield, Ill.: Charles C Thomas, 1961.

Lazarus, R. S., & McCleary, R. A. Autonomic discrimination without awareness: A study of subception. *Psychological Review,* 1951, *58,* 113–122.

Lewin, K., Dembo, T., Festinger, L., & Sears, P. S. Level of aspiration. In J. McV. Hunt (Ed.), *Personality and the behavior disorders.* New York: Ronald Press, 1944.

Lindsley, D. B. Psychophysiology and motivation. In M. R. Jones (Ed.), *Nebraska Symposium on Motivation* (Vol. 5). Lincoln: University of Nebraska Press, 1957.

Littig, L. W., & Yeracaris, C. A. Achievement motivation and intergenerational occupational motility. *Journal of Personality and Social Psychology,* 1965, *1,* 386–389.

Lovaas, O. I. The relationship of anxiety level and shock on a paired-associate verbal task. *Journal of Experimental Psychology,* 1960, *59,* 145–152.

Lowell, E. L. *A methodological study of projectively measured achievement motivation.* Unpublished master's thesis. Wesleyan University, 1950.

McClelland, D. C. Methods of measuring human motivation. In J. W. Atkinson (Ed.), *Motives in fantasy, action, and society.* Princeton, N. J.: Van Nostrand-Reinhold, 1958.

McClelland, D. C. *The achieving society.* Princeton, N. J.: Van Nostrand-Reinhold, 1961.

McClelland, D. C. Toward a theory of motive acquisition. *American Psychologist,* 1965, *20,* 321–333.

McClelland, D. C., Atkinson, J. W., Clark, R. A., & Lowell, E. L. *The achievement motive.* New York: Appleton-Century-Crofts, 1953.

McClelland, D. C., & Winter, D. G. *Motivating economic achievement*. New York: Free Press, 1969.

MacCorquodale, K., & Meehl, P. E. Edward C. Tolman. In W. K. Estes, S. Koch, K. MacCorquodale, P. E. Meehl, C. G. Mueller, Jr., W. H. Schoenfeld, & W. S. Verplanck (Eds.), *Modern learning theory: A critical analysis of five examples*. New York: Appleton-Century-Crofts, 1954.

McDougall, W. Outline of psychology. New York: Scribner's, 1923. (a)

McDougall, W. Purposive or mechanical psychology? *Psychological Review*, 1923, *30*, 273–288. (b)

McGinnies, E. Emotionality and perceptual defense. *Psychological Review*, 1949, *56*, 244–251.

Mahone, C. H. Fear of failure and unrealistic vocational aspiration. *Journal of Abnormal and Social Psychology*, 1960, *60*, 253–261.

Mandler, G., & Sarason, S. B. A study of anxiety and learning. *Journal of Abnormal and Social Psychology*, 1952, *47*, 166–173.

Marcel, A. J. Explaining selective effects of prior context on perception: The need to distinguish conscious and pre-conscious processes. In J. Requin (Ed.), *Anticipation and behaviour*. Paris: Centre National de la Recherche Scientifique, 1980.

Marcel, A. Conscious and unconscious reading: The effects of visual masking on word perception. *Cognitive Psychology*, in press.

Markus, H. The effect of mere presence on social facilitation: An unobtrusive test. *Journal of Experimental Social Psychology*, 1978, *14*, 389–397.

Marshall, G. D., & Zimbardo, P. G. Affective consequences of inadequately explained physiological arousal. *Journal of Personality and Social Psychology*, 1979, *37*, 970–988.

Maslach, C. Negative emotional biasing of unexpected arousal. *Journal of Personality and Social Psychology*, 1979, *37*, 953–969.

Matlin, M. M., & Zajonc, R. B. Social facilitation of word associations. *Journal of Personality and Social Psychology*, 1968, *10*, 435–460.

Mednick, M. T. Mediated generalization and the incubation effect as a function of manifest anxiety. *Journal of Abnormal and Social Psychology*, 1957, *55*, 315–321.

Meehl, P. E. On the circularity of the law of effect. *Psychological Bulletin*, 1950, *47*, 52–75.

Mehrabian, A. Male and female scales of tendency to achieve. *Educational and Psychological Measurement*, 1968, *28*, 493–502.

Meyer, D. R., & Noble, M. E. Summation of manifest anxiety and muscular tension. *Journal of Experimental Psychology*, 1958, *55*, 599–602.

Meyer, W. U., Folkes, V. S., & Weiner, B. The perceived informational value and affective consequences of choice behavior and intermediate difficulty task selection. *Journal of Research in Personality*, 1976, *10*, 410–423.

Mineka, S., Suomi, S. J., & Delizio, R. Multiple separations in adolescent monkeys: An opponent-process interpretation. *Journal of Experimental Psychology: General*, 1981, *110*, 56–85.

Mosher, D. L. Measurement of guilt in females by self-report inventories. *Journal of Consulting and Clinical Psychology*, 1968, *32*, 690–695.

Moulton, R. W. Effects of success and failure on level of aspiration as related to achievement motives. *Journal of Personality and Social Psychology*, 1965, *1*, 399–406.

Mueller, J. H. Anxiety and encoding processes in memory. *Personality and Social Psychology Bulletin*, 1979, *5*, 288–294.

Murray, H. A. *Explorations in personality*. New York: Oxford University Press, 1938.

Nagel, E. *The structure of science*. New York: Harcourt, Brace & World, 1961.

Nisbett, R. E., & Schachter, S. Cognitive manipulation of pain. *Journal of Experimental Social Psychology*, 1966, *2*, 227–236.

Nisbett, R. E., & Wilson, T. D. Telling more than we can know: Verbal reports on mental processes. *Psychological Review,* 1977, *84,* 231–259.

O'Connor, P., Atkinson, J. W., & Horner, M. Motivational implications of ability grouping in the schools. In J. W. Atkinson & N. T. Feather (Ed.), *A theory of achievement motivation.* New York: Wiley, 1966.

Pepler, R. D. Warmth and lack of sleep: Accuracy of activity reduced. *Journal of Comparative and Physiological Psychology,* 1959, *52,* 446–450.

Perin, C. T. Behavior potentiality as a joint function of the amount of training and the degree of hunger at the time of extinction. *Journal of Experimental Psychology,* 1942, *30,* 93–113.

Perry, R. B. Docility and purposiveness. *Psychological Review,* 1918, *25,* 1–21.

Perry, R. B. A behavioristic view of purpose. *Journal of Philosophy,* 1921, *18,* 85–101. (a)

Perry, R. B. The cognitive interest and its refinement. *Journal of Philosophy,* 1921, *18,* 365–375. (b)

Perry, R. B. The independent variability of purpose and belief. *Journal of Philosophy,* 1921, *18,* 169–180. (c)

Peters, R. S. *The concept of motivation.* London: Routledge & Kegan Paul, 1958.

Pittman, T. S., Cooper, E. E., & Smith, T. W. Attribution of causality and the overjustification effect. *Personality and Social Psychology Bulletin,* 1977, *3,* 280–283.

Posner, M. I. *Chronometric explorations of mind.* Hillsdale, N. J.: Erlbaum, 1978.

Poulton, E. C. Continuous intense noise masks auditory feedback and inner speech. *Psychological Bulletin,* 1977, *84,* 977–1001.

Poulton, E. C. Composite model for human performance in continuous noise. *Psychological Review,* 1979, *86,* 361–375.

Poulton, E. C. Not so! Rejoinder to Hartley on masking in continuous noise. *Psychological Review,* 1981, *88,* 90–92.

Premack, D. Toward empirical behavioral laws: I. Positive reinforcement. *Psychological Review,* 1959, *66,* 219–233.

Premack, D. Rate differential reinforcement in monkey manipulation. *Journal of the Experimental Analysis of Behavior,* 1963, *6,* 81–89.

Premack, D. Reinforcement theory. In M. R. Jones (Ed.), *Nebraska Symposium on Motivation* (Vol. 13). Lincoln: University of Nebraska Press, 1965.

Rachlin, H., Green, L., Kasel, J. H., & Battalio, R. C. Economic demand theory and psychological studies of choice. In G. H. Bower (Ed.), *The psychology of learning and motivation. Advances in research and theory* (Vol. 10). New York: Academic Press, 1976.

Raynor, J. O. Future orientation and motivation of immediate activity: An elaboration of the theory of achievement motivation. *Psychological Review,* 1969, *76,* 606–610.

Raynor, J. O. Relationships between achievement-related motives, future orientation, and academic performance. *Journal of Personality and Social Psychology,* 1970, *15,* 28–33.

Raynor, J. O. Future orientation in the study of achievement motivation. In J. W. Atkinson & J. O. Raynor (Eds.), *Motivation and achievement.* New York: Wiley, 1974.

Raynor, J. O., & Rubin, I. S. Effects of achievement motivation and future orientation on level of performance. *Journal of Personality and Social Psychology,* 1971, *17,* 36–41.

Reuter-Lorenz, P., & Davidson, R. J. Differential contributions of the two cerebral hemispheres to the perception of happy and sad faces. *Neuropsychologia,* 1981, *19,* 609–613.

Revelle, W., & Humphreys, M. *Personality, motivation, and performance: A theory of individual differences and information processing.* Unpublished manuscript, Northwestern University, 1980.

Revelle, W., Humphreys, M. S., Simon, L., & Gilliland, K. The interactive effect of personality, time of day, and caffeine: A test of the arousal model. *Journal of Experimental Psychology: General,* 1980, *109,* 1–31.

Ryan, T. A. *Intentional behavior.* New York: Ronald Press, 1970.

Ryle, G. *The concept of mind.* London: Hutchinson's University Library, 1949.

Schachter, S. The interaction of cognitive and physiological determinants of emotional state. In L. Berkowitz (Ed.), *Advances in experimental social psychology* (Vol. 1). New York: Academic Press, 1964.

Schachter, S. Nicotine regulation in heavy and light smokers. *Journal of Experimental Psychology: General,* 1977, *106,* 5–12.

Schachter, S., Kozlowski, L. T., & Silverstein, B. Effects of urinary pH on cigarette smoking. *Journal of Experimental Psychology: General,* 1977, *106,* 13–19.

Schachter, S., Silverstein, B., Kozlowski, L. T., Herman, C. P., & Lieblin, B. Effects of stress on cigarette smoking and urinary pH. *Journal of Experimental Psychology: General,* 1977, *106,* 24–30.

Schachter, S., Silverstein, B., Kozlowski, L. T., Perlick, D., Herman, C. P., & Liebling, B. Studies of the interaction of psychological and pharmacological determinants of smoking. *Journal of Experimental Psychology: General,* 1977, *106,* 3–4.

Schachter, S., & Singer, J. E. Cognitive, social and physiological determinants of emotional state. *Psychological Review,* 1962, *69,* 379–399.

Schachter, S., & Singer, J. E. Comments on the Maslach and Marshall–Zimbardo experiments. *Journal of Personality and Social Psychology,* 1979, *37,* 989–995.

Schachter, S., & Wheeler, L. Epinephrine, chlorpromazine, and amusement. *Journal of Abnormal and Social Psychology,* 1962, *65,* 121–128.

Scheier, M. F. Self-awareness, self-consciousness, and angry aggression. *Journal of Personality,* 1976, *44,* 627–644.

Scheier, M. F., & Carver, C. S. Self-focused attention and the experience of emotion: Attraction, repulsion, elation and depression. *Journal of Personality and Social Psychology,* 1977, *35,* 625–636.

Schmalt, H.-D. *Die Messung des Leitstungsmotivs.* Göttingen, West Germany: Hogrefe, 1976.

Schwartz, G. E., Ahern, G. L., & Brown, S. L. Lateralized facial muscle response to positive and negative emotional stimuli. *Psychophysiology,* 1979, *16,* 561–571.

Schwartz, S. Arousal and recall. Effects of noise on two retrieval strategies. *Journal of Experimental Psychology,* 1974, *102,* 896–898.

Seamon, J. G., Brody, N., & Kauff, D. M. Feeling and thinking: Tests of a model of independent processing of affect and cognition. *Journal of Experimental Psychology: Human Learning and Memory,* 1983, in press.

Seltzer, R. A. Simulation of the dynamics of action. *Psychological Reports,* 1973, *32,* 859–872.

Seltzer, R. A., & Sawusch, J. R. A program for computer simulation of the dynamics of action. In J. W. Atkinson & J. O. Raynor (Eds.), *Motivation and achievement.* New York: Halsted/Wiley, 1974.

Silverman, L. H. Psychoanalytic theory. The reports of my death are greatly exaggerated. *American Psychologist,* 1976, *31,* 621–637.

Silverman, L. H., Bronstein, A., & Mendelsohn, E. The further use of the subliminal psychodynamic activation method for the experimental study of the clinical theory of psychoanalysis. *Psychotherapy: Theory, Research and Practice,* 1976, *13,* 2–16.

Silverman, L. H., Martin, A., Ungaro, R., & Mendelsohn, E. Effect of subliminal stimulation of symbiotic fantasies on behavior modification treatment of obesity. *Journal of Consulting and Clinical Psychology,* 1978, *46,* 432–441.

Silverman, L. H., Ross, D. L., Adler, J. M., & Lustig, D. A. Simple research paradigm for demonstrating subliminal psychodynamic activation: Effects of oedipal stimuli on dart-throwing accuracy in college males. *Journal of Abnormal Psychology,* 1978, *87,* 341–357

Silverman, L. H., & Spiro, R. H. The effects of subliminal, supraliminal and vocalized aggression on the ego functioning of schizophrenics. *Journal of Nervous and Mental Disease,* 1968, *146,* 50–61.

Silverstein, B., Kozlowski, L. T., & Schachter, S. Social life, cigarette smoking, and urinary pH. *Journal of Experimental Psychology: General,* 1977, *106,* 20–23.

Skinner, B. F. *The behavior of organisms. An experimental analysis.* Englewood Cliffs, N. J.: Prentice-Hall, 1938.

Skinner, B. F. *Science and human behavior.* New York: Macmillan, 1953.

Skolnick, A. Motivational imagery and behavior over twenty years. *Journal of Consulting Psychology,* 1966, *30,* 463–478.

Smith, C. P., & Feld, S. How to learn the method of content analysis for n achievement, n affiliation, and n power. In J. W. Atkinson (Ed.), *Motives in fantasy, action, and society.* Princeton, N.J.: Van Nostrand-Reinhold, 1958.

Solomon, R. L. Recent experiments testing an opponent-process theory of acquired motivation. *Acta Neurobiological Experimentalis,* 1980, *40,* 271–289. (a)

Solomon, R. L. The opponent-process theory of acquired motivation. The costs of pleasure and the benefits of pain. *American Psychologist,* 1980, *35,* 691–712. (b)

Solomon, R. L., & Corbit, J. D. An opponent-process theory of motivation: I. Temporal dynamics of affect. *Psychological Review,* 1974, *81,* 119–145.

Spence, J. T., & Spence, K. W. The motivational components of manifest anxiety: Drive and drive stimuli. In C. D. Spielberger (Ed.), *Anxiety and behavior.* New York: Academic Press, 1966.

Spence, K. W. *Behavior theory and conditioning.* New Haven, Conn.: Yale University Press, 1956.

Spence, K. W. A theory of emotionally based drive (D) and its relation to performance in simple learning situations. *American Psychologist,* 1958, *13,* 131–141.

Spence, K. W. Anxiety (drive) level and performance in eyelid conditioning. *Psychological Bulletin,* 1964, *61,* 124–139.

Spence, K. W., Farber, I. E., & McFann, H. H. The relation of anxiety (drive) level to performance on competitional and noncompetitional pained-associates learning. *Journal of Experimental Psychology,* 1956, 52, 296–305.

Spence, K. W., Taylor, J. A., & Ketchel, R. Anxiety (drive) level and degree of competition in paired-associates learning. *Journal of Experimental Psychology,* 1956, *52,* 306–310.

Spielberger, C. D., & Smith, L. H. Anxiety (drive), stress, and serial-position effects in serial-verbal learning. *Journal of Experimental Psychology,* 1966, *72,* 589–595.

Staddon, J. E. R. Regulation and time allocation: Comment on conservation in behavior. *Journal of Experimental Psychology: General,* 1979, *108,* 35–40.

Standish, R. R., & Champion, R. A. Task difficulty and drive in verbal learning. *Journal of Experimental Psychology,* 1960, *59,* 361–365.

Starr, M. D. An opponent-process theory of motivation. VI. Time and intensity variables in the development of separation-induced distress calling in ducklings. *Journal of Experimental Psychology: Animal Behavior Processes,* 1978, *4,* 338–355.

Storms, M. D., & Nisbett, R. E. Insomnia and the attribution process. *Journal of Personality and Social Psychology,* 1970, *2,* 319–328.

Taylor, C. *The explanation of behavior.* New York: Humanities Press, 1964.

Taylor, J. A. The relationship of anxiety to the conditioned eyelid response. *Journal of Experimental Psychology,* 1951, *41,* 81–92.

Taylor, J. A. A personality scale of manifest anxiety. *Journal of Abnormal and Social Psychology,* 1953, *48,* 285–290.

Taylor, J. A. The effects of anxiety level and psychological stress on verbal learning. *Journal of Abnormal and Social Psychology,* 1958, *57,* 55–60.

Taylor, J. A., & Chapman, J. P. Anxiety and the learning of paired-associates. *American Journal of Psychology,* 1955, *68,* 671.

Taylor, R. *Action and purpose.* Englewood Cliffs, N. J.: Prentice-Hall, 1966.

Thorndike, E. L. *Animal intelligence.* New York: Macmillan, 1911.

Timberlake, W. A molar equilibrium theory of learned performance. In G. H. Bower (Ed.), *The psychology of learning and motivation* (Vol. 14). New York: Academic Press, 1980.

Timberlake, W., & Allison, J. Response deprivation: An empirical approach to instrumental performance. *Psychological Review,* 1974, *81,* 146–164.

Tolman, E. C. Instinct and purpose. *Psychological Review,* 1920, *27,* 217–233.

Tolman, E. C. A new formula for behaviorism. *Psychological Review,* 1922, *29,* 44–53.

Tolman, E. C. The nature of instinct. *Psychological Bulletin,* 1923, *20,* 200–216.

Tolman, E. C. Behaviorism and purpose. *Journal of Philosophy,* 1925, *22,* 36–41. (a)

Tolman, E. C. Purpose and cognition: The determiners of animal learning. *Psychological Review,* 1925, *32,* 285–297. (b)

Tolman, E. C. A behavioristic theory of ideas. *Psychological Review,* 1926, *33,* 352–369.

Tolman, E. C. *Purposive behavior in animals and men.* New York: Century, 1932.

Tolman, E. C. The determiners of behavior at a choice point. *Psychological Review,* 1938, *45,* 1–41.

Tolman, E. C. Cognitive maps in rats and men. *Psychological Review,* 1948, *55,* 189–208.

Tolman, E. C. Principles of performance. *Psychological Review,* 1955, *62,* 315–326.

Triplett, N. The dynamogenic factors in pacemaking and competition. *American Journal of Psychology,* 1898, *9,* 507–533.

Trope, Y. Seeking information about one's own ability as a determinant of choice among tasks. *Journal of Personality and Social Psychology,* 1975, *32,* 1004–1013.

Trope, Y., & Brickman, P. Difficulty and diagnosticity as determinants of choice among tasks. *Journal of Personality and Social Psychology,* 1975, *31,* 918–926.

Turvey, M. T. On peripheral and central processes in vision: Inferences from an information-processing analysis of masking with patterned stimuli. *Psychological Review,* 1973, *80,* 1–52.

Underwood, B. J., & Schulz, R. W. *Meaningfulness and verbal learning.* Philadelphia: Lippincott, 1960.

Velten, E. A laboratory task for induction of mood states. *Behavior Research and Therapy,* 1968, *6,* 473–482.

von Wright, G. H. *Causality and determinism.* New York: Columbia University Press, 1974.

Wardlaw, K. A., & Kroll, N. E. A. Autonomic responses to shock-associated words in a nonattended message: A failure to replicate. *Journal of Experimental Psychology: Human Perception and Performance,* 1976, *2,* 357–360.

Watson, J. B. *Psychology from the standpoint of a behaviorist* (2nd ed.). Philadelphia: Lippincott, 1919.

Weber, M. *The protestant ethic and the spirit of capitalism.* New York: Scribner's Sons, 1958. (Originally published, 1904.)

Weiner, B. The effects of unsatisfied achievement motivation on persistence and subsequent performance. *Journal of Personality,* 1965, *33,* 428–442.

Weiner, B. The role of success and failure in the learning of easy and complex tasks. *Journal of Personality and Social Psychology,* 1966, *3,* 339–344.

Weiner, B. *Theories of motivation: From mechanism to cognition.* Chicago: Rand McNally, 1972.

Weiner, B. (Ed.). *Achievement motivation and attribution theory.* Morristown, N. J.: General Learning Press, 1974.

Weiner, B. *Human motivation.* New York: Holt, Rinehart and Winston, 1980.

Weiner, B., & Sierad, J. Misattribution for failure and enhancement of achievement strivings. *Journal of Personality and Social Psychology,* 1975, *31,* 415–421.

Weiss, R. F., & Miller, F. G. The drive theory of social facilitation. *Psychological Review,* 1971, *78,* 44–57.

Wilkinson, R. T. Rest pauses in a task affected by lack of sleep. *Ergonomics,* 1959, *2,* 373–380.

Wilkinson, R. T. Sleep deprivation. In O. G. Edholm & A. L. Bacharach (Eds.), *The physiology of human survival.* London: Academic Press, 1965.

Williams, S. B. Resistance to extinction as a function of the number of reinforcements. *Journal of Experimental Psychology,* 1938, *23,* 506–521.

Wilson, T. D., & Linville, P. W. Improving the academic performance of college freshmen: Attribution theory revisited. *Journal of Personality and Social Psychology,* 1982, *42,* 367–376.

Wilson, W. R. Feeling more than we can know: Exposure affects without learning. *Journal of Personality and Social Psychology,* 1979, *37,* 811–831.

Winter, D. G. *The power motive.* New York: Free Press, 1973.

Winter, D. G., & Stewart, A. J. Power motive reliability as a function of retest instructions. *Journal of Consulting and Clinical Psychology,* 1977, *45,* 436–440.

Winterbottom, M. R. *The relation of childhood training in independence to achievement motivation.* Unpublished doctoral dissertation, University of Michigan, 1953.

Winterbottom, M. R. The relation of need for achievement to learning experiences in independence and mastery. In J. W. Atkinson (Ed.), *Motives in fantasy, action, and society.* Princeton, N. J.: Van Nostrand-Reinhold, 1958.

Wright, L. *Teleological explanations.* Berkeley: University of California Press, 1976.

Yerkes, R. M., & Dodson, J. O. The relation of strength of stimulus to rapidity of habit formation. *Journal of Comparative Neurology and Psychology,* 1908, *18,* 459–482.

Zajonc, R. B. Social facilitation. *Science,* 1965, *149,* 269–274.

Zajonc, R. B. Attitudinal effects of mere exposure. *Journal of Personality and Social Psychology Monograph,* 1968, *9*(Part 2), 1–28.

Zajonc, R. B., & Sales, S. M. Social facilitation of dominant and subordinate responses. *Journal of Experimental Social Psychology,* 1966, *2,* 160–168.

Zimbardo, P. G. *The cognitive control of motivation.* Glenville, Ill.: Scott, Foresman and Co., 1969.

Zimbardo, P. G., Cohen, A., Weisenberg, M., Dworkin, L., & Firestone, I. The control of experimental pain. In P. G. Zimbardo, *The cognitive control of motivation.* Glenville, Ill.: Scott, Foresman and Co., 1969.

Zuckerman, M. *Sensation seeking: Beyond the optimal level of arousal.* Hillsdale, N. J.: Erlbaum, 1979.

AUTHOR INDEX

Numbers in italics refer to the pages on which the complete references are listed.

A

Adams, N. E., 190, *212*
Adler, J. M., 156, *219*
Ahern, G. L., 151, *219*
Allison, J., 116, 117, 118, 119, *211, 221*
Allport, F. H., 27, *211*
Anderson, K. G., 54, *211*
Aronson, E., 73, *211*
Atkinson, J. W., 60, 61, 71, 72, 73, 74, 76, 77, 78, 84, 86, 95, 97, 98, 99, 102, 103, *211, 212, 218*

B

Bacon, S. J., 39, *212*
Bandura, A., 188, 189, 190, 191, *212*
Battialio, R. C., 120, *218*
Beit-Hallahmi, B., 65, 68, *212*
Berkowitz, L., 176, *212*
Beyer, J., 190, *212*

Bindra, D., 18, *212*
Birch, D., 77, 97, 98, *211*
Blanchard, E. A., 189, 190, *212*
Blaney, P. H., 196, 197, *213*
Blank, A., 164, *216*
Blank, T. O., 28, *212*
Blankenship, V., 104, *212, 216*
Boden, M. A., 3, *212*
Bolles, R. C., 10, *212*
Bongort, K., 102, *211*
Bootzin, R. T., 178, *212*
Brehm, J. M., 170, *212*
Brickman, P., 76, *221*
Broadbent, D. E., 36, 44, 49, 53, 170, *212*
Broadhurst, P. L., 32, *212*
Brody, N., 26, 46, 47, 141, 145, 150, 151, 202, *212, 219*
Bronstein, A., 158, 160, *219*
Brown, J. S., 45, *213*

Brown, S. L., 151, *219*
Buckert, U., 81, *213*
Bunge, M., 2, *213*
Bursill, A. E., 34, *213*
Buss, A. H., 194, *214*

C
Cartwright, D., 86, *211*
Carver, C. S., 193, 194, 196, 197, *213, 219*
Champion, R. A., 22, *220*
Chanowitz, B., 164, *216*
Chapman, J. P., 20, *221*
Child, I. L., 24, *213*
Church, R. M., 121, *213*
Clark, C., 65, *213*
Clark, L., 4, *216*
Clark, R. A., 60, 61, *217*
Cohen, A., 171, 175, *222*
Cohen, A. R., 170, *212*
Cooper, E. E., 204, *218*
Corbit, J. D., 121, 135, 136, *220*
Corcoran, D. W. J., 49, *213*
Cortell, N. B., 29, 30, *213*
Coteen, R. J., 146, 147, *213*
Covington, M. V., 185, *213*
Craig, M. J., 53, *213*
Crockett, H. J., Jr., 62, *213*

D
Daee, S., 43, *213*
Danto, A. C., 3, *213*
Davidson, R. J., 151, *218*
Davies, D. R., 49, *214*
Dawson, M. E., 146, 148, *214*
Day, U., 3, *214*
deCharms, R., 66, *214*
Deci, E. L., 205, *214*
Delizio, R., 125, *217*
Dembo, T., 70, *216*
Dodson, J. O., 32, *222*
Duffy, E., 45, *214*
Duncan, J. W., 177, 178, *214*
Dunn, D., 146, 147, *213*
Dworkin, L., 171, 175, *222*

E
Easterbrook, J. A., 32, 34, *214*
Edward, C., 5, *216*
Eisenberger, R., 117, *214*
Entwisle, D. R., 101, *214*

Epstein, S., 121, 129, 130, 131, 132, *214*
Eriksen, C. W., 35, 47, 142, *214, 216*
Eyseneck, M. W., 45, 51, *214*

F
Falk, J. L., 132, *214*
Farber, I. E., 21, *220*
Feather, N. T., 70, 76, 82, 84, 86, *211, 214*
Fedorchak, O., 20, *216*
Feld, S., 60, *220*
Fenigstein, A., 194, *214*
Festinger, L., 70, 170, *214, 216*
Firestone, I., 171, 175, *222*
Flew, A., 4, *214*
Folkard, S., 45, 51, *214*
Folkes, V. S., 76, 79, *217*
Fowler, C. A., 153, 154, 203, *214*
Franks, C. M., 25, *214*

G
Gainotti, G., 151, *215*
Gange, J. J., 27, *215*
Geen, R. G., 27, *215*
Gibbons, F. X., 177, *215*
Gilliland, K., 45, 51, *215, 218*
Glucksberg, S., 36, *215*
Goldiamond, I., 142, *215*
Goulet, L. R., 21, 22, *215*
Green, L., 120, *218*

H
Hamilton, P., 40, 41, 42, 57, *215*
Harrison, A. A., 144, *215*
Hartley, L., 53, *215*
Hebb, D. O., 45, *215*
Hempel, C. G., 2, *215*
Herman, C. P., 54, 178, *212, 219*
Hilgard, E. R., 19, *215*
Hockey, B., 40, 41, 42, 57, *215*
Hockey, G. R. J., 37, 44, 54, *211, 215*
Hockey, R., 48, 49, *215*
Hoffman, H. S., 124, *215*
Hörmann, H., 43, *215*
Horner, M., 84, *218*
Howes, D. H., 141, *215*
Hull, C. L., 7, 8, 10, 12, 13, 112, *215*
Humphreys, M. S., 45, 49, 50, 51, 53, *213, 215, 218*

J

Jones, D. M., 49, *214*
Jones, L. V., 19, *215*

K

Kahnemann, D., 50, *216*
Kamin, L. J., 20, *216*
Kaplan, S. J., 19, *215*
Karpman, M., 117, *214*
Kasel, J. H., 120, *218*
Kauff, D. M., 145, 150, 151, *219*
Kausler, D. H., 24, *216*
Ketchel, R., 21, *220*
Kolb, D., 68, *216*
Korch, S., 4, *216*
Kozlowski, L. T., 54, *219, 220*
Kroll, N. E. A., 146, 147, *221*
Kuethe, J. L., 35, 47, *216*
Kuhl, J., 104, *216*
Kunst-Wilson, W. R., 144, *216*

L

Lacey, J. L., 45, *216*
Laird, J. D., 177, 178, *214, 216*
Langer, E. J., 164, *216*
Lazarus, R. S., 141, *216*
Lewin, K., 70, *216*
Lieblin, B., 54, *219*
Lindsley, D. B., 45, *216*
Linville, P. W., 187, *222*
Littig, L. W., 62, *216*
Litwin, G. H., 74, 78, *212*
Lolordo, V., 121, *213*
Lovaas, O. I., 21, *216*
Lowell, E. L., 60, 61, 62, *216, 217*
Lustig, D. A., 156, *219*

M

McCleary, R. A., 141, *216*
McClelland, D. C., 59, 60, 61, 63, 64, 65,
    66, 68, 69, 73, 78, *217*
MacCorquodale, K., 5, *216*
McDougall, W., 5, *217*
McFann, H. H., 21, *220*
McGinnies, E., 141, *217*
Mahone, C. H., 74, 79, *216*
Mandler, G., 72, 105, *217*
Marcel, A. J., 153, 154, *217*
Markus, H., 30, 31, *217*
Marshall, G. D., 169, *217*

Martin, A., 157, *219*
Maslach, C., 169, *217*
Matlin, M. M., 28, *217*
Mednick, M. T., 18, *217*
Meehl, C. G., 5, *216*
Meehl, P. E., 112, *217*
Mehrabian, A., 77, 80, *217*
Mendelsohn, E., 157, 158, 160, *219*
Meyer, D. R., 47, *217*
Meyer, W. U., 76, 79, 81, *213, 217*
Miller, F. G., 28, *222*
Miller, M., 117, 118, 119, *211*
Mineka, S., 125, *217*
Moeller, G. H., 66, *214*
Mosher, D. L., 177, *217*
Moulton, R. W., 78, 82, 83, *217*
Mueller, J. H., 43, *217*
Murray, H. A., 59, *217*

N

Nagel, E., 2, *217*
Nicassio, P., 178, *212*
Nisbett, R. E., 169, 174, 178, 202, *217,
    218, 220*
Noble, M. E., 47, *217*

O

O'Connor, P., 84, *218*
Omelich, C. L., 185, *213*
Oppenheim, P., 2, *215*
Osterkramp, U., 43, *215*
Overmier, J. B., 121, *213*

P

Patterson, A. L., 18, *212*
Pepler, R. D., 45, *218*
Perin, C. T., 12, *218*
Perlick, D., 54, *219*
Perry, R. B., 5, 12, *218*
Peters, R. S., 2, 4, *218*
Peterson, E., 26, 46, 47, *213*
Pittman, T. S., 204, *218*
Posner, M. I., 146, *218*
Poulton, E. C., 53, *218*
Premack, D., 112, 113, 114, *218*
Price, L. H., 102, *211*

R

Rachlin, H., 120, *218*
Raynor, J. O., 88, 89, 90, 91, 92, *218*

Rejman, M., 40, 41, 42, 57, *215*
Reuter-Lorenz, P., 151, *218*
Revelle, W., 45, 49, 50, 51, 53, *213, 215, 218*
Ritter, B., 189, 190, *212*
Rittle, R. H., 29, 30, *213*
Rocklin, T., 53, *213*
Ross, D. L., 156, *219*
Rubin, I. S., 88, 90, 91, *218*
Ryan, T. A., 3, *219*
Ryle, G., 139, *219*

S
Sales, S. M., 28, *222*
Sarason, S. B., 72, 105, *217*
Sawusch, J. R., 96, *219*
Schachter, S., 54, 166, 168, 169, *217, 219, 220*
Scheier, M. F., 193, 194, 196, 197, 199, 200, 201, *213, 214, 219*
Schell, A. M., 146, 148, *214*
Schmalt, H. D., 81, *213, 219*
Schulz, R. W., 21, *221*
Schunk, D. H., 191, *212*
Schwartz, G. E., 151, *219*
Schwartz, S., 41, *219*
Seamon, J. G., 145, 150, 151, *219*
Sears, P. S., 70, *216*
Sekarak, G. J., 29, 30, *213*
Selzer, R. A., 96, *219*
Sierad, J., 181, *222*
Silverman, L. H., 156, 157, 158, 160, 203, *219*
Silverstein, B., 54, *219, 220*
Simon, L., 45, 51, *215, 218*
Singer, J. E., 166, *219*
Skinner, B. F., 112, *220*
Skolnick, A., 63, 68, *220*
Slade, R., 153, 154, 203, *214*
Smith, C. P., 60, *220*
Smith, L. H., 22, 23, 24, *220*
Smith, T. W., 204, *218*
Solomon, R. L., 121, 124, 132, 133, 134, 135, 136, 141, *213, 215, 220*
Spence, J. T., 18, *220*
Spence, K. W., 16, 18, 19, 20, 21, 50, *220*
Spielberger, C. D., 22, 23, 24, *220*
Spiro, R. H., 159, *219, 220*
Stabile, R., 26, 46, 47, *213*
Staddon, J. E. R., 119, *220*

Standish, R. R., 22, *220*
Starr, M. D., 124, *220*
Stewart, A. J., 102, *222*
Storms, M. D., 178, *220*
Strzelecki, J., 18, *212*
Suomi, S. J., 125, *217*

T
Tassinary, L., 153, 154, 203, *214*
Taylor, C., 2, *220*
Taylor, J. A., 15, 20, 21, *220, 221*
Taylor, R., 2, *221*
Thorndike, E. L., 112, *221*
Timberlake, W., 116, 117, 119, *221*
Tolman, E. C., 4, 5, 31, 70, *221*
Trapp, E. P., 24, *216*
Trattner, J., 117, *214*
Triplett, N., 27, *221*
Trope, Y., 76, 77, *221*
Turner, L. H., 121, *213*
Turvey, M. T., 153, *221*

U
Underwood, B. J., 21, *221*
Ungaro, R., 157, *219*
Upton, M., 26, 46, 47, *213*

V
Velten, E. A., 195, *221*
vonWright, G. H., 2, *221*

W
Wack, D. L., 29, 30, *213*
Wardlaw, K. A., 146, 147, *221*
Watson, J. B., 7, *221*
Weber, M., 64, *221*
Weiner, B., 54, 55, 76, 79, 86, 87, 180, 181, 183, 184, 185, *217, 221, 222*
Weisenberg, M., 171, 175, *222*
Weiss, R. F., 28, *222*
Wheeler, L., 168, *219*
Wilding, J. M., 43, *213*
Wilkinson, R. T., 45, 49, *222*
Williams, S. B., 12, *222*
Wilson, T. D., 174, 187, 202, *218, 222*
Wilson, W. R., 145, *222*
Winter, D. G., 68, 69, 102, *217, 222*
Winterbottom, M. R., 63, 64, *222*
Wolford, A., 153, 154, 203, *214*
Wood, B., 146, 147, *213*
Wozny, M., 117, 118, 119, *211*

Wright, L., 3, *222*
Wright, R. A., 177, *215*

Y
Yeracaris, C. A., 62, *216*
Yerkes, R. M., 32, *222*

Z
Zajonic, R. B., 28, 144, *216, 217, 222*
Zimbardo, P. G., 169, 170, 171, 175, *217, 222*
Zuckerman, M., 46, *222*

SUBJECT INDEX

A

n Achievement, 60–85, 180–187
  academic success, 68–69
  attribution theory, 180–187
  economic development, 63–70
  Mehrabian test, 76–80
  misattribution, 181–183
  occupational mobility, 62–63
  performance, 61–62
  persistence, 82–84
  reliability of, 100–103
  risk-taking model, 70–85
  scoring rules, 60
  training, 68–70
Action, theory of, 93–110
  computer simulation, 96–99
  difficulty level of repeated choice,
    104–106
  inertial tendency, 99–100
  reliability, 101–103
  substitution, 106–108
Affective contrast, see Opponent process
  theory
Affective habituation, see Opponent process
  theory

Affective withdrawal, see Opponent process
  theory
d-Amphetamine, 46–47
Anxiety, drive theory of, 15–27, see also
  Drive; Manifest Anxiety Scale; Test Anxiety Questionnaire
  eyeblink conditioning, 15–19
  paired associate learning, 19–22
  serial learning, 22–24
Arousal, 45–46, 49–53
  diurnal variations, 51–52
  indices of, 45–46
Attention, 32–33, 37–39, see also Cue
  utilization
Attribution theory, 187–188, see also n
  Achievement; Misattribution
Automata, 3

C

Caffeine, 51, 54
Cognitive reappraisal, 174–176, see also
  Dissonance theory; Two-factor theory of
  emotion
Contingent goal, 88–93

Cue utilization, 32–34
Cybernetics, 2

D
Dissonance theory, 170–175
Drive, 10–13, 27, 44–56
    additivity of sources, 47–53
    irrelevant sources of, 11, 13
    multiplicative influence, 10–12
    threshold of response evocation, 25–27
    width of cognitive map, 31–32
Drive stimulus, 7, 24, 53
Dual task
    heat, 34
    noise, 37–39

E
Easterbrook's generalization, *see* Cue utiliza-
        tion; Yerkes–Dodson Law
Efficacy, 189–193, 204, 207
    phobia, 189–191
    proximal goal, 191–193, 207
Electric shock, 35–36
Epiphenomenalism, 139, 202, 207
Evaluation apprehension, *see* Social
        facilitation
Expectancy, 5–6
Exposure effect, *see* Unconscious

F
Financial incentive, 36–37
Fractional anticipatory goal response, 9

H
Hull's theory, *see* Anxiety, drive theory of;
        Drive; Drive stimulus; Fractional antic-
        ipatory goal response

I
Imprinting, *see* Opponent process theory
Impulsivity, 49–51
Incentive, 36–37, 48–50, 70–71
Inertial tendency, 86–88
Intrinsic motivation, *see* Overjustification
        effect

L
Lateralization of affect, 150–153
Lay theory of action, 104, 209–210
Level of aspiration, 70, 73–75, 82

M
Manifest Anxiety Scale (MAS), 15–27,
        46–47
    complex task, 19–24
    eyeblink conditioning, 16–19
    serial learning, 22–24
MAS, *see* Manifest Anxiety Scale
Memory, 39–43
    clustering, 41–43
    noise, 40–43
Mindlessness, 164–165
Misattribution, 169–170, 176–178
    aggressive behavior, 176–177
    placebo, 178–179
    sexual guilt, 177
Muscular tension, 47–48

N
Nicotine, 54
Noise, 36–39, 53

O
Opponent process theory, 121–137
    action theory, relation to, 134–137
    adjunctive behavior, 132–134
    affective contrast, 122–123
    affective habituation, 122–123
    affective withdrawal, 123–124
    imprinting, 124–126
    parachute jumping, 129–132
    separation response, 125–128
Overjustification effect, 204–206

P
Perceptual defense, *see* Unconscious
Perceptual–response confound, 34–37
Persistence, *see* n Achievement
Phenomenal enhancement, *see* Self-directed
        attention
Premack's principle, *see* Reinforcement
        theory
Proximal goal, *see* Efficacy
Psychoanalytic theory, *see* Unconscious
Purposive explanation, 4–10
    Hull's view, 6–10
    Tolman's view, 4–6

R
Reaction potential, 6
Reinforcement theory, 111–121
    circularity of definition, 112

economic analogy, 119–121
elasticity of demand, 120–121
Premack's principle, 112–116
response deprivation, 116–119
Response deprivation, *see* Reinforcement
    theory
Response variability, 26–27, 35
response sequence, 26–27
word associate, 26
Reticular arousing system, *see* Arousal

S
Self-directed attention, 193–202
aggression, 199–202
mirror, influence of, 193–202
outcome expectancy, 196–199
phenomenal enhancement, 194–196
Sleep deprivation, 44
Social facilitation, 27–31
drive theory, 27–31
evaluation apprehension, 29–30
Subception, *see* Unconscious

T
TAT, *see* Thematic Apperception Test
Taylor scale, *see* Manifest Anxiety Scale
Teleological explanation, 2–4, 10

Test Anxiety Questionnaire, 72–73, 77–79,
    80, 105
Thematic Apperception Test (TAT), 55–56,
    59, 60, 62, 105, 157, *see also* n
    Achievement
Threshold of response evocation, *see* Drive
Two-factor theory of emotion, 166–170

U
Unconscious, 4, 140–164
exposure effect, 144–146
hemispheric asymmetries, 147–153
masking, 153–156
obesity modification, 157–158
oedipal conflict, 156–157
perceptual defense, 141
psychoanalytic theory, 156–164
purposive explanation, 4
subception, 141–143
supraliminal comparison, 161–164

V
Voluntary response, 3

Y
Yerkes-Dodson Law, 32–34, 44, 51